ESSAYS AND LECTURES

ON

INDIAN HISTORICAL SUBJECTS

ESSAYS AND LECTURES

ON

INDIAN HISTORICAL SUBJECTS.

BY COLONEL G. B. MALLESON, C.S.I.

GYAN

Published by

GYAN

Gyan Publishing House
5, Ansari Road
Daryaganj, New Delhi-110002
Phone: 011-47034999, 9811692060
E-mail: books@gyanbooks.com

Distribution Network
gyanbooks.com
India, USA, Canada, UK, Australia

ISBN: 978-81-212-4752-8 (HB)
First Published, 1866

2nd Impression 2024

Printed at: Gyan Press, Delhi.

ESSAYS AND LECTURES ON INDIAN HISTORICAL SUBJECTS
Author: G. B. MALLESON

ESSAYS AND LECTURES

ON

INDIAN HISTORICAL SUBJECTS.

ESSAYS AND LECTURES

ON

INDIAN HISTORICAL SUBJECTS.

By COLONEL G. B. MALLESON, C.S.I.,

GUARDIAN TO HIS HIGHNESS THE MAHARAJAH OF MYSORE; AUTHOR OF "HISTORY OF THE FRENCH IN INDIA."

"To believe in the heroic makes heroes."—*Disraeli.*

"I am convinced it was the force of will, the sense of duty, and the determination not to give in, that enabled him to make himself a model for all of us who yet remain to follow him with feeble and unequal steps in the performance of some of the duties which it fell to his lot to discharge."—*Gladstone, on "Lord Palmerston."*

SECOND ISSUE.

LONDON:

TRÜBNER & CO., 57 AND 59, LUDGATE HILL;

AND

W. NEWMAN & CO., CALCUTTA.

1876.

TO

THE RIGHT HONORABLE

SIR BARTLE EDWARD FRERE, K.C.B., G.C.S.I.,

These Pages are Dedicated

NOT LESS IN TESTIMONY OF ADMIRATION FOR
HIS PUBLIC CHARACTER AND OF REGARD FOR HIS PRIVATE VIRTUES,
THAN IN HUMBLE APPRECIATION OF
THE GENEROUS SYMPATHIES, THE EARNEST ENDEAVOURS
TO OBLITERATE ALL DISTINCTIONS OF RACE
WHICH HAVE MARKED HIS CAREER.

CONTENTS.

ESSAYS AND LECTURES

ON

INDIAN HISTORICAL SUBJECTS.

LECTURE ON A NATIVE STATE AND ITS RULERS.*

[DELIVERED IN THE DALHOUSIE INSTITUTE, CALCUTTA, 20TH FEBRUARY, 1865.]

THE impression, I believe, very generally prevails, that a Native State, that is, a State administered and governed solely by Natives, must necessarily be ill governed; that the vices of lying, of corruption, and of venality, must flourish in it to a considerable, even to an alarming, extent. Whether such a state of things actually exist or not, it is nevertheless certain that its existence is taken for granted. The mis-government and corruption of Native States, the effeminacy, the sloth, the immorality, the untrustworthiness of their rulers, have formed the text for many a homily, and the pretext for a great deal of "sanctimonious rhetoric." The indignation roused by some well authenticated instances of mal-administration and oppression,

* That portion of this Lecture, commencing with the rise of the Affghan family, and ending with the death of Nuzzer Mahomed Khan, has been taken chiefly from Sir John Malcolm's narrative of Bhopal. The remainder has been compiled from documents in the Calcutta Foreign Office, for liberty to examine which the writer was indebted to the courtesy of the then Secretary, Colonel Durand, C.B.

B

has, too often, found its vent in the denunciation of an entire community; and in contemplating the vices of a Sooraja Dowlah and a Sambajee, the energy and the talents of a Baber and an Akbar have been often forgotten. In fact, the truth of the old proverb, has, in their case, also been attested :—

> Men's evil manners live in brass; their virtues
> We write in water.

And yet, it is impossible for any man to study the history of India, without being struck by the many instances of the attainment of power, of prosperity, and of influence, by Native States under the rule of their own Chiefs. This power, this prosperity, and this influence, have been acquired, too, by the display and exercise of those qualities and those virtues, which specially commend themselves to a manly mind,—by valour in the field, as well as by prudence in the cabinet,—by a strict and impartial administration of justice,—by a wise foresight in the direction of foreign affairs,—and, above all, by a resolute good faith in all things. I have said that many instances have occurred of such results having been achieved, but, perhaps, of all that are upon record, there is not one case more striking, certainly not one,—regard being had to the very circumstances of its existence,—more interesting, than that of the State, which will form the subject of my lecture this evening; and that State is—Bhopal.

That a small Mahomedan Principality surrounded by powerful Hindoo Sovereigns, should simply exist for one hundred and seventy years, would be deemed, under any circumstances, no small marvel; but the marvel increases almost to the proportion of a miracle when we recollect, that those hundred and seventy years comprehend the most stirring periods of modern Indian History—that in the interval, the Mahratta power attained and fell from its greatest height—the Pindarrees exercised and lost a dominion, which if predatory, yet caused itself to be felt—that Scindia and Holkar reached the very zenith of their renown; and, finally, that a foreign power, beginning with small things, gradually spread itself over Hindustan; striking down, disabling, and always partially, if not entirely, absorbing those who ventured to oppose its resistless course. There must have been something remarkable in the Rulers of that small Mahomedan State; there must have been a consistency and an honesty in the course of conduct, by which the country they governed emerged from the chaos and conflagration of the eighteenth century, and of the first twenty years of its successor, not only uninjured but even consolidated; by which, whilst it saw the Mahrattas broken, Scindia struck down, Holkar all but annihilated, it was itself enabled to remain intact. Yes, there was something indeed! Not long since, one of the greatest of living orators and statesmen, speaking of our own country, made use of these remarkable words:—"Our Empire is now unrivalled in its extent; but the material basis of that Empire is by no means equal to its colossal superstructure. It is not our iron ships, it is not our celebrated regiments, it is not these that have created, or indeed really maintained our Empire. It is the character of the people." Now, I think that this remark is extremely applicable, in principle, to the Rulers of Bhopal. The safety of that State, during the last hundred and seventy years, did not consist in its army, for that was small; it did not depend upon the square miles of its territory, for they were few; but it did depend upon the character of its rulers; upon the character of those, who, whether as Nawabs, or Dewans, or Begums,—and not least as Begums,—guided its destinies: and I think I shall be able to shew you this night, that it was because the character of the great majority of those to whom authority was intrusted had been moulded by a sense of what was right and just, that Bhopal itself has been able to defy the march of time, and to survive the changes by which almost all the neighbouring States have been more or less injuriously affected.

The principality of Bhopal was founded at the close of the seventeenth century by Dost Mahomed Khan, an Affghan nobleman, who had taken service under the Emperor Aurungzebe. In the last decade of the administration of that great prince, Dost Mahomed Khan was detached at the head of a body of his countrymen into Malwa, on the service of his Sovereign. It was just at the period when the overgrown empire of the Moguls had begun to shew the first symptoms of decay,—when the eye of the great Emperor himself had grown too dim, and his hand too feeble, to observe and to repress all the commotions and self-seekings which had arisen in some of the more remote provinces of his dominions. It was just the occasion, in fact, which an adventurer of noble birth, more able, more ambitious, more daring, and not more scrupulous than his neighbours, might use to his own advantage. And thus Dost Mahomed Khan did use that occasion. Partly by force, partly as a reward for services rendered, partly by stratagem, and partly also, it is asserted, by treachery, Dost Mahomed Khan gradually gained possession of a territory, some 4,000 square miles in extent, containing five or six large towns, and nearly three thousand villages; and inhabited by a population of about half a million. This territory he formed into a principality which he named Bhopal, after the chief town within its limits. But this principality lay in a very dangerous neighbourhood. On the north, west, and south, it was hemmed in by the great Mahratta powers, then rising into reputation, of Scindia and Holkar; whilst, on the east and south-east, Bundelkund and Berar were under the sway of princes who sympathised with the Affghan neither in policy nor in faith. But Dost Mahomed Khan had all the large views of a founder of a dynasty that was to endure. Like other rulers of our own days, he considered that the principality would survive, if only the capital could be kept sacred from an enemy. With this view he erected a fort, which he called Futtehgurh, within the limits of the town of Bhopal, and surrounded both with a strong wall. He was prescient even in this undertaking, for the time did come when these fortifications proved the safety of his descendants.

Dost Mahomed Khan had commenced his career of conquest and acquisitions at the close of the 17th century, but it was not till after the death of the Emperor Aurungzebe (on the 22nd February, 1707) that he ventured to consolidate them into one principality, and to assume the title of Nawab. And he not only assumed, but held that title, and held it till his death. He died in 1723, leaving the government of the principality he had acquired secure in his own family,—leaving too behind him a reputation, which, if not immaculate, may fairly challenge comparison with the reputation of most conquerors and founders of dynasties. "Whatever may have been his defects," writes Sir John Malcolm, "there can be no doubt of his talents. He was deemed, even in a tribe where valour is a common quality, a man of remarkable courage. His life was for more than thirty years one scene of warfare; he had received in action about thirty wounds; and his memory, as a soldier, is still fondly cherished by the family of which he was the founder."

The death of Dost Mahomed was the signal for a struggle between two parties who claimed to succeed him. One of these was headed by his elder though illegitimate son, Yar Mahomed; the other by the partisans of his younger but legitimate son, Sooltan Mahomed. The elder son triumphed, and Sooltan was compelled to renounce his pretensions for a time. He renewed them on the death of Yar Mahomed, but having been defeated in a pitched battle, he finally withdrew his claims, on the condition of receiving, in a free grant, the hill-fort of Rathgurh and its dependencies. It is necessary that I should thus allude to the fate of this claimant to the succession, for two reasons. The first is, that the decision by which Sooltan Mahomed acquired Rathgurh was mainly caused by the interference of Mahjee Sahibah, the widow of Yah Mahomed, and in that interference we have the first glimpse of the pressure exercised by the delicate hand of Woman, almost always for good, on the affairs at Bhopal; and the second, that, some years later, one of this man's descendants came from Rathgurh to play an important, though not a very honourable, part in the history of Bhopal.

The immediate descendants of the founder of the Affghan dynasty in Bhopal formed no exception to the idea prevailing regarding men born in the purple. Yar Mahomed the son, and Feyz Mahomed and Yassein Mahomed, the grandsons, were men in no way distinguished by ability of any sort. Feyz Mahomed, indeed, was a man of singularly weak intellect, and, during the thirty-eight years he reigned as Nawab of Bhopal, he acted the part more of a religious recluse than of a sovereign prince. Yet, even during his reign, Bhopal attained a very high degree of prosperity. And this was owing to a very simple cause.

Probably there is no nation in the world that carries pride to a higher extent than the Affghans. They are, as a rule, proud of their descent, proud of their daring courage, proud of their independence, proud also of—whilst strongly, perhaps even fanatically, attached to—their religion. Now, though some people may adopt the arguments of the Puritans, and may condemn all pride in the abstract, yet I cannot but regard the pride of which I have spoken as not only a very wholesome, but as a very noble and a very stimulating quality, in the heart of the uncultivated man. If these Affghan nobles gloried in their descent, it was because they gloried in ancestors who never knew what it was to turn their backs before numbers; if they were proud of their valour, they at least felt that "what men dared they would dare;" if they were proud of their independence, they had at least achieved it; and, as for their religion,—the religion which made them go forth with sword on their thigh, and to smite the infidel,—why, at all events, they would die for it. There was thus something that was very sincere, and honest, and noble in this pride. It was a pride which, at least, they could justify. It was a pride in what they could do, and not in what they could not do. It was a pride, which, whilst it stimulated them to excellence in the performance of those deeds which they felt they could perform, yet held them back from rushing on those paths which, distrusting their windings, "they feared to tread." Thus it was, that, whilst exclusive in many matters, they kept the government in their own family, they did not think that it trenched upon their prerogative, or detracted from their influence, to commit those offices of State, for which they felt they had neither leaning nor capacity, to men, not only of another family, but of another creed. Proud though they were of being Affghans, they were ready enough to acknowledge that they had not been endowed, solely in virtue of their Affghan birth, with every talent, every virtue, and every acquirement. Many offices, therefore, they made over to Hindoos. And if there were one department of which, more than another, they carefully avoided the handling, it was that of Finance. This they willingly yielded to trained financiers of Hindoo origin. Capacity, talent, and honesty, were the three chief requisites for this office; and any individual, gifted with these qualities, might have fairly aspired to a financial career.

The financial ministers in the reigns of Yar and Feyz Mahomed were Byjeeram, Gassyram, and Raja Keesoree, and it was owing to their able administration that Bhopal, though forced for a moment to affect submission to the Mahrattas under Bajee Row, and even to yield a portion of its territory, preserved the independent position that had been acquired for it by its founder.

Their financial administration, or, to speak more correctly, the balance sheet between the Nawab and his ministers, was conducted, in those days, on a very simple plan. The annual revenue was estimated at about two hundred thousand pounds; of this a portion, equal to fifty thousand pounds' value in land, was set apart for the Nawab, under his sole control; the remaining three-fourths were administered by the Dewan, and from this latter sum alone were the expenses of the State defrayed.

The last-mentioned Dewan of Nawab, Feyz Mahomed Khan,—the Rajah Kessoree,—lost his life in consequence of a Court scandal with which he was concerned, and was succeeded, for the moment, by the brother of the Nawab, Mahomed Yassein. The death of the Nawab elevated this brother to the sovereignty; but he, in his turn, died, before any permanent arrangements for the office of Dewan could be made. His death made way for his brother, Nawab Hyat Mahomed Khan.

This prince was about forty-four years old when he ascended the throne, and he sat upon it twenty-nine years,—twenty-nine years of most stirring events. He himself took but little part in affairs, devoting himself almost entirely to religious exercises. There was one in the family, however, who was well able to supply his place. This was the Mahjee Sahibah, or Lady Mother, the widow or principal lady of the deceased Nawab Yar Mahomed. This lady had long exercised a silent though powerful influence in the Councils of Bhopal, and, on the accession of Hyat Mahomed, she came forward even more prominently to lighten the toils with which his feeble nature was unequal to grapple. Her first care was to provide him with a Dewan or chief minister. It so happened that, prior to his accession to the throne, Hyat Mahomed, having at the time no children of his own, had adopted four Hindoos, two of them Brahmins, and had converted them to the Mahomedan faith. The eldest of these, under the name of Fowlad Khan, was alone of a fit age to be appointed minister, when Nawab Mahomed Yassein died. He was accordingly nominated. But with a careful prescience, and with a view to be prepared for any events that might happen, the Lady Mother selected the most promising of the remaining three adopted children of the Nawab, and gave him, under the name of Chutta Khan, the very best education it was in her power to bestow.

I would pause for an instant to dwell upon the character of this Princess. She was born in Upper Hindustan, of obscure parentage. Her name was Mumullah. She had been united, at an early age, to Nawab Yar Mahomed, son of the founder of the family, by the tie of Nikah.* She had no children of her own, but the best proof of the estimation in which she was held may be derived from the fact that all members of the family addressed her as Mahjee Sahibah (Lady Mother). Sir John Malcolm tells us, that "from the account given of her conduct, under the most trying circumstances, it seems difficult to pronounce whether she was most remarkable for the humanity of her disposition or the excellence of her judgment. She was beloved and respected by all. Her memory is still cherished by the natives, both Hindoo and Mahomme-

* This engagement, though inferior to marriage, is still respectable. It is common where the condition of the parties is too unequal to admit of one more legitimate.—*Sir John Malcolm.*

dan, of Bhopal; and it is consoling to see, in the example of her life, that, even amid scenes of violence and crime, goodness and virtue, when combined with spirit and sense, maintain that superiority which belongs alone to the higher qualities of our nature, and which, without these, can be permanently conferred by neither title nor station."

The Lady Mother must have been upwards of sixty years old when Fowlad Khan, the adopted convert to Mahommedanism, entered upon his office as chief minister at Bhopal. It was during the administration of this man—memorable for little else—that an event occurred, slight perhaps in itself, but which proved in reality the foundation-stone of a new era in the fortunes of Bhopal. This event was the first contact of the Affghan principality with the British. The occasion of this contact I will now proceed to relate.

The shameful convention of Wurgaum, entered into between Colonels Egerton and Carnac on one side, and Scindia and Nana Furnuvese on the other, in the month of January, 1778, had so much endangered the English settlements at Bombay, that the very safety of the Presidency seemed to depend upon the opportune arrival of a force of between 4000 and 5000 men which Warren Hastings, with the wonderful prevision for which he was distinguished, had despatched, in anticipation of disturbances on the coast, from Bengal. This force had originally been placed under the orders of Colonel Leslie, but, on Leslie's death in May of that year, the command devolved upon Colonel Goddard. As this officer advanced from the Jumma the obstacles thrown in his way were literally all but insurmountable. The various powers of Central India, accustomed to regard the

Mahrattas as their most dreaded enemies, and being most obnoxious to their blows, were fearful of provoking, by favours to the English, the certain vengeance of the nearer foe. To advance further, under such circumstances, would have seemed madness to most commanders. But Goddard persevered, and in this case, also, perseverance and determination were synonymous with safety and success. When everything seemed at its worst, one independent Power stood forward to offer a friendly hand to the stranger. Not only did this Power afford the English a passage through its territory, but it furnished them abundantly with supplies. It did this too in defiance of threats freely lavished upon it by the Mahrattas. Its nobles and people seemed to vie with one another in ministering to the wants of the warriors of the West. This Power was Bhopal.

The friendly feelings engendered on this occasion were never forgotten by either party; indeed, it was to the recollection of them, many years later, that Bhopal owed its first connection by treaty with the Government of India.

The death of Fowlad Khan, who had rebelled against the authority of the Lady Mother, not long after these events, gave the latter the wished-for opportunity of elevating her protégé, Chutta Khan, the convert from Brahminism, to the vacant post of Minister. This man did full justice to the education he had received. He curbed the power of the nobles, suppressed numerous plots to subvert his authority, established an efficient police, maintained internal quiet, and by his tact and decided measures, cleared Bhopal of freebooters. His ministry was eminently advantageous to the Principality, for it secured for it peace and good government at an epoch when both those commodities were rare.

But death too soon put a stop to the career of this able administrator. The Lady Mother had gone before him, and it seemed as though the power, but lately so well exercised, was now to be scrambled for. Intrigue succeeded intrigue, each one using the State for his own purpose, until Bhopal, bled from within and threatened from without, appeared likely to fall a prey to the first powerful enemy that should march against it.

But the hereditary qualities of their race had not been extinguished in every member of this Affghan family. When, after a series of internal disorders, the authority of the State had again centred in the grasp of a woman, —though that woman, the favourite lady of the reigning Nawab, wanted strength and purpose for her task;— when she, the real ruler, to save the State from one enemy, committed the fatal error of calling in another power, likely at any moment to become an enemy, to assist her; when it seemed only a question to which of the two great predatory powers of Central India Bhopal should fall a prey,—there suddenly appeared upon the stage a youth, lineally descended from the founder of the dynasty, who, by his strong character, his daring courage, and by the possession of some of the greatest qualities that have been allotted to man, succeeded not only in saving his country from the destruction that threatened it, but in indicating a line of policy, by a strict adherence to which Bhopal has been placed behind a barrier, secure for ever against the storms of Fortune. He became, in fact, the second founder of the Principality.

This youth was Wuzeer Mahomed, son of Sheriff

Mahomed, cousin of the Nawab. During the administration of Chutta Khan, Sheriff Mahomed and his son had rebelled against the Nawab; but Sheriff Mahomed had been slain, and his son had taken refuge in flight. That son now came, habited as a soldier of fortune, and attended by a few well-mounted adherents, to the gate of the city. When stopped by the guards, he proclaimed himself to be Wuzeer Mahomed, son of Sheriff Mahomed, the cousin of the Nawab, with whom he demanded an interview. The interview was granted. In the course of it, Wuzeer Mahomed admitted that, having been banished from his country by Chutta Khan, he had been compelled to earn his livelihood by serving a neighbouring predatory Rajpoot chief. He had learned, he said, the profession of a soldier, and the reports he had received as to the dangers which threatened his native land, had made him determine, at all hazards, to offer his services, and to give his life (it was all he had), for his country. The old Prince was roused from his usual state of abstraction by the frank honesty of this offer, and by the noble bearing of the youth who made it. He gave to the youthful stranger the endearing title of son, and hailed him as the future saviour of the country. Wuzeer Mahomed was at once placed at the head of the forces of Bhopal, and, in this capacity, showed himself, in a very short time, worthy of the trust that had been reposed in him. In less than eight months the depredations of the Pindarees had been repressed, whilst the Rajah of Berar had been compelled to relinquish the siege of Hoshungabad. His praises were in every one's mouth; he extorted commendation even from his enemies; and he was universally looked upon as the fittest man, in that time of war and tumult, to fill the office of Dewan, then recently become vacant.

But in those days, as in the present, praise, too loudly and too generally administered, was the reverse of beneficial to its object. It is impossible to praise any one man to a very great extent, without indirectly reflecting upon those to whom the same opportunities had been vouchsafed, but who had neglected to use them. In this instance, the universal expression of admiration of Wuzeer Mahomed grated rather too harshly on the ear of Ghous Mahomed, son of the reigning Nawab. To the small mind of this man, who, in virtue of his position, might have led the army of Bhopal to battle,—though scarcely perhaps to victory,—this excessive laudation of one who had been so successful, appeared positively dangerous. One thing he was determined upon, and that was that Wuzeer Mahomed should never become Dewan.

To accomplish this resolve, it was necessary that he should be able to produce a candidate of his own, whose pretensions should, in some respects, equal the claims of Wuzeer Mahomed. No mere Hindoo would be considered fit for such a purpose. But there was a man,—a man of high birth, great pretensions, unlimited professions of obedience, and a lineal descendant too of the founder of the house. This man was Mooreed Mahomed Khan, hereditary Lord of Rathgurh, and a descendant of that Sooltan Mahomed, whom we found in rebellion against the two first successors of the first Nawab of Bhopal.

And now the two candidates stood together, waiting for the decision of the Nawab. There could not have been a greater contrast. The one, in the flush of manly youth, noble and handsome in appearance, possessing an open, generous, trustful nature, and master of the divine art of managing his fellow-men. He made no great professions, no splendid promises. This one thing alone he said,—that he was ready to fight, and work, and die, for his sovereign and his country.

But the other. More like a Hindoo merchant than an Affghan Chief, he creeps submissively into the presence of the Nawab. He addresses him in language as humble as fulsome; calls him his more than father; on the heir apparent, Ghous Mahomed, he lavishes the most exaggerated praise, praise of his accomplishments of mind and body, of his abilities, his courage, his acquirements; to the Beebee, or Lady Mother, whom he next visits, and who, by her influence with the Nawab, is the real dispenser of gifts, he is equally submissive. He calls her his aunt, declares to her that he will hear with her ears, and see with her eyes; that her opinions shall be his opinions, her enemies his enemies.

The next day he acts even a more extraordinary part. When waited upon by the Hindoo merchants and bankers of the city, he refuses their usual offerings of money, makes them presents of clothes, and calls them his cousins. To the poor everywhere he distributes considerable sums in charity.

The commonalty are delighted. Such a man, so meek, so humble, so charitable, so religious,—for he had sighed away one whole day at the tomb of his ancestor,—such a man was a marvel in that rude age, —so beneficent a mortal had never been seen.

The Court were equally pleased. His promises, his professions were still ringing in their ears. This man was to be their apt tool, their willing instrument, their slave in all things—a better substitute for the popular soldier. Mooreed Mahomed Khan was accordingly appointed minister.

I need scarcely add that he was a miserable hypocrite, "a mean, base, fawning, parasite." Let us condemn him for that by all means, but before we include his nation in the condemnation, let us ask ourselves if we have never witnessed similar conduct amongst our own people; if we have never known or heard of men giving up their own convictions, merely to curry favour with their superior; advising him, not according as he ought to be advised, but according as they knew he would like to be advised,—doing this too without even the aim, which this man had, to become minister, but simply with a view to stand high in the graces of a great man. If we have heard of such amongst our people, we ought not surely to charge the vice on any nation in particular, though we may well regard the perpetrators of it as the offscourings of their kind,—as the Pariahs of the human race.

Deceit and hypocrisy gained for Mooreed Mahomed the office of minister: the same qualities led likewise to his destruction. He soon shewed his true character. In less than a month, the man who, when bidding for office, had refused the customary presents from those who visited him, had commenced a system of extortion, unprecedented in Indian history. No class escaped his avarice. The relations of former ministers were openly fleeced: contributions were forced from the inhabitants in proportion to their supposed wealth: no pleas of poverty were accepted. Commencing, with the meanness common to his class, with those who were powerless to protect themselves, he enlarged by degrees the circle of his exactions; till at last, grown bold with success, he demanded money from the Beebee. This was the woman of whom he had promised to be the slave, whose opinion and wishes he had declared he would accept as his own; and she, weak woman, on the strength of these flattering promises, had raised him to power. But no deceiver can be regarded as having accomplished his destiny, until he have smitten the hand that extended to him its bounty. Mooreed Mahomed was no exception to the rule. The Beebee refused to disgorge. The minister therefore caused her to be assassinated, and at once enriched himself by the plunder of the property she had amassed. The Nawab and his wretched son were completely in his power, and dared not even remonstrate against his authority. One man alone he feared, and him he was determined to destroy. This was Wuzeer Mahomed, "the saviour of Bhopal," who had been his rival candidate for the office of Dewan.

His rejection for that office had caused no change in the conduct of Wuzeer Mahomed. He had accepted the decision of the Nawab without a murmur, and, with the innate loyalty of his nature, had striven ever since to serve the State in the manner he was best able to serve it. And in every undertaking he had added to his reputation. Sent with inadequate means against the Pindarrees, his valour and judgment had supplied the place of numbers, and he had everywhere triumphed. His appearance was often sufficient to put his enemies to flight. In one of his expeditions the tail of his horse had been cut off, and thenceforth, horse and rider were associated together. It is asserted that the cry of *Banda ghora ka Sowar* (Cavalier with the cut-tail horse) was always certain to cause a panic in the ranks of the Pindarrees. Finding his rival's reputation thus increasing, whilst his own had sunk to the lowest ebb, Mooreed Mahomed attempted to cut him off by treachery. His letter, however, was intercepted, and his plans defeated. The minister then threw off the mask, and had the incredible baseness to invite the Mahrattas to aid him in the destruction of the best general of his sovereign. Hearing that the Mahrattas were in Bhopal, Wuzeer Mahomed advanced, though with a very disproportionate force, to oppose them. In several skirmishes his valour gave him the advantage; but he would not have been able long to avert the downfall of his country, if a disturbance in Scindia's own dominions had not caused the recall of the Mahratta force. It was then that deceit and treachery met with a righteous retribution. The Mahrattas, forced to leave, were yet unwilling to depart empty-handed. They, therefore, compelled Mooreed Mahomed, whose immense wealth was notorious, to accompany them to the last town in the frontier. Here charges were trumped up against him, and he was threatened with torture unless he should give up his treasures. The fear of being himself treated as he had treated so many others brought on an illness which terminated in his death. Yet so entirely had he acquired the reputation of being a "Living Lie," that even his death was supposed to be counterfeited, and it was not till decomposition had set in, that the Mahratta chief allowed the body to be buried. But though he died, his reputation still survives him, and, we are told, "that when a Patan of Bhopal visits Seronge to pay his devotion at a shrine sacred to Murtiza Ali, it is deemed an essential part of the pilgrimage to bestow five blows with a slipper on the tomb of Mooreed Mahomed Khan, to mark at once the contempt and indignation which his memory excites."

The death of Mooreed Mahomed made way for the youthful hero whom he had in vain endeavoured to destroy. But though he had become minister, Wuzeer Mahomed found that the office was no bed of roses. The treasury was empty, the revenue, formerly 200,000*l.*, had declined under Mooreed's administration to 5000*l.*, and enemies were on every side of him. But by his valour in the field, and his administrative abilities, Wuzeer Mahomed soon repaired the losses the State had sustained, and Bhopal would then have been placed upon a permanent basis of prosperity, had not the imbecile Ghous Mahomed, the heir apparent, jealous of Wuzeer's reputation, intrigued with the Pindarrees to supplant him. The attempt failed, but another, aided by the whole power of Scindia, was more successful; and Wuzeer was, for the moment, powerless to offer any successful opposition.

Just at this crisis the Nawab died, and was succeeded by Ghous Mahomed. The first act of this imbecile was to invite Sadick Ali, the general of Ragojee Bhonsla, Rajah of Berar, one of the most persistant enemies of the country, to the capital, to secure his authority. Seeing this, and powerless to prevent it, Wuzeer Mahomed withdrew to the fortress of Gunnour. But it was only the one step backwards which so often precedes a resolute advance. Watching his opportunity, he marched, after the departure of Sadick Ali, upon Bhopal, expelled the Mahrattas, reproached the imbecile Nawab for his perfidy, and reassumed the reins of power. From that moment Ghous Mahomed was but a cypher in the State; all the real power was in the hands of Wuzeer Mahomed, and even the title of Nawab was transmitted by him to his descendants.

The nine years that elapsed from this period to his death in 1816 were years of constant warfare, but it was a warfare of the noblest kind. Twice, however, in that interval Bhopal was in imminent peril. In the year 1809, a British force had been sent under Sir Barry Close to operate with the Rajah of Nagpore against the Pindarrees, and as Wuzeer Mahomed had been compelled, in self-defence, to ally himself with these depredators, and even to give them an asylum, he had thus drawn upon himself the hostility of the British power. But Wuzeer Mahomed was far too acute to commit himself to a contest which must be hopeless. He therefore endeavoured by all the means in his power to avert hostilities: he sent an agent to Sir Barry Close to describe the necessity under which he had acted in allying himself with the Pindarrees; to urge the claims of the family of Bhopal on the British nation for the aid formerly given to Colonel Goddard; to state that the feeling of confidence with which Bhopal regarded the British Power was an heriditary feeling, a feeling incapable of being turned into hostility, and he finally professed himself ready to enter into any arrangement the British general might dictate.

The difficulties under which Wuzeer Mahomed had laboured were but little known to Sir Barry Close, and the fact of his alliance with the Pindarrees, pressed into service on every occasion by the emissaries in the British camp of Holkar, Scindia, and the Rajah of Berar, might have led to his destruction, but for the discovery by the English commander of the little dependence to be placed on the active co-operation of his professed allies. The British force did not therefore attack Bhopal, but, still uncertain of the real character of its ruler, the British Government then and afterwards declined to enter into any engagement of protection or alliance. Wuzeer Mahomed, however, to the end of his career lived in hope of effecting this great object, and shaped all his policy with that end in view.

The second peril to which Wuzeer Mahomed was exposed was far more direct, and he was enabled to ward it off only by the display of courage and endurance and high purpose, such as could have only emanated from a man moulded and born a hero. In 1813, four years after his negociations with Sir Barry Close, one of Scindia's armies of 40,000 men combined with the army of the Rajah of Berar, 30,000 strong, to besiege Wuzeer Mohamed in Bhopal. This city was defended on three sides by a wall, and on the south side by the citadel of Futtehgurh, but it had no ditch or other fortifications. The forces by which it was garrisoned consisted altogether of 11,000 men, of whom 5000 were Pindarrees and levies of neighbouring zemindars. These, however, being unable long to support the hardships of the defence, and the deficiencies of food and forage, Wuzeer Mahomed was left with his own army of 6000 men. This disproportion in numbers was, however, amply compensated for by the fact that Wuzeer Mahomed, and his gallant son, Nuzzer Mahomed, father of Her Highness the present Begum, were within the walls. The description of this siege has been written by a merchant who was on the spot at the time; and the detail he gives of the gallantry, readiness, fertility of resource, and immense energy of the two leaders are most interesting. Time will only allow me to give the result.

The siege lasted from October, 1813, to May, 1814. On the latter date, the numbers of the besieged had diminished, by casualties and desertions, to 200 fighting men. They had been for some time forced to live on pounded tamarind-stones and carrion, and these were at famine prices. Still, however, in this case as in so many others, perseverance gained her end. It so happened that in one great attack, the enemy, through the treachery of one of Wuzeer Mahomed's officers, had penetrated within the walls, and it was owing only to the daring valour of Wuzeer Mahomed and his son, and to the spirit with which they inspired their followers, that he was finally driven back. But the repulse of this attack had such an effect upon Sadick Ally, leader of the Nagpore forces, that he withdrew his army from Bhopal, under the pretext that he had heard a voice in a dream uttering against him maledictions for allying himself with infidels against a true believer. Scindia, dispirited by this example, broke up likewise a fortnight later, and thus, this peril, the last that really threatened the existence of Bhopal, happily passed away. It is true that at the close of the year Scindia's troops, reinforced by eight battalions under Jean Baptiste Filoze, threatened to renew the siege, but the allied commanders quarrelled, and at the same time the British agent called upon Scindia to refrain from prosecuting hostilities against Bhopal.

Eighteen months later, Wuzeer Mahomed died. He was then only fifty-one, but he had spent his whole life in a turmoil of activity. He left behind him the reputation of being the greatest warrior, the most skilful and dashing leader, and the wisest politician of that part of India. He had amply justified the title with which old Hiyut Mahomed had saluted him on his first entrance into Bhopal, of, "Saviour of his country." He alone could have saved it. A great French writer has remarked that "where nothing great is to be done, the existence of a great man becomes impossible," but Wuzeer Mahomed's career is but one example, out of many, of the truth of the converse proposition, *viz.*, that where great things are to be achieved, the existence of a great man is assured. Of his exploits I have been able to give in this place but a very faint outline. Those, however, who would care to read what one man, a native of this country, having had no European education, but wholly self-taught, may be capable of accomplishing, will find Sir John Malcolm's account of the career of Wuzeer Mahomed as interesting as it is instructive. To many it will doubtless convey some new ideas.

The son, Nuzzer Mahomed, who succeeded him as Dewan, was worthy of his father. Though he filled the office less than four years, his administration had lasting consequences for Bhopal. He succeeded, the year after his accession, in concluding an engagement with the British, whereby Bhopal was guaranteed to himself, on condition of his aiding the British army with a contingent, and co-operating with it against the Pindarrees, —a condition which was faithfully observed. He was thus recognized as ruler of Bhopal, though Ghous Mahomed remained for his lifetime nominal Nawab. The finances, too, met with his earnest attention, and the revenue, under the influence of his benign rule, soon recovered its elasticity. The districts likewise which had been lost in former wars were re-united to Bhopal. In fact, a new era of prosperity had commenced for the principality, when the accidental discharge of a pistol in his harem, by his nephew Foujdar Mahomed, a boy of eight years old, deprived the State of the skilful ruler who was so well guiding its destinies.

By that shot Nuzzer Mahomed lost his life. Though he had reigned only three years and a half, he had given proofs of great ability, tempered by a sound discretion, and guided by a mature wisdom. He was one of the most virtuous and enlightened men of his time. Though a Mahomedan he had but one wife, and his favourite companion and minister was a Christian. His merits were so acknowledged, that the elder branch of the family of Bhopal and his own elder brother acquiesced in his elevation, and it has been said of him—what can be recorded of so few in his position—that "his memory is unstained by the reproach of a single act of tyranny."

Nuzzer Mahomed left behind him but one child, a daughter, Her Highness Secunder Begum, the present Ruler of Bhopal. This lady was then but an infant, and it was therefore arranged that she should be betrothed at the proper age to her cousin Mooneer Mahomed Khan, the son of the elder brother of Nuzzer Mahomed, and that meanwhile the regency should be confided to his widow, Koodsia Begum.

This lady, who is still alive, was only seventeen years old when she assumed the office of Regent. She commenced her reign by continuing in office the ministers of her husband, and by guiding herself by their advice. The possession of power has its effect, however, even upon ladies, and very often develops instincts and passions which, otherwise, might have lain dormant. Koodsia Begum was no exception to this rule. Her character, scarcely formed when she assumed the regency, soon shewed a power of will and a consistency, for which, up to that time, few had given her credit. This was first displayed by her firm persistent support of Balthazar Bourbon, the Christian minister who had possessed the confidence of her husband, notwithstanding many intrigues against him, both inside and outside the circle of her own family. But six years later a circumstance occurred, which shewed her character in a still stronger light.

In 1827, Mooneer Mahomed, having attained an age when he thought he might exert his authority, claimed the hand of his promised bride, Secunder Begum, and demanded that he should be invested with the sovereign authority. But Koodsia Begum, not wishing to give up the power she had wielded for nine years, and distrusting the character of the youth, refused to accede to the request; and, urging the unfitness of Mooneer Mahomed for the position to which he aspired, declared the engagement cancelled. Mooneer at once took up arms to support his rights, but the Begum was firm. The case was finally referred to the Council of Nobles, and by them it was decided, that Koodsia Begum should be considered as absolute Ruler in her own right, with succession to her daughter; and that Mooneer Mahomed should resign his title to that daughter's hand in favour of his younger brother, Jehangir, on receiving immediate possession of a jaghire of Rs. 40,000, guaranteed to him by the British Government.

Mooneer having thus been got rid of, Koodsia Begum

began to intrigue to defer, if not to prevent, the marriage of Jehangir with her daughter. She feared that this union would be the term of her power, and power was too sweet to be lightly given up. She was so far successful, that the celebration of the marriage was deferred, in spite of all the efforts of Jehangir, for seven years. It was then only brought about, partly by the interference of the British agent, and partly by the arts of the young princess, Secunder Begum, herself. It would seem that the spark of ambition had been already lighted in her bosom. Hence she bound herself to consent to the immediate solemnization of the ceremony, if the prince would sign a paper binding himself to certain conditions. Of these, the principal were:—the acknowledgment on his part that he derived his rights solely from her; his engagement to obey her in all things; never to marry another woman;—and to allow her free liberty to remain outside the Purdah. Anxious for the marriage, he signed the paper, though with a mental reservation, and the ceremony was solemnized on the 28th April, 1835.

It could not be expected that engagements so hollow would last long. There were now three parties in the State, intriguing for supreme power. There was Koodsia Begum, the Regent, striving openly to prolong her tenure of office; Jehangir Mahomed, now titular Nawab, struggling also openly to gain the power as well as the title; and Secunder Begum, his wife, secretly determined to become herself the ruler. It so happened that, at this period, Koodsia Begum had disgusted many even of her own party by her caprices, and the nobles of Bhopal had become weary of the domination of a woman. The British agent also had expressed himself in favour of the claims of the Nawab. Jehangir Mahomed had therefore only to wait. Power was fast coming to him, if he had only stood still to take it. Every day augmented his chances, and it was only requisite for him to maintain a cautious silence. This seemed the more easy, as it was certainly the natural course for a man to take in a contest with the more impulsive sex. But Jehangir was not more than half a man. He did not possess the divine faculty of knowing when to speak and when to be silent. He could not restrain the ambitious longings of his soul. Thirsting for power, and despairing of obtaining it by other means, he resolved therefore upon a *coup d'état.*

It was the month of August, 1836, when the Nawab Jehangir and his wife Secunder Begum gave a grand entertainment to Koodsia Begum, her brothers, and all the nobility of Bhopal. Suspicion was asleep, and the utmost cordiality and good humour prevailed amongst the guests. Yet it was this evening, and this occasion, that Jehangir had chosen, with a view to carry out his purpose of seizing Koodsia Begum. The troops in the fort of Futtehgurh and in Bhopal itself were at his disposal, and he had only to give the word to ensure success. Yet, though the matter had been well thought over,—though Sadoolla Khan—his St. Arnaud—had been summoned, and was actually present with his troops in the palace, yet, the signal to act was not given. Jehangir was barely nineteen; his heart was not yet hardened; he had never yet committed himself to actual bloodshedding; and, as he surveyed that banqueting room, crowded with the nobility of Bhopal, some of them his kinsfolk, many of them his friends, and the others, though devoted to the Begum, not personally hostile to himself, the thought could not but strike him that the attempt to seize the Begum in such an assembly would change the sounds of cheerfulness into shouts of anger, and could be accomplished only at the cost of the best blood in Bhopal. This idea paralysed and unnerved him. He ordered back his troops, and left the deed undone. Meanwhile the secret had transpired. One of the Nawab's chief instruments, furious at his master's weakness, had divulged it to save himself. The Begum and her daughter at once retired; and next morning, the Nawab was besieged in his own house by the very troops who, the evening before, had been devoted to his person. "Men and soldiers," says Carlyle, "love intrepidity and swift inflexible decision, even when they suffer by it." Infirmity of purpose is the one crime they cannot pardon.

Time will not allow me to do more than give an outline of the events that followed this unlucky attempt. The Nawab was for a time blocked up in his house, but escaping from it, he raised a force, and took possession, through the treachery of the commandant, of the fort of Ashta. Furious at this, the Begum sent her troops against him. The two armies met in June, 1837, and, after a desperate encounter, the Nawab was defeated, and driven within the fort. Here he was besieged for two months, and at the end of that period, both parties, weary of the contest, consented to accept the mediation of the British Government. It was finally arranged that the executive power should be made over to the Nawab,—a jagheer, of the value of three lakhs, being assigned to Koodsia Begum. The Nawab was accordingly formally invested on 29th November, 1837, Koodsia Begum assisting.

From this moment, we hear no more of Koodsia Begum as a candidate for power, but her retirement only brought into greater prominence the efforts of Secunder Begum to take part in affairs. Her quarrels with her husband were incessant, and reached at last such a pitch, that at the end of 1838 she retired with her mother to the fortress of Islamnugger, having previously, in July, given birth to a daughter, the Princess Shahjehan. From this place she watched, without attempting to disturb, the weak rule of the Nawab. Her ambition to rule was great, but her patience and self-restraint were greater. She knew the character of the Nawab, and she knew herself, and she felt that in the end she must win the game. Her calculations were correct. After six years of inglorious rule, the Nawab Jehangir died, expressing in his last moments his dislike to his wife by a will in which he attempted to deprive his daughter by her of her succession to the throne.

The character of Secunder Begum is well illustrated by an incident which followed this event. Ignorant of her talents, the British agent, not quite in the spirit of the orders he had received, intimated that her mother's brother, Foujdar Mahomed, was to be sole regent, whilst Secunder Begum was to be intrusted with the education of her daughter, the future ruler. This arrangement was not at all consonant to the wishes of that lady, and when the agent, in a bland manner, attempted to explain to her the important nature of her duties as guardian to her daughter, she turned furiously to him, and exclaimed:—"Am I then a *Dhaee* (wet-nurse)?"

Notwithstanding her opposition, the arrangement was,

with some slight modifications, persisted in. It proved, however, a failure. Foujdar Mahomed had neither strength of will, force of character, nor any just idea of the principles of administration. The British agent found that the Begum possessed all three. Foujdar himself, sensible of his unfitness for the position, became nervous and despondent, and finally resigned the regency at the beginning of 1847. Secunder Begum was at once appointed sole regent in his place.

In that capacity, she had a large field for her talents, and she fully justified all the expectations that had been formed regarding her. Her administration was remarkable for vigour and ability. In six years she was able to report to the British Government that she had paid off the entire public debt of the State; that she had abolished the system of farming the revenue, and had made her own engagements with the heads of villages; that monopolies of trades and handicrafts had ceased; that she had re-organized the police; brought the mint under her own management, and effected many other improvements. She had displayed, in fact, in all departments of the State, an energy, an assiduity, and an administrative ability, such as would have done credit to a trained statesman.

She had originally been appointed regent till her daughter should attain the age of eighteen, but on the occasion of Shahjehan's marriage to the commander of her forces, Bukshee Bakee Mahomed Khan, the period was extended for three years. It was the desire of Secunder Begum, however, that she should be regarded as ruler in her own right, and though this request was not complied with at that time, events soon after occurred, which gave her a real claim on the British Government.

The storm of the mutiny in 1857 did not leave Bhopal uninjured. So early in that year as April, hundreds of copies of a lithographed proclamation urging the overthrow and destruction of the English, sent from Delhi, had been circulated throughout the principality. As soon as this fact became known to the Begum, she communicated it to the political agent, and issued orders to search for and apprehend those who were circulating the document.

In the month of June she expelled from the city a jemadar whom she had caught in the act of raising troops for some unavowed purpose. In July she afforded shelter to the British officers who had been driven from Indore by the mutinous troops of Holkar. She did this too, in spite of a strong opposition on the part of her own subjects, and under a sense of her inability to render aught but a passive aid to her allies. Even the contingent had mutinied, and some of her own relatives had proclaimed a religious war. Yet under all these circumstances, Secunder Begum, though standing almost alone, never swerved from the traditional policy of Bhopal. Her mother was a bigot, her uncles were weak-minded men, yet she never faltered. She caused the British officers to be safely escorted to Hoshungabad; then, with infinite tact, allayed the excitement in her capital; put down the mutinous contingent with a strong hand; and finally restored order in every part of the Bhopal territory. In consequence of these measures, there was little for the British authorities to do, when, at the close of the year, British supremacy was restored in that part of Central India. Rewards were dealt out by the Begum with a liberal hand to those ministers who had so efficiently supported her in her measures, whilst condign punishment was inflicted on her rebel relatives and 149 men of the contingent.

In the campaign of the following year, the Begum assisted the army which, under the personal command of Sir Hugh Rose, re-conquered Central India; not only by amply supplying it with provisions, but by furnishing a contingent of 800 men.

As an acknowledgment of her great services at this crisis, the British Government, with the full consent of her daughter, recognized her, in December, 1859, as ruler in her own right of the State of Bhopal, with succession to her daughter; in May, 1860, four guns were presented to her; the Pergunnah of Bairseea, which had been taken from the Dhar State, was, in December, 1860, added to Bhopal; in March 1862, the right of succession according to Mahomedan Law was conceded to her; and on the 1st September, 1863, Her Highness was invested, in the Viceroy's public Durbar at Allahabad, with the Exalted Order of the Star of India.

Subsequently, in November 1863, Her Highness left Bhopal with her suite on a pilgrimage to Mecca. It had been at one time her intention to proceed to Medina, and thence to England, but the annoyances to which she was subjected in Arabia induced her to return at once to her dominions, after an absence of about a year. Before she left Bhopal, she wrote a letter to Colonel Durand, whom she had known both as agent at her Court and agent for Central India, which shews at least that she is not deficient in warmth of feeling and gratitude. After commending her daughter to his care, she added—"It is a custom of long standing, for an individual of the Mahomedan faith, when on the eve of proceeding on a pilgrimage, to solicit forgiveness at the hands of their former acquaintances. For five or six years you were in Bhopal, and a partaker of my happiness and grief. As mortals are prone to err, I beg that, if I have ever done anything which was not agreeable, you will pardon such acts. As far as I could help, I wish to undertake this sacred mission with as much purity as possible, because life is uncertain, and this world without stability."

On the occasion of her being invested with the order of the Star of India, after having been led up by the most lately created knight—H. E. Sir Hugh Rose,—and by Colonel Durand, she turned to the Viceroy, and expressed her gratification at the honour done her by the investiture,—an honour the greater, as no Lady but Her Majesty possessed the Order. She then added: "Other Governments can praise and reward men, but the British Government stands alone in thinking of awarding praise, honour, and distinction to a woman like myself for any humble services she may have rendered."

And thus I conclude this slight sketch of a Native State and its Rulers. Yet, slight though it be, I would fain hope that it may suggest some truths which we may ponder over, and some conclusions which we may not entirely ignore. I would first call attention to the remarkable assimilation in the feelings and policy of the rulers of Bhopal to English feelings and English policy, as evidenced by the resolute good faith with which they adhered to their early alliance with our own nation, and to the high place and free action they accorded to women. This course of conduct would seem to be the development of a national character, which, not born of the civilization which we acknowledge, has yet been strong enough to overcome the prejudices of custom, and to recognise the power and virtue inherent in truth and justice.

Then again, with respect to individual character:—we notice not only the workings, always interesting, always instructive, of its various phases, but we are brought face to face with the consequences which, sooner or later, must follow the adherence to, or the departure from, certain fixed principles. Thus, in Moreed Mahomed, we see the type of the fawning yet designing hypocrite, of the man who is willing to undergo any humiliation to obtain power and place, and whose guile, nevertheless, not only involves himself in destruction, but recoils upon those who trusted him. There may be different developments of this species: one may be sneaking, complaisant, timorous; another cruel and malignant; yet the consequences of their conduct are almost always the same, and, as a race, they are abhorrent alike to gods and men. In Wuzeer Mahomed, again, we see the gallant warrior, the undaunted defender of his country, the man who was ready to die,—for men can die but once,—rather than surrender, and whose energy and perseverance triumphed—as energy and perseverance, directed to a right end, always will triumph—over myriads of obstacles. In Nuzzer Mahomed we have an example of the wise and virtuous ruler, of the autocrat whose administration was "unstained by a single act of tyranny." In many of the others we see the various forms of irresolution and firmness, loyalty and disloyalty, petty motives and mean actions, common in the world, and therefore, not inviting on this occasion, special attention. But something must be said regarding Her Highness, the reigning Begum. In her we see the type not only of a very remarkable woman, but of a woman who joins to the strong constancy and deep feeling of woman's character, the energy, the daring, the longsighted perseverance, which are generally supposed to be more peculiarly the property of the rougher sex. Her career has proved many things; but to my mind, it has brought into strongest light, this old truth,—not less true because it is as old almost as the world,—that, all other circumstances being equal, no man, and no body of men, can hope to contend successfully with a woman who is at once clever and ambitious, strong-willed and daring. It may be said of her that she never propounded a scheme, never aimed at an object, but that whatever were the obstacles, she ultimately succeeded in carrying them out.

One word more. Let me ask now, taking a retrospective glance at this Native State during the hundred and seventy years of its existence, what is the conclusion that must be drawn? As we notice the working of the springs which set its rulers in action, do we not instinctively feel that we,—we Englishmen,—are liable to be acted upon by the same causes, that we are subject to the same impulses,—that we, according to our different natures, are to be equally moved by the passions of ambition, of avarice, of love, of hatred, of revenge? Do we not feel, in fact, that we and they are shaped in the same mould and formed of the same clay? Recollect, for a moment, that civilization, as we know it, was unknown to those men; that education, as we regard it, was, to them, as though it had never existed. Keeping sight of this fact, dare any of us who are here this evening, and who may have the boldness to examine himself,—to delve into his own heart,—dare any of us say, that he would have been braver and more politic than Wuzeer Mahomed, more virtuous than his successor, more loyal and resolute than the present able ruler, more prescient than the series of men who adhered, through good and evil report, to the wise policy which Bhopal has followed? Dare any even stand up and declare that he would not have succumbed like some of the others? I, for one, having known and felt how true is the saying of one of our greatest statesman, that "not to aspire is to grovel," I, for one, feel confident, that there are few indeed who know themselves, who, recollecting all the circumstances of their position, would dare to stoop down deliberately in order to cast a stone at this Native State and its Rulers.

LORD LAKE.

[From the 'Calcutta Review,' May, 1866.]

Of all the great warriors who contributed to establish British supremacy in India, not one earned a higher reputation for chivalry and daring than did Lord Lake; not one ever combined, to a higher extent, the most undaunted courage with that clear-headedness and presence of mind, which in him were never so remarkable as amid the roar of artillery and the whistling of bullets. He was not much of a tactician. Indeed, for manœuvring, as such, he had always a sort of lofty contempt. His principle of war was to ascertain where the enemy was, then to close with him quickly and rapidly, never to let go his hold till he had beaten him. He had all the natural qualifications for a general of this class. It has been recorded of him, that to judgment and quickness of perception he united courage, decision, and a remarkable capability of bearing fatigue. He possessed, in an eminent degree, the art of conciliating the confidence and attachment of those under his command. In all his great Indian battles the mutual confidence felt by the soldiers in his leadership, and by himself in his soldiers, is clearly visible, and to this feeling, and to his wonderful presence of mind under all circumstances, may be attributed his success against numbers greatly superior. And this indicates another peculiarity in his mode of warfare. Although general of the army, he always led on his men in person. The greater the danger, and the more difficult the position, the more surely was he to be seen at the head of his troops, whether cavalry or infantry, leading them to the charge or to the assault. Whatever may be thought of such conduct in the abstract, it is certain that its effect on his soldiers was electric, and, considering the circumstances in which he was placed, fighting at the head of an extremely small force against an enemy strong in prestige and in numbers, it may be doubted whether any other tactics would have been equally successful.

The adoption by Lord Lake of this daring, dashing, system of warfare may be attributed not less to his early education than to his natural character. Both as a very young and as a middle-aged man, he had enjoyed peculiar opportunities of observing that the very fact of moving on to an attack imbued the advancing troops with a moral power which gave them a great superiority over a standing enemy, and that, although a larger immediate loss of life might sometimes result from such tactics, it often had the effect of putting an end to the war. Thus, in his first campaign, as an ensign in the Foot Guards, during the seven years' war in Germany, he had become familiar with the tactics of the great Frederick, and had noticed how he, by acting up to this dashing principle, succeeded in confounding his numerous enemies. He himself was serving in that war, with the rest of the English contingent, under Prince Ferdinand of Brunswick, and it was in the year after he joined* that he gave the first indication of the

* It may be necessary to state here that Lord Lake was born on the 27th July, 1744, at Ashton Clinton, in the county of Buckingham, that

possession of that spirit and presence of mind to which we have alluded. It was at the combat of Williamstadt near Cassel. The French army was already almost beaten and was retiring, when a portion of their cavalry, making a detour, came upon the right of the allied army, and caused a sudden panic amongst the troops stationed there. Of these young Lake's regiment formed a part, and the men composing it, with the exception of a very few, joined in the flight. No sooner did Lake see this than he waved the colours, which he was carrying that day, and, forming up the few men who remained with him, shewed a bold front to the enemy. This conduct had such an effect upon the fugitives, that they at once rallied to his support, and the French were beaten off.

The experience he gained in the next war in which he took a part,—the war caused by the revolt of the American colonies,—only confirmed his early impressions. It is true that he joined the army under Lord Cornwallis but a short time before its humiliation at York Town, yet, before the surrender, he seized the opportunity of particularly distinguishing himself by attacking and storming one of the enemy's batteries, in such a manner as to obtain the warmest thanks of the Commander-in-chief. From the spectacle here afforded him of this army compelled to capitulate, he drew a very practical deduction regarding the loss of moral spirit and physical power almost inevitably produced by inaction.

But his third campaign, against revolutionary France,

he joined the army as an ensign in the 1st Regiment, Foot Guards, in 1758, and the English contingent under the Marquess of Granby in Germany in 1760.

in 1793, probably had the greatest effect in forming his character as a general. He was then nearly fifty years old, and was serving as Brigadier-General in command of the brigade of Guards, the entire army being under the direction of the Duke of York. Although this campaign opened with some success for the allies, yet its conclusion was disastrous. The allies took Valenciennes, and Brigadier-General Lake himself contributed to the success of the battle in which Dampierre was killed, and afterwards beat the French at Lincelles. This action may be regarded as a type of the battles he was about to fight in India, and he displayed in it the same tactics. The enemy were superior in numbers, were very strongly posted,—but they were stationary. Though the position was extremely strong, General Lake resolved to storm it. He accordingly formed his men up, and led them himself against the enemy under a heavy fire. The French fought well, but the impetus of the attack was too much for them. They were completely dislodged, with the loss of their guns.

Such victories, however, were exceptional. In that war the French were generally the attacking, and, therefore, the victorious party; and it concluded, so far as the Duke of York's army was concerned, by a retreat from the Waal to the mouth of the Elbe, which, in the intensity of suffering from cold, and, in its disastrous results to the soldiers engaged, has been surpassed only by the terrible retreat of the French from Moscow in 1812. It deserves to be recorded, however, that throughout that retreat the rear-guard of the British army performed wonders, and that General Lake made himself conspicuous on several occasions. At Bois d'Alkmaer his personal exertions contributed materially to the safety of his brigade.

From the close of that campaign, in 1794, to the date of his appointment as Commander-in-chief in India, in 1800, General Lake saw no foreign service. He was employed, however, in 1798, in crushing the rebellion in Ireland,—a service he performed most effectively, by the exercise of his favourite tactics, first at Vinegar Hill, and afterwards at Ballinamuck, where the French general, Humbert, surrendered to him with the eleven hundred men at whose head he had too rashly invaded the country.

We have thus briefly referred to the services of Lord Lake in Europe, under the idea that his character can be better appreciated by a glance at the schools in which he served his apprenticeship. There can be little doubt, we think, that the contemplation of the daring campaigns of the great Frederick, who won battles with his soldiers' legs, and for whom no position was too strong to assault,—in the first place,—and the experience of the triumph of revolutionary onward-moving France against her methodic and stationary enemies,—in the second,—contributed not a little to influence his after career. Considering the country he was coming out to, and the enemies he was to encounter, he could scarcely have had a better training.

It was in the year 1801, he being then fifty-six years of age, that General Lake came out to India as Commander-in-chief. He proceeded almost immediately to Cawnpore, which was then our frontier station, and busied himself there with a constant exercise of his men. To the tactics of the cavalry especially he paid very great attention. The great use that might be made of this arm, especially by combining its movements with the movements of artillery, in a flat country like India, did not escape him. It was during the exercise-months that followed his arrival that, on the plains about Kanouge to the north of Cawnpore, he devised and put into execution a scheme, which he afterwards found of incalculable use, viz., that of attaching to each regiment of cavalry two light six-pounder guns, splendidly horsed. These guns, which were called "galloper guns," formed, in fact, a part of each cavalry regiment, and the combined movements of the two arms were conducted with the most perfect exactness, and the most wonderful effect. It was during these exercises that General Lake had the first opportunity of displaying in India that courage and coolness which were afterwards so conspicuous in the field. An officer of his staff, Major Nairne, had speared a tiger, when riding out with the Commander-in-chief in the jungle. The infuriated animal at once turned upon him, and was in the act of making a spring, when General Lake, with imperturbable presence of mind, coolly drew a pistol from his belt, and shot the tiger dead upon the spot.

For about a year after the arrival of the new Commander-in-chief, nothing occurred to demand his presence in the field. In the beginning of 1802, however, he was called upon to chastise the rebellious spirit of some zamindars, whose territories, in virtue of an agreement made with the Nawab Wuzer of Oudh, had been made over to us, but who had refused to submit. Against these General Lake marched with a small force. The resistance he experienced was very obstinate, and it was not until after he had lost many lives that their strongholds were carried.

Peace had scarcely been restored in these districts, when rumours of a contest with the Mahrattas began to circulate very freely in the camp. We will not enter here into the causes which had tended to raise that power into the formidable position it occupied after the downfall of Tippoo Sultan. Fortunately the Mahratta power was not directed by one ruling mind: it was a confederacy, divided into five heads, all jealous of one another; and of these five heads, the wise policy of the Governor-General of India, the illustrious Marquess Wellesley, had succeeded in the interval between the fall of Tippoo and the time of which we are writing, in reducing two,—the Peshwa and the Guikwar,—into a state of dependence on the British. The three that remained, Scindia, Holkar, and the Bhonsla, viewed with a jealous dread the gradual progress of the British arms. They accordingly banded together to overthrow us. But when all their preparations had been completed, Holkar stood hesitatingly aloof, leaving his two allies to bear the brunt of the contest which their preparations had made unavoidable, waiting apparently the first results of the campaign to determine in what manner he should act. But Scindia and the Bhonsla alone were most formidable enemies. Between them they possessed actually, if not nominally, the whole of Berar and Bundlecund, a portion of Malwa and Rajpootana, the imperial cities of Delhi and Agra, and the country known as the Doab, north of the town of Cöel,—the fortress of Allygurh, two miles from that town, constituting the frontier fortification.

The Mahrattas were very famous warriors. Originally

their great strength consisted in their numerous cavalry, capable of any amount of endurance, able to subsist without a commissariat, without tents, without organisation. Taking with them but sufficient for the provision of the day, a spare blanket and a spare horse,* they subsisted on the country through which they passed, until a great victory or some unlooked for prize gave them the opportunity of loading themselves with plunder. With the advance of time they had submitted to a rude sort of discipline, without in any way impairing their hardihood or their efficiency. They possessed, too, numerous guns, the use and value of which they had learned from the French. Their valour had been proved on many a field and over many a foe. Though almost annihilated by Ahmed Shah Abdallee at Paniput in 1761, they had gradually recovered their strength, until, under the greatest prince of the House of Scindia, Madhajee, they had gained possession of the whole of Central India, and, at the period to which we refer, were using the authority of the Emperor Shah Alum, who was a State prisoner in their hands, still further to cement their power.

But to bring about this order of things the Mahratta chieftains had not depended upon their swarms of cavalry and their splendid artillery alone. Madhajee Scindia had noted that the battles which the French and English had gained against their native enemies, had been won chiefly by the infantry. To discipline this arm, therefore, his greatest efforts had been directed. He had invited adventurers from all parts of the world. One of these, a Savoyard, named De Boigne, a man of superior attainments, rose gradually to the command of the

* *Grant Duff.*

troops, which he himself had disciplined after the European fashion, and when, in 1797, he resigned his command into the hands of his master, Dowlut Rao, the successor of Madhajee, he left him thirty-two disciplined battalions, many of them commanded by Frenchmen, and all imbued by a confidence in themselves, and in the discipline they had acquired, such as was possessed by no other soldiers in the country, except the British and Anglo-Indian.

In the command of these troops De Boigne was succeeded by Perron, a Frenchman, who had come out to India, nearly fifty years before, as a common sailor. Perron was in many respects a superior man. He was indefatigable, energetic, attentive to his duties, brave, and a first-rate organiser. At the time to which we are referring, he commanded the troops on the frontier, having his head-quarters at Allygurh. But his master Scindia, probably distrusting him, had, on the outbreak of hostilities, appointed a Mahratta, Ambajee Inglia, to take his place. The supersession, however, had not taken effect, when, on the 28th August, 1803, General Lake, at the head of an army numbering 5000 infantry, 2500 cavalry, with the usual proportion of artillery, crossed the frontier, about four miles to the south of Cöel.

The plan adopted by Lord Wellesley, when the outbreak of hostilities could be no longer doubtful, had been worthy of his comprehensive mind and strong practical intellect. To strike and strike at the heart, with a force that would be irresistible; to break for ever the power of the Mahratta confederacy; to deprive Scindia on the one side, of all prospects of extending his possessions towards the south, and to rescue from his grasp, on the other, not only the imperial cities of Delhi and Agra, but the person of the captive emperor,—were the great objects he proposed to himself. The first of these movements he entrusted to the vigorous arm of his brother, General Wellesley; the second was confided to the tried experience of the Commander-in-chief.

It was then, in pursuance of instructions received from the Governor General, that General Lake organised a force at Cawnpore, in July, moved from that station with it on the 5th August, and crossed the frontier on the 28th, to attack the enemy at Cöel.

Though General Perron commanded at Cöel, he had there a very small portion of his infantry. These, to the number of 2000, he had thrown into the fort of Allygurh, which place he considered capable of sustaining a protracted siege. His plan was to attack the English force as it was moving upon Allygurh, with 8000 Mahratta horse, and, should he fail to beat them, to move rapidly upon Delhi, collect his infantry there, and march upon the English whilst they should be yet engaged in the siege of Allygurh. It was a bold and well-conceived plan, but, in drawing it up, he had not made sufficient allowance for the fact, that the troops to whom he was opposed were either English, or officered by Englishmen, and that the name of their general was Lake.

At four o'clock in the morning, the English left their camping ground, and at seven o'clock they came in sight of the Mahratta cavalry, drawn up in the plain in a strong position, their right resting on the fort of Allygurh, their front protected by a deep morass, and their left by two detached villages, in which they had placed some matchlock-men. General Lake at once carefully examined the position, and determined to attack the enemy on their weakest point—their left flank. He accordingly formed his cavalry in columns of regiments, and placing himself at their head, moved off to the right, supported by the infantry. On taking up a position on the enemy's left flank, the general formed his cavalry into two lines, and moved on to the two villages, behind which the Mahratta cavalry slowly retired. The matchlock-men in these villages, however, poured in so annoying a fire that General Lake halted the cavalry, and sent a battalion of sepoys to drive them out. This was effected in gallant style, and the cavalry again advanced. But they had scarcely cleared the villages, when the Mahratta horse was seen coming up in two lines, prepared to charge. But before they could carry out this intention, the galloper guns, attached to our cavalry, opened upon them. This fire was evidently a surprise; yet had Perron at that moment continued his movement, and ordered a charge, he might have taken the English cavalry, separated as they were from the infantry, at great disadvantage. But the artillery fire so confounded him, that he was incapable of giving any definite orders. The natural result followed. Indecision spread through the ranks, and, in a moment, the Mahratta horse fled in all directions. They were followed by our cavalry close to the walls of the fort, under the fire of which Perron withdrew them from the field.

He had still, however, left 2000 men in Allygurh, under the command of Colonel Pedron, a brave and resolute officer. It had been calculated that this place could hold out for six weeks at least. The importance with which it was regarded by the French commander may be estimated by the letter which he wrote on the occasion to Colonel Pedron, and which ran thus:—

"You will have received the answer you are to make to the propositions of General Lake. I never could have believed for an instant you could have thought of a capitulation. Remember, you are a Frenchman; and let no action of yours tarnish the glory of your nation. I hope in a few days to send back the English general as fast as, or faster than he came. Make yourself perfectly easy on this subject. Either the Emperor's army or that of General Lake shall find a grave before the fort of Allygurh."

The first act of the British general was to summon the fort to surrender, but Colonel Pedron gave him the answer that became a brave man; General Lake, therefore, resolved to lose no time in attacking it.

To attack it, however, by regular approaches, would, he soon saw, occupy sufficient time to enable the enemy to assemble in such force as seriously to compromise his army. Yet it was equally impossible for him to march to Delhi, leaving Allygurh in the hands of the Mahrattas. There was one other chance,—a desperate one,—and that was to attempt it by a *coup-de-main*.

The defences of Allygurh were particularly strong; and not only that, but the country had been levelled for a mile round it, and the fire of the fort guns covered the entire intermediate space. There was but one passage across the ditch into the fort, and at the entrance to this was a strong gateway. Three other gateways had also to be forced before the body of the place could be entered.

It was, nevertheless, that passage, strengthened as it had been to meet such an attempt, which the British general resolved to force. At three o'clock on the morning of the 4th September, therefore, he detached, under the command of Colonel Monson, a storming party, consisting of four companies of the 76th Regiment, the 1st battalion 4th Native Infantry, and four companies of the 17th Native Infantry. These were afterwards reinforced by the 2nd battalion 4th Native Infantry. This party moved at once to within 600 yards of the gateway, and then halted. On the booming of the morning gun,—the signal previously agreed upon,—two batteries of four 18-pounders each, which had been erected for the purpose the previous evening, opened fire on the defences, and under cover of their fire, the storming party advanced to within a hundred yards of the gate before they were perceived. On recognising the advancing line, the enemy hastily abandoned a traverse that had been thrown up in front of the first gateway, and retired within the fort. Noting their retreat, Colonel Monson hastened to follow them with two companies of the 76th, hoping to enter with them, but he was too late. The gate was shut, and the entrance to it defended by a tremendous cross-fire. Nor was an attempt at escalading made by Major McLeod and some grenadiers of the 76th more successful, for the enemy's pikemen crowded the walls in such numbers, that success was impossible. A 6-pounder gun was then brought up to force open the gate, but as it did not succeed, it was followed by a 12-pounder, and from this four or five rounds were ineffectually fired. All this time, a period of twenty minutes, our troops were exposed to a tremendous fire of grape and musketry, and, not content with that, some of the enemy clambered down the scaling-ladders, and attacked our men with their pikes. By one of these Colonel Monson was wounded, and here six officers and several men were killed. Just, however, as matters were getting very critical, the first gateway was forced open, and our troops, pouring through it along a narrow causeway, quickly mastered the second gate,* then advancing with a rush, passed through the third simultaneously with the enemy's fugitives. There remained yet one more, the gateway leading into the body of the place. The artillery officer having been killed, some delay occurred in bringing up the 12-pounder, and when it came, the gate had been too strongly secured to be forced. Major McLeod, of the 76th, however, succeeded in opening the wicket, and dashing through it, followed by his men, he ascended the ramparts, and drove the enemy from the place, or forced them to surrender. Our loss in killed and wounded was 260; that of the enemy much greater.

The capture of Allygurh,—an event which elicited the strongest eulogiums from Marquis Wellesley, and which, by the panic it struck into the minds of the natives, gave them an overwhelming idea of European daring, and contributed probably to the inaction of Holkar,—enabled General Lake to attempt the other object he had in view, *viz.*, to pursue and to encounter the main body of the enemy's forces, before they could receive any reinforcement from Scindia. Accordingly, having detached a party of cavalry to look after a French partisan of the name of Fleury, who had attacked Etawah, and having restored and improved the fortifications of Allygurh, the general marched on the 7th September towards Delhi, and encamped that same evening at

* The advance of our troops was much facilitated by the guidance of an adventurer, Lieutenant Lucan, who had quitted the service of Scindia on the declaration of war. He was killed on the first day of Colonel Monson's retreat, noticed further on.

Soomna. Here he received a letter from Perron, intimating that he had resigned the service of Scindia, and soliciting safe conducts for himself and two of his officers into British territory. These were readily granted, and overjoyed at this signal proof of the injured *morale* of the enemy, the Commander-in-Chief pushed forward on the following morning to meet their new general, also a Frenchman, M. Louis Bourquin. On the night of the 11th September, Bourquin, at the head of twelve battalions of infantry, five thousand cavalry, and seventy guns, crossed the Jumna, with the express purpose of attacking the English force. Our army, much fatigued after a long march, had but just reached at eleven o'clock in the morning the banks of the Jehna Nullah, six miles from Delhi, when Bourquin with his whole force was upon them. The British troops, 4500 strong, had already grounded their arms, many were undressed, and all scattered, General Lake, however, with his usual alacrity, hastily collected the 27th Light Dragoons, and the 2nd and 3rd Regiments of Native Cavalry, and pushed on within cannon-shot of the enemy, to reconnoitre. He found them halted in a position which had been previously selected with great care, each flank being covered by a swamp, their front by a line of intrenchments, and their numerous guns almost hidden from view by a high grass jungle. The fire of the enemy was instantly directed upon this large body of cavalry, which, however, continued stationary, in order to give time to the infantry to come up and attack the intrenchments. It was more than an hour before this could be done, and in the interval, the enemy's fire caused us great loss in men and horses, the Commander-in-Chief himself having a horse shot under him.

At length, perceiving that the infantry had begun to move to the front, and having had time to notice how very strong was the position of the enemy, General Lake resolved upon a movement, which should at the same time entice them from their strong position, and cover the advance of his infantry. Accordingly, he gave orders to his cavalry to retire slowly from the front of the enemy's position, and to move in the direction of the infantry. No sooner had they begun this movement, than the enemy, conceiving them to be beaten, advanced with loud shouts from their intrenchments,—their artillery in the front,—to convert the retreat into a rout. Still the cavalry continued their retrograde movement, until they found themselves on the infantry. The cavalry then opened from the centre, and the infantry marching through, advanced steadily with sloped arms towards the enemy, led by the Commander-in-Chief in person. On arriving within eighty yards of their guns, which all this time were pouring upon them showers of grape and round shot, the line halted to give one volley; then, bringing their muskets to the charge, they rushed forward with such impetuosity, General Lake leading them, that the enemy gave way, and fled precipitately. On this taking place, the line halted, and formed into column of companies, upon which, as had been before arranged, the cavalry, and the galloper guns rushed through the intervals, and rendered the victory complete. The enemy were pursued to the Jumna, in which many of them perished. Their loss was enormous; ours amounted to 486 killed and wounded. All their artillery and stores fell into our hands, and, what was of a moral importance still stronger, the imperial city of Delhi, within sight of which the battle had been fought, was occupied two days later by the conqueror. It deserves to be recorded that Bourquin and the French officers were the first to quit the field, and Bourquin himself, and four others, surrendered the day after the action to the English general.

The battle of Delhi may justly be regarded as one of the most brilliant feats of arms ever performed by a British general and an Anglo-Indian army. The skill, the daring, the intrepidity of the Commander-in-Chief were not more worthy of notice than the discipline and gallantry of the soldiers, European and native. From Marquess Wellesley all the actors in it received well-earned eulogiums. "The decisive victory gained in the battle of Delhi, on the 11th September," he wrote in his general order, "justified the firm confidence reposed by the Governor-General in Council, in the bravery, perseverance, and discipline of the army, and in the skill, judgment, active spirit, and invincible intrepidity of their illustrious commander. The glory of that day is not surpassed by any recorded triumph of the British arms in India, and is attended by every circumstance calculated to elevate the fame of British valour, to illustrate the character of British humanity, and to secure the stability of the British empire in the East."

On the 14th September, General Lake entered Delhi, and liberated from confinement the unhappy blind old king, Shah Alum, who had been so long, not only a state prisoner, but subjected to tyranny and insult. By him, and by all the inhabitants of Delhi, the English army were hailed as deliverers, and they showed their title to that designation, by observing the strictest discipline during their occupation of the imperial city. Having made the necessary arrangements for the security of the capital and the tranquillity of the surrounding country, as well as for the peaceful enjoyment by the Emperor Shah Alum of his freedom and dignities, General Lake left Delhi with his army, on the 24th September, for Agra, which place it was his intention to besiege. He arrived there on the 4th October, and encamped within long cannon-shot of the fort. The garrison of Agra consisted of 4500 fighting men, under the nominal command of an English adventurer, Colonel George Hessing; but, distrusting him and their other English officers, six in number, the troops had mutinied and made them prisoners. Besides these troops, there were encamped under the walls of the fort, three battalions of the army that had been defeated at Delhi, and four battalions of Perron's fifth brigade, just arrived from the Dekkan, under the command of Major Brownrigg, with twenty-six pieces of cannon. The garrison had refused to admit these troops into the fort, because there were within its walls twenty-five lacs of rupees, their share of which, they feared, would be lessened by a further accession of troops. They, therefore, occupied the city and glacis. In addition to these, twelve battalions of regular troops had taken up a position in the rear of the besieging army, on the Delhi road, with the view, should the siege be protracted, of attempting to recover the imperial city. The Commander-in-Chief, having noted this state of things, resolved, with his accustomed skill and energy, to dislodge those battalions on the glacis and in the city before commencing the siege. Accordingly, on the morning of the 10th October, he detached two battalions of sepoys, under Brigadier General Clarke, to attack the city; one battalion, under Colonel M'Collough, to attack the enemy on the western face of the fort; and a fourth battalion, under Captain Worsley, to attack them on the southern face. These three attacks completely succeeded, though not till after a long and severe resistance, costing us 213 men killed and wounded. The loss of the enemy was computed at 600, besides which, all their guns, twenty-six in number, were captured, and they were so dispirited by the defeat, that two days after, 2500 of them surrendered in a body to the English general, the conditions being that they should be taken into the Company's service, on the same pay they received from Scindia.

This difficulty being removed, the general prepared in earnest for the siege, and on the 16th opened his batteries. The next day, however, the garrison demanded terms of capitulation. These were, after some discussion, agreed to, and the fort was evacuated on the 18th. By this surrender, 25 lakhs of rupees and 162 pieces of cannon fell into our hands. But, what was of infinitely more importance, a line of defence along the left bank of the Jumna was secured, and the British were left at liberty to pursue Scindia's brigades into his own territory.

It has been mentioned, that whilst the army was encamped before Agra, twelve of Scindia's battalions, with some cavalry and guns, had taken up a position on the Delhi road in their rear. These consisted of seven battalions, which had come up from the Dekkan, styled the Dekkan Invincibles, reinforced by five others which had escaped from Delhi, of 1500 cavalry and 74 guns, about 9000 men in all. This force was commanded by Abajee, a Mahratta, and was officered entirely by natives. To pursue and destroy this, representing as it did the last remnant of the force disciplined by De Boigne, was the object General Lake proposed to himself after the fall of Agra. Accordingly, after making the necessary preparations for its defence, and for the care of the wounded, he started on the 27th October at the head of three regiments of dragoons, five of native cavalry, one European regiment of infantry (the 76th), and four battalions of Sepoys, in pursuit. He soon ascertained that the Mahrattas had moved off in the direction of the Jyepore country. Thither, accordingly, he followed them. The heavy state of the soil, saturated with rain, having compelled him to leave the greater part of his artillery behind him, he pressed on by forced marches, and arrived, on the night of the 31st, on the ground which the enemy had only quitted that morning. As this ground was but thirty-three miles from the hilly country of Mewât, the only pass into which could have been easily made almost impregnable, the general resolved to push on with his three cavalry brigades, and try the effect upon the enemy with that arm alone.

Accordingly, at twelve o'clock that same night, he set off, leaving the infantry to follow. At sunrise, next morning, he came up with the enemy at the village of Laswarrie. Here they were very strongly posted, their right thrown back on a rivulet, "the banks of which were extremely difficult of access; their left rested on the village of Laswarrie, whilst their entire front, which lay concealed from view by long grass, was defended by a most formidable line of artillery."* Owing partly to the long grass, and partly to the clouds of dust which were blown from the enemy, the strength

* *Thorn.*

of their position was not at once apparent to General Lake; and as it appeared to him that their movements indicated an intention to retreat to the Mewâtee hills, from which they were then but eight miles distant, he resolved to attack them without waiting for the infantry. Accordingly, he formed up his cavalry, and, as usual, placing himself at their head, ordered successive charges to be made by the advanced guard and the first and second brigades on the left of their position, whilst the third should turn their right. The charges on the left were most gallantly executed; the enemy were driven back into the village, several guns were taken, and their line in some instances penetrated, but owing to the attack being unsupported by the infantry, the guns could not be carried off, and, on the cavalry retiring, they were recovered by the enemy. In this attack our loss was heavy, Colonel Vandeleur, commanding the brigade, received a mortal wound. But the charge of the third brigade was even more desperate, and, if possible, more daring. This brigade, consisting of the 29th dragoons and the 4th Native Cavalry had been directed to turn the right of the enemy's line. To obtain a position from which to effect this, they moved along the front of that line, exposed to the fire of seventy-four guns, which lay concealed by the long grass. Heedless of this fire, however, they moved on to the position that had been marked out for them, formed up as steadily as if on parade, and charged the hostile batteries. Here, however, their success was but transient; for though they rode through the guns, they failed to reach the infantry, who were posted behind an intrenchment, from which they poured in a musketry-fire most galling to our men. In this unequal conflict they were some time engaged, making heroic efforts to get at the infantry. But it was in vain, the steady fire from the enemy's line made terrible havoc amongst them; and at last the general, perceiving the inutility of farther persevering in a fruitless attack, drew off all his cavalry, resolving to watch the enemy till the infantry should arrive.

At noon the infantry came up, eager for the attack; but, having made a forced march of twenty-five miles, the general ordered refreshments to be served out to them before leading them into action. After an hour's respite for this purpose, during which the enemy entered into negotiations to surrender their guns,—but which came to nothing,—he formed them into two columns, the first of which was to turn the enemy's right, now concentrated round the village of Mohaulpore. The second was to support it, whilst one portion of the cavalry should draw off the enemy's attention by threatening his left, and another should hold itself in readiness to take advantage of any confusion in the hostile line.

These dispositions having been effected, the first column moved on; but their advance was no sooner perceived by the enemy, than they threw back their right, and concentrated on the advancing column the whole fire of their artillery. So great was the slaughter, especially in the leading regiment, the 76th, that the general who was with them, resolved not to wait for his supports,—the advance of which had been delayed,—but to press on at once to the enemy's guns. But the enemy's resistance was so determined, and the fire so hot, that but little impression was made even by this advance. At this moment, too, our advancing column was charged by the enemy's cavalry. Although this charge was repulsed, yet the position was altogether so critical, that orders were sent to our cavalry to make a counter attack. As they were forming up for this purpose,* the horse of the Commander-in-Chief was shot under him; and his son,† whilst in the act of tendering to him his own, was shot by his side and severely wounded. This affecting incident was not lost upon the troops; it appeared to inspire them with enthusiasm. Just at that moment the order to charge sounded, whilst seventy pieces of canon opened on our line. The advance of our men, however, was irresistible; again they drove back the gunners; and the Commander-in-chief, this time, having infantry with him, brought them up at the right moment, and secured the greater part of the guns. Both arms then pressed forward. The enemy however, fought with the most determined courage, and did not quit the field until they had been driven from every position, and had lost every gun.

This was the most desperate and well fought battle in which our force had yet been engaged. "From the commencement of the conflict early in the morning," says the historian‡ of that period, "to the close of the general action in the evening, the enemy discovered a firmness of resolution and contempt of death which could not fail to command the admiration of their

* At this point of the action a matchlockman pointed his matchlock close to the side of the general; but just as the piece was discharged, the Commander-in-Chief turned involuntarily, and the contents passed under his arm, burning only his coat.—*Thorn.*

† This son, the Honourable G. A. F. Lake, became afterwards Lieutenant-Colonel of the 29th Foot. He was killed at the battle of Roleia, on the 17th August, 1808, just when, at the head of his regiment, he had forced the pass, the possession of which decided the victory.

‡ *Major Thorn.*

opponents." Let it never be forgotten that those who constituted that enemy were the warlike sons of Hindostan. Here they were unaided by the presence of European officers, though trained in a European school; they were left solely to their own resources; and though superior in numbers, the superiority was by no means strongly marked. Yet here they fought with a gallantry, a resolution, an energy, that would have done honour to any troops in the world.

In this obstinately contested battle, it has been very generally* conceded that the credit of the victory was due not less to the unsurpassed valour of our troops than to the character, the presence of mind, and the personal exertions of the general himself. His influence with the soldiers, their confidence in his generalship and resources, his coolness in danger, the reliance he had in himself, were never more conspicuous than on

* The following observations on this battle are from the pen of Marquess Wellesley:—"The victory, however, must be principally attributed to the admirable skill, judgment, heroic valour, and activity, of the Commander-in-Chief, General Lake, whose magnanimous example, together with the recollection of his achievements at Cöel, Allygurh, Delhi, and Agra, inspired general confidence and emulation. In the morning General Lake led the charge of the cavalry, and, in the afternoon, conducted in person, at the head of the 76th regiment, all the different attacks on the enemy's line; and on their reserve, posted in and near the village of Mohaulpore. On this day two horses were killed under the Commander-in-Chief. The shot showered around him in every direction. In the midst of the danger and slaughter which surrounded him, he displayed not only the most resolute fortitude and ardent valour, but the utmost degree of professional ability and knowledge, availing himself, with admirable promptitude, of every advantage presented by the enemy, and frustrating every effort of the enemy's obstinacy and boldness. His masterly plans of attack during the action were carried into instantaneous execution by his unrivalled personal activity; and he appeared, with matchless courage and alacrity, in front of every principal charge, which he had planned with eminent judgment and skill."

this occasion. The imperturbable coolness with which, after repulsing the enemy's cavalry, he halted his own columns to allow the dragoons to come up to make a way for the infantry, has never been surpassed on any field; whilst the touching incident by which it was marked gave to it a romantic colouring by which its effect on the troops was greatly heightened.

The victory was the most important of the war. The last remnant of the disciplined battalions of Scindia, raised with so much care by De Boigne, were in this action destroyed; whilst seventy guns and numerous stores of all sorts fell into our hands. Our loss was in proportion, amounting to 823 killed and wounded, or nearly one man out of every five engaged. The loss in the 76th regiment was especially great; and the general, as he rode through their ranks after the battle, could not refrain from dropping a tear at the terrible reduction in their numbers.

On the 8th November the force left Laswarrie, and on the 14th treaties were concluded with the Rajah of Ulwar, as well as with the Rajas of Jyepore and Joudhpore, the object being the exclusion of the Mahratta power from their territories. A treaty was concluded about the same time with Begum Sumroo; and her troops, 2000 strong, joined our army in December, after a long and difficult march from the Dekkan. The force then proceeded to Canoare,—where the Commander-in-chief had an interview with Runjeet Singh, Rajah of Bhurtpore,—and thence by slow marches to Biana, opposite the pass leading into the territories of the Rajah of Jyepore, where it remained halted from the 27th December, 1803, to the 9th February following.

Meanwhile, whilst these events were progressing in

the north-west, English arms had been no less successful in the south. At Assaye, on the 24th September, and at Argaum, on the 28th November, the combined armies of Scindia and the Raja of Berar had been signally defeated. Such, indeed, was the consternation produced by these defeats that, on the 7th December, the Raja of Berar withdrew from the confederacy; and, on the 30th, Scindia, deserted by him, and abandoned before the outset of hostilities by Holkar, signed a treaty of peace * with General Wellesley.

This treaty put a stop to the further operations of General Lake against Scindia. We have seen, in detail, how completely successful he had been, how utterly he had destroyed the ambitious projects formed by that chieftain. With a force, at no time exceeding 5000 foot, 2500 horse, and a small proportion of artillery, he had, between the 29th of August and the 1st November,—a short period of little more than two months,—destroyed the thirty-one battalions which the French adventurers had disciplined with so much care for the service of Scindia; he had stormed the fort of Allygurh, captured Agra, and entered as a conqueror the imperial city of Delhi; he had taken four hundred and twenty-six pieces of cannon,—and, more than all, he had proved the soundness of the theory, that a British general, possessing the confidence of his troops, may dare almost anything in India. Thus Lake, at Allygurh, stormed a fortress which was apparently as proof against the chances of a *coup-de-main* as any fortress in the world; at Delhi, finding the position of the enemy so strong that a direct attack upon him must be attended with enormous loss, he tried an experiment, which can only

* The treaty of Surjee Arjengaum.

be successful when troops have confidence in their commander, and their commander in the troops,—that of enticing him from his intrenchments by a feigned defeat. At Agra again, deeming the possession of that fortress of the last importance to the success of his operations, he deliberately sat down before it, although, in addition to the garrison within its walls, a second hostile force had possession of the city, and a third was marching on his rear. Beating one force, frightening another into quiescence by his fearless attitude, and compelling the fort to surrender, he dashed then hastily in pursuit of the last remnant of the enemy, making for the hilly country of Mewât. These he encountered and brought to bay only eight miles from their destination; then, with his cavalry alone, keeping them in position till his infantry could come up, he launched upon them his well-tried veterans, and after a conflict which, in the desperate valour evinced by both sides, has never been surpassed, destroyed or forced into surrender the entire force. What a career! Wonderful not less in the magnitude of the events, than in the rapidity, in the completeness, with which they were executed,—a rapidity and a completeness for the solution of which we must look to the quick, decided, energetic character of General Lake.

It was not considered improper or detrimental to military discipline in those days for the officers of the army to express publicly their sense of the high qualities of the Commander-in-Chief, even during his tenure of office. During the campaign we have described General Lake had enjoyed very many opportunities of displaying other qualities besides those of a daring and successful general. His conciliatory and genial manners, his care of the troops, and his attention to the comfort alike of officers and soldiers, had, not less than his lofty contempt of death, the dashing manner in which he had led his troops into action, his imperturbable coolness under fire, won for him the regard of all ranks. He had shown himself essentially a fair man. In his treatment of the officers in the immediate service of the King, and those in the employ of the East India Company, he had made no distinction. Those only had obtained his patronage who had merited it by their character and their actions. At the close of this campaign, therefore, and when it seemed, for a moment, as though it only remained to guard the conquests that had been won, the officers of both services belonging to the army he commanded determined to present to General Lake a testimonial of their attachment and esteem. The sum of four thousand pounds having been subscribed, a committee was appointed to offer to the Commander-in-Chief a service of plate of that value,* with an appropriate letter. This was accordingly done.† General Lake replied the same

* The inhabitants of Calcutta also presented General Lake with a sword of the value of 1500*l.*, and one to General Wellesley, valued at 1000*l.* It was to commemorate these two campaigns, that the marble statue of Marquess Wellesley, now in Government House, was subscribed for.

† The following is the text of the letters referred to, dated 21st December, 1803:—"We, the officers of the British Indian army, who have had the honour of serving under your Excellency's personal command, during the present campaign, impressed with sentiments of high respect towards your Excellency, and admiration of those exalted talents by which we have been led to a series of brilliant victories, confirming the superiority of British arms in this remote quarter of the globe, and yielding to us a soldier's best reward, the approbation of Government, beg leave to request your Excellency's acceptance of a service of plate of the value of four thousand pounds, in testimony of our attachment and esteem.

"Zealously devoted to the service of our King, our country, and the day, accepting the testimonial as coming from "officers of an army whose meritorious services throughout this campaign must ever entitle them to the highest respect and honour." Although the practice of giving and receiving testimonials whilst the recipient is in active service would not be tolerated in the present day, it is impossible not to respect the genuine feeling which prompted the officers of that gallant force, thus at the close of the campaign, to dedicate a large proportion of their prize money to do honour to the general, to whose daring leadership and never-failing self-reliance they felt so greatly indebted for the success they had achieved.

Before proceeding to describe the course of action which, after a very brief interval of rest, forced the British general into warlike measures against another

Government under which we have the honour to serve, it only remains for us to express our sincere and ardent hope, that we may long enjoy the advantage of being placed under your Excellency's guidance and command; and that, wherever the interests of the State may require our services, inspired by your animating example, and cherished by your applause, we may continue to follow you to victory and renown."

General Lake replied thus:—"I receive with sentiments of the most lively gratitude the valuable testimony of the esteem and attachment of the army with which they have honoured me.

"This mark of regard is peculiarly flattering from the officers of an army whose meritorious services throughout this campaign must ever entitle them to the highest respect and honour.

"In the hour of severe trial, next to that Providence who protects us, I have trusted to the invincible firmness, steady support, and unexampled gallantry of my army; and the distinguished success which has, in every instance, crowned our exertions, has fully justified my entire confidence and firm reliance.

"I shall with pride and pleasure reflect upon those situations in which we have together maintained the honour of our King and the glory of our country.

"The possession of this valuable testimony of your attachment will serve to awaken those sentiments of esteem, gratitude, and affection, which are already too deeply imprinted on my mind ever to be forgotten."

Mahratta power, it may be convenient to refer very briefly to the operations by which, at the time of the campaign against Scindia, Bundelkund and the fortress of Gwalior were brought under subjection to British arms. The Peshwa had, in 1802, escaped from the state of vassalage in which he had been held by Scindia and Holkar, by throwing himself, as we have intimated, under the protection of the British. By the treaty made on that occasion,* certain territories south of the Taptee, and between the Taptee and the Nerbudda, had been ceded by the Peshwa to his protectors. But it was afterwards agreed that in lieu of a portion of this ceded territory, the greater part of the province of Bundelkund, over which the Peshwa held a nominal sovereignty, but which lay at an inconvenient distance from Poona, should be made over to the British. It was to carry out this arrangement that on the 6th September, 1803, a detachment of British troops under Lieutenant-Colonel Powell crossed the Jumna, and, on the 14th, joined the native troops of Himmut Bahadoor, the chief representative of the Peshwa's authority in the provinces on the borders of Bundelkund. The cession of that territory was, however, disputed by another chieftain, Shumsheer Bahadoor, and it was not until Colonel Powell and his native allies had bombarded Calpee into surrender † that Shumsheer realised the folly of further resistance. He continued, however, to negotiate until the offer of an annual pension of four lakhs to him and his family induced him to submit entirely to the arrangements made with the Peshwa. About the same time the

* Treaty of Bassein, dated 31st December, 1802.

† 4th December, 1803.

Subadar of Jhansie entered into an alliance, offensive and defensive, with the English.

There was one other chieftain upon whom the progress of British arms in Bundelkund had an important effect. This was Ambajee Inglia, the Mahratta chieftain, who, it will be recollected, had been selected by Scindia to supplant the Frenchman Perron, in the government of his dominions in the north-west, just previous to the outbreak of hostilities. The English had not yet come to an arrangement with Shumsheer Bahadoor when Ambajee, noting their progress in Bundelkund, offered to transfer his allegiance from Scindia, in lieu of a guarantee of the more important of his possessions. So long, however, as Shumsheer remained unsubdued, Ambajee carefully avoided entering into any positive engagement; but when the fortunes of that chieftain had sunk to their lowest ebb, Ambajee, bent on securing himself, entered into conditions with the Commander-in-Chief, whereby he abandoned all his territory north of Gwalior, and that fortress itself, to the British, on condition of being assured independent possession of the remainder.*

But although he had agreed to these terms, Ambajee sent private instructions to the commandant of the fortress to refuse to surrender it. Standing on the summit of a very steep hill, about a mile and a half in length, with a width of 300 yards in its broadest part, well-fortified, abundantly supplied with stores, and regarded by the natives as impregnable, Gwalior, he probably thought, would successfully defy the small force of native troops that had been detached by the Com-

* There were some trifling exceptions for which, however, Ambajee was to receive indemnification.

mander-in-Chief under the orders of Colonel White to take possession of it.

But he had not sufficiently considered the character of the English commander. No sooner did General Lake hear of the unexpected resistance than he detached reinforcements of Europeans to Colonel White, and gave him authority to call up the contingent employed in Bundelkund. Colonel White, thus strengthened, opened fire on the fortress, effected a practicable breach on the 4th February, and, on the 5th, accepted the offer of the garrison to surrender on the condition that the value of certain stores were made over to them.

The capture of Gwalior and of some intermediate forts of secondary importance completed the line of defence against the Mahrattas, and assured the Commander-in-Chief against the chances of an invasion of the country lying to the north or north-east of the line he had obtained. The possession of a great part of Bundelkund secured the country between Mirzapore and Midnapore. No enemy could even threaten that line without exposing his left flank in such a manner as to court destruction. Calpee on the right, and Etawah on the left, of the Jumna, secured the country between Allahabad and Agra, whilst the possession of Gwalior and Dutteeah,* and the alliance with Jhansie, rendered any direct attack from the south-west impossible. Never had British India occupied a position at once so safe and so commanding.

We must now turn for a brief interval to those proceedings of the Mahratta powers, especially of Holkar, which led to the renewal of hostilities. By the treaty †

* One of the forts of secondary importance referred to.

† The treaty of Surjee Arjengaum, 30th December, 1803.

concluded with Dowlut Rao Scindia, that prince had ceded to the British all his positions in the provinces of the north-west, and all the territories he had held south of the Ajunta hills, with the exception of a few hereditary villages; and he had besides resigned his claims on his former feudatory rajahs, with whom the British Government had made treaties. Subsequently to the signing of that treaty, alarmed at some hostile demonstrations made by Jeswunt Rao Holkar, Scindia had agreed to become a party to the defensive alliance subsisting between the British Government, the Peshwa, and the Nizam, on condition that the British should maintain a subsidiary force of six battalions, to be paid for out of the revenues of the ceded territories, for his defence. This arrangement was ratified in a fresh treaty signed on the 27th February, 1804, and in this it was agreed that the six battalions should be stationed near Scindia's boundary but within British territory.*

It has already been stated that when the movements of Scindia, in the early part of 1803, left to Marquess Wellesley no alternative between an ignominious admission of Mahratta supremacy and war, that chieftain had entered into an offensive alliance with the Rajah of Berar and Jeswunt Rao Holkar, but that after hostilities had been actually entered upon Jeswunt Rao had held aloof and had watched with complaisance the overthrow of his two confederates. This conduct on the part of Jeswunt Rao is susceptible of easy explanation. Himself an illegitimate son, having seen one legitimate brother, Mulhar Rao, massacred by Scindia, and the other, Kashee Rao, a man of weak intellect, kept a prisoner by that prince, and used as a puppet by whose means

* *Aitchison.*

his ancestral territories might be annexed, Jeswunt Rao had early perceived that his sole chance of safety and independence rested on the use he might make of the talents and energies with which had been gifted. These were neither few nor inconsiderable. High-spirited, of daring courage, a splendid horseman, the leader in every charge, a Mahratta of Mahrattas, Jeswunt Rao was designed by nature to be a leader of men, a king amongst nobles. Immediately after the murder of his brother, therefore, he entered upon the one course which appeared to present to him at once a chance of vengeance and a prospect of sovereignty. Escaping the fury of his enemy, he rallied round him the adherents of the house of Holkar, and called upon them to acknowledge him as their chief. Many responded to the call, and he soon found himself at the head of a force which, if not equal to the large armies of Scindia, was still respectable even in numbers. The comparative deficiency in numbers, too, was more than compensated for by the vigour, the energy, and the skill of its leader. In the first encounter between the two rivals all the advantages rested with Holkar. Encouraged by this, he determined to contest with Dowlut Rao the supremacy in the Mahratta confederacy—a post which, long held by the Peshwa, had now come, by the gradual decline of the power of that potentate, to be regarded as the property of the chieftain who should exercise the greatest amount of influence at Poona. Pursuing this course Jeswunt Rao marched at once upon that city, defeated Scindia in a bloody battle near it on the 29th October, 1802, and entered Poona * a few days later.

* Sir John Malcolm relates that in this battle, Jeswunt Rao "led the charge on Scindia's guns, and being wounded, and pulled from his

It is unnecessary that we should refer at any length to the course adopted by Marquess Wellesley at this conjuncture. It was a course remarkable for the combined daring and wisdom by which all the public acts of that great statesman were characterised. Without irritating Holkar into war, he not only restored the Peshwa to his capital, but brought him, as well as the Guikwar, into a state of dependence on the British. By a masterly political stroke, in fact, supported by the equally masterly military movement of his brother, General Wellesley, the great Marquess cast off from the Peshwa's neck the iron yoke which Scindia, Holkar, and the Bhonsla, had each, as the power of each predominated, fixed upon him; deprived those three powers of the prestige attaching to intimate alliance with the possessor of Poona, and then presented himself ready to meet them, isolated as they were, on the field he had chosen.

The first result of this policy we have already shown. Scindia and the Bhonsla, shorn of a great portion of their territories and a great portion of their power, had been completely humiliated. But Holkar had been untouched. It is probable, that having tested his superiority over Scindia at Poona, he was not sorry to see him weakened by the British, feeling that he would thus become even an easier prey to his own arms. He himself believed more in sweeping charges of Mahratta cavalry than in the slower attacks of disciplined infantry. But he showed by his subsequent acts that he felt at this period master of the situation, and that he was

horse by an artillery soldier of great strength, he wrestled with his enemy on foot, until one of his attendants came to his aid, and, after slaying his antagonist, re-mounted him."

waiting only an indication of the result of the war to declare himself.

He was, however, little prepared for the rapid movements of the two English generals. Cöel, Delhi, Agra, and Laswarrie on the one side, and Assaye and Argaum on the other, all fought within a period of little more than two months, took him somewhat by surprise, and for a moment he appeared undecided as to his action. Even after peace had been signed with Scindia and the Bhonsla at Surjee Arjengaum, he long hesitated as to whether he should plunder the former, weakened by his losses, or, cementing an alliance with him, turn his arms against the British.

For a moment he seemed inclined to the former course, and it was from a real apprehension of his aggressions that Scindia made that application for the British contingent, to which reference has been made. But soon other counsels prevailed. Before proceeding against Scindia he felt that he must either have a guarantee for his own territories from the British, or he must show himself their master. He tried for both ends about the same time. Whilst the envoy whom he sent to Scindia had instructions to induce that prince to enter into an alliance for the destruction of the British, the agents he accredited to these latter were commissioned to make demands,* which, if acquiesced in, would have left him free to rebuild the Mahratta power on a basis more powerful than before.

But in both these attempts he over-reached himself.

* These were,—(1) leave to collect chout according to the custom of his ancestors, to obtain possession of Etawah and other territories in the Doab, Bundelkund, and Hurriana, formerly possessed by his ancestors; the guarantee of the country he then possessed; and a treaty similar to that concluded with Scindia.—*Thorn's War in India.*

Scindia, smarting under the blows, the severity of which he attributed mainly to the treachery of Holkar, informed the British Government of the overtures thus made to him, although, to maintain Jeswunt Rao in his delusion, he sent a return embassy to his camp, charged with professions of devotion. The letters * which, at the same time, Holkar despatched by the hands of his agents to the British generals, breathed a spirit so haughty, and a confidence in his own power so resolute, whilst, at the same time, his demands were so preposterous, that little doubt was left on the minds of either the Governor-General or the Commander-in-Chief that he was really bent on war.

We left General Lake encamped at Biana, opposite the pass leading into the dominions of the Rajah of Jyepore. He had taken up this position because, ever since the conclusion of the war with Scindia, the movements of Holkar had indicated an intention to make an incursion into those territories. Hence, before the receipt of the communications above referred to, he despatched a letter to Holkar warning him of the consequences of making war on any ally of the British nation, and advising him to remain within his own frontier. But Holkar cared little for such advice. Indeed, his first act after the receipt of this letter showed but too clearly that he had resolved to break altogether with the English. He at once sent for an English adventurer in his service, named Vickers, informed him

* In his letter to General Wellesley, he intimated that a war with him would not be without its perils, "that countries of many hundred miles should be overrun and plundered, General Lake shall not have leisure to breathe for a moment; and calamities shall fall on thousands of human beings by the attacks of my army which overwhelm like the waves of the sea."

of his resolution to fight, and asked him as to his willingness to join in a campaign against his own countrymen. On receiving from Vickers a positive refusal, he called up two others, Tod and Ryan, and put the same question to them. They also having declined, the three were simultaneously beheaded.* The heads were then fixed on lances in front of Jeswunt Rao's camp, and a public crier proclaimed that such would be the fate of every European who should fall into the hands of Holkar.

This barbarous murder,—the discovery about the same time of a correspondence with the Rohillas and Sikhs, having for its object a combination against us,—and the threatening position assumed by the forces of Holkar against Jyepore,—determined General Lake to break up from Biana, and advance into that territory. This resolution he carried out on the 9th February, after having sent back his heavy guns to Agra. He marched thence leisurely to Hindown, and annoyed only by the marauding propensities of the Mewatties, who lost no opportunity of plundering the baggage-carts and murdering all stragglers who fell in their way,† arrived there on the 20th. Here he received reinforcements, consisting of the two flank companies of the 22nd Regiment, the flank companies of the 1st Europeans, and five companies of the 16th Native Infantry. Here, too, negotiations were re-opened with Jeswunt

* The excuse privately alleged by Holkar was that he had detected these men in correspondence with the British general, and under Tod's head, he affixed a letter which, he pretended, that officer had received from General Lake. Vickers was one of his best officers, and had contributed greatly to the defeat of Scindia at Poona.

† Amongst these was an officer of the 15th Native Infantry, Lieutenant Tyson, murdered not far from the outposts.

Rao. No progress, however, having been made tending to a peaceful result, the army moved on the 8th March from Hindown to Ramgurh. It was here that the British Commander-in-Chief received the haughty and defiant letters to which we have already alluded. The agents, who were the bearers of these messages, showed likewise, by their arrogant language, a spirit not less haughty and self-confident. They openly avowed the connection of their master with the Rohillas and the Rajah of Bhurtpore; they stated that a war with Holkar could never be attended with any profit to his opponents, since he was a marauder by profession, and disposed of 150,000 cavalry, at whose head he could inflict terrible injury on our territories, whilst defeat in one place would not prevent his re-appearance in another. They also added that Scindia was with them, and that a powerful French army had already landed on the coast, and was marching to their aid.

The Commander-in-Chief contented himself with the dismissal of these envoys from the camp, with advice to Holkar to be more moderate in his demands, and continued his advance. Arriving on the 23rd at Ballaheera, he received a copy of the letter addressed by Jeswunt Rao to General Wellesley.* No further doubt remained on his mind as to the intentions of that chieftain, and learning a few days later that he had actually plundered the territories of the Jyepore Rajah, he applied for and obtained the orders of the Government to act against him as an enemy.

On the 16th April, Marquess Wellesley issued instructions to the officers commanding in the Dekkan to

* Vide note to page 74.

co-operate with the movement against Holkar, which the Commander-in-Chief had been instructed to make from the side of Hindostan. General Lake, meanwhile, had marched from Ballaheera, and, on the 17th of April, reached Dowsa, about fifty miles from Jyepore. From this place he resolved to detach three native regiments under the command of Colonel Monson to protect that city, and to observe the movements of Jeswunt Rao.

Colonel Monson was a very gallant soldier. He had particularly distinguished himself at the capture of Allygurh, where he led the storming party, and received a severe wound. This wound had not only caused him much suffering, but it had prevented him from taking part in the subsequent actions of the campaign. It was, therefore, to compensate him for his enforced absence from the fields of Delhi and Laswarrie, and to give him a second opportunity of distinction, that the Commander-in-Chief entrusted to him the command of the detachment destined to bear the first brunt of the encounter with Jeswunt Rao.

The force commanded by Colonel Monson consisted of both battalions of the 12th Native Infantry, the 2nd battalion 2nd Native Infantry, a detachment of European artillery, and some native cavalry levies commanded by Lieutenant Lucan and the Baraitch Nawab, with a Mahratta contingent under Bapoojee Scindia, a relation of Dowlut Rao. Pushing on towards Jyepore, Colonel Monson encamped near the city on the 21st, and found Holkar's army occupying a threatening position to the south of it. On the morning of the 23rd, however, Holkar, without making any demonstration against the city or the British force, broke up from his encampment and marched to the south. But as it did not appear to be his intention to evacuate the country north of the Chumbul, the Commander-in-Chief directed Colonel Monson to continue his advance, he himself following with the bulk of the army. As the British army approached, Holkar still continued to retreat, but it was not apparently until Rampoora, a strong fort in the district of Tonk, had been gallantly stormed by Colonel Don, at the head of a force* detached from the main army, that he abandoned all hopes of maintaining himself on the northern bank of the Chumbul. On the fall of that place he retreated precipitately to the south.

Satisfied with the disappearance of the enemy to the southward, and anxious to recruit the European portion of his army, then suffering extremely from the heat, General Lake resolved to postpone any serious operations until after the rainy season. He accordingly reinforced Colonel Monson with two native battalions under Lieutenant-Colonel Don, thus raising his numbers to about 4000 men, and instructed him to cover the Jyepore country, whilst he should move with the main body upon Agra and Cawnpore. There was not the smallest idea that Colonel Monson's force would be attacked. Hitherto Holkar had shown but one disposition,—to flee,—and it was believed that the movement ordered by General Wellesley, and entrusted to Colonel Murray, to march from Guzerat upon Indore, would effectually prevent Holkar from attempting to recover ground in the north.

To open communications with this force, Colonel

* This force consisted of five companies of the 8th Native Infantry, the flank companies of the 2nd battalion 21st Native Infantry, the 3rd regiment Native Cavalry, and some guns.

Monson, after the departure of the Commander-in-Chief, moved* on from Kotah, where it was previously encamped, through the Mokundra Pass to Sonara. Having detached hence one regiment to take possession of the small but strong fort of Hinglaizghur, he marched on, notwithstanding bad roads and very rainy weather, to the village of Peeplah. Here he received information that Holkar had suddenly retraced his steps, and was encamped with a strong force of all arms on the river Chumbul, some five-and-twenty miles distant, covering the town of Rampoora,† and guarding the only ford across the river by which it could be approached.

Colonel Monson had with him but three days' provisions, and he had experienced the greatest difficulty in obtaining supplies from the people of the country. He might indeed expect, could he reach Rampoora, to victual his camp, but between him and that place lay the river Chumbul and the numerous army of Holkar. To stay at Peeplah with but three days' supplies was impossible. To retreat to Hinglaizghur or to the Mokundra Pass before an enemy who had always hitherto fled before him, was not to be thought of. Rumours, too, reached him that the movement of Holkar indicated great infirmity of purpose, inasmuch as he had re-crossed the river, and appeared half-inclined once more to retreat. Nothing seemed so likely, in the judgment of Colonel Monson, to compel him to such a movement, as a daring and resolute advance. Notwithstanding, then, the heavy rain that fell all that night,

* This movement was made by Colonel Monson on his own authority, and was rather opposed to the general instructions he received from General Lake. The Commander-in-Chief, in fact, blamed him for having made it.

† Not the fort Rampoora previously referred to.

Colonel Monson resolved to act as a soldier bred in the school of Lake, and to move forward.

Onward, then, he marched, on the 7th July, to Gooree, within six or eight miles of the enemy. But he had not been long on this encamping ground when intelligence reached him of a nature to shake his resolution. First he learned that Holkar had crossed the Chumbul, then that he had re-crossed; but finally, at nine o'clock in the evening, it was affirmed that he had passed the river with his whole army, and was himself sitting on the left bank, with two lakhs of rupees before him, from which he was distributing largesses to his army. This at least seemed to indicate action. Orders were therefore issued to the troops to remain under arms all night, ready for any contingency that might occur.

But if Colonel Monson, in his advance from Peeplah to Gooree had been mindful of the example of his great leader, now, when difficulties increased upon him, he showed that he did not possess that deliberate coolness, that imperturbable presence of mind under all circumstances, which constituted one of the secrets of the success of General Lake. Instead of taking counsel only from his own brave heart, and making that forward movement which, in all probability, would have induced Holkar to retreat without an action, he took the advice tendered to him by Bapoojee Scindia, who was in secret correspondence with Jeswunt Rao, and resolved to retreat. He was confirmed in this view by a rumour which reached him about the same time, and which was probably invented by the enemy, that Colonel Murray had found the difficulties to his advance too great to be surmounted, and had resolved to fall back on the river Mhye. In vain did his best officers entreat him to advance. In vain did Lieutenant Lucan beg him, on his knees, to attack Holkar, offering himself to encounter that chief with his own few levies. Colonel Monson had made up his mind. Telling Lieutenant Lucan that he, if he chose, might stay to encounter the whole Mahratta army, he gave orders for a retrograde movement. Holding his ground only during the night, he despatched at four o'clock in the morning his baggage and camp equipage in the direction of Sonara, following at 9 A.M. with the infantry and guns, leaving the cavalry under Lucan to cover the retreat. His hope was to reach the Mokundra Pass before the enemy could overtake him. Once there, he calculated on being able to obtain supplies from his rear, and to defend the pass against all the force that Holkar could bring against it.

We have been careful to detail the movements of Colonel Monson up to the moment when he decided upon this retrograde movement in front of a barbarian enemy, because it affords an illustration of the great difference between the action of a master and that of a pupil, who, though trained in that master's school, lacks the qualities which, in him, makes boldness almost synonymous with safety. The world's history abounds with such instances. The pupils and successors of that Frederick, who for seven years had made head against combined Europe, were crushed in a single campaign by only one of the powers which, when united with others, he had long baffled. The troops were the same, the principles of warfare he adopted were well known, the difference was simply that he possessed the power of knowing how to apply those principles, and they did not. It was the difference of the organization of one man's brain. So it was with Monson and Lake. Trained in the school of the latter, having seen what wonderful successes had attended him from merely advancing, Monson resolved to follow out that principle himself. When, therefore, he heard that the enemy were but twenty miles distant from him on the Chumbul, he advanced to within eight. Then, according to his calculations, the enemy ought to have retreated. But as they did not retreat, as they even showed a disposition to advance, Monson, possessing no creative power of his own, no innate evidence to force upon himself conviction, being but a copier without the talent to originate, became helpless as a babe. He had pursued Lake's system up to a certain point, then dropped it at the very moment when not to pursue it to the end was to court failure and destruction. If Lake had advanced so far he would have advanced further. He would, in such a difficulty,—and, no doubt, it was a great difficulty,—have made up for the superior numbers of the enemy by the superior *morale* which the act of advancing would have given to his troops. His forward movement would have inspired confidence in his own men, have diminished it in the soldiers of Holkar, already distrustful of themselves, and half-demoralised by repeated retreats. The difference between the two men was simply this, that the greater the danger, the more cool, the more self-possessed, the more daring, was General Lake; Colonel Monson, on the contrary, though possessing equal courage, could not see that in war, as in most other contingencies, when circumstances are more than usually threatening, boldness is prudence.

Into the full details of the unfortunate retreat it is unnecessary that we should enter. The outline we give will be sufficient to show the infinitely greater dangers likely to be encountered by the general who retreats from, than by him who advances to attack, a barbarian enemy. The infantry had not left their ground three hours, before the Mahratta cavalry, 20,000 in number, flushed with the sense of superiority, and inspirited by the thought that they were the attacking party, dashed upon the Anglo-Indian horse. In the short but desperate contest that followed Lieutenant Lucan * and the Baraitch Nawab were completely overpowered. After fighting with all the energy of despair, they were both wounded and taken prisoners. Their combined squadrons were cut up, the galloper guns were taken, whilst the traitor Bapoojee Scindia went over to the enemy. Meanwhile, the infantry and guns retreated, the first day, 29 miles, to Soonara, the second day, nearly 20 miles, to the entrance of the Mokundra Pass. Here Monson was attacked, after having refused a summons to surrender, by the whole force of the enemy, but after a contest which lasted from eleven o'clock in the morning to six o'clock in the evening, he succeeded in driving them back in confusion.

It had been Colonel Monson's intention to hold the Mokundra Pass, the entrance to which was strongly fortified, and to wait there provisions and reinforcements. But fearing, on his arrival, that the enemy might cut him off from Kotah, he resolved to retreat at once to that place, leaving Colonel Don, with one battalion, to defend the pass till the morning.

Three days of heavy marching brought the force, re-united by the junction of Colonel Don, who had suc-

* He died soon afterwards at Kotah.

cessfully performed the part allotted to him, to Kotah; but as the Rajah of that place showed himself hostile, refusing provisions, and even retaining some stores that had been left in his charge, it moved, at 9 P.M. of the 12th, to Gunneas Ghât on the Chumbul. This place was reached, after a most fatiguing march, on the 13th, and the river crossed with much difficulty on the 14th. in the midst of pouring rain. On the 15th the retreat was continued, the men marching through a very heavy country, the black soil of which was sticky with rain, from 10 A.M. to 7 P.M., taking refuge then, without order, discipline, or regard for rank, but crowding promiscuously together, in the huts of a deserted village. On the 16th, the ground becoming from incessant rain even heavier, the guns were spiked and left; our troops, notwithstanding, though marching eight hours, only accomplished as many miles. On the 17th, the force reached the Chumbullee Nullah, near the entrance of the Lackerie Pass. Here, in consequence of the swollen state of the nullah, it was compelled to halt till the 26th, in great distress from want of food, and harassed by attacks from the enemy's parties. On the evening of that day the troops commenced crossing, but during the operation a great portion of their baggage-cattle were carried off by the enemy's horse. However, on the morning of the 27th, the entire force had crossed over, and had begun its march towards the Lackerie Pass, Colonel Don bringing up the rear. In this difficult march, the rear-guard suffered much from the attacks of the Menahs, and the entire remnant of the baggage had to be abandoned. On joining the main body that evening Colonel Don found a letter from Colonel Monson, announcing that he had resolved to precede the force to Rampoora.* The command, therefore, temporarily devolved upon Colonel Don.

On the 30th, after two dreadful marches, with but little food available, the force reached Rampoora. Here, after many orders and counter-orders, Colonel Monson, who re-assumed command, resolved to halt until he should receive the reinforcements which his urgent requisitions to the Commander-in-Chief had led him to expect.

These reinforcements, consisting of the 2nd battalion 9th Native Infantry, and the 1st battalion 14th Native Infantry, with six guns and a corps of irregular cavalry, arrived on the 14th, but brought with them no supplies. Between this date and the 21st August, the force halted at Rampoora, threatened by Holkar on the one side, and by Bapoojee Scindia on the other. There can be little doubt that Colonel Monson might have made a successful stand at this place, as the fort of Rampoora was very strong, and the Tonk country favourable for the supply of his army. He had, too, received letters from General Lake, informing him of his having ordered, on the first news of his retreat, all the infantry in Agra to march to his assistance. But, to use his own expression, "his mind was so distracted," he could not think coolly upon any point. Instead, therefore, of remaining halted at Rampoora, he resolved to retreat to Kooshalgurh, where he expected he might be joined by a considerable detachment of Scindia's troops. Before doing this, he informed the commanding officers of his intention, adding that it would be for them to make their way to Agra as best they could.

* The fort in the Tonk district.

To retreat to Kooshalgurh Colonel Monson had to cross the river Bunass, and, in attempting this on the 24th, after having left one battalion in garrison at Rampoora, he was attacked in force by Holkar, and was most severely handled. Colonel Monson himself behaved with conspicuous bravery, but the 2nd battalion 2nd regiment was almost annihilated, several of his best officers were killed or wounded, one howitzer was lost, and the spirits of native officers and men received a terrible shock. He succeeded, however, in reaching Kooshalgurh on the night of the 25th, after marching 36 miles, during which he was exposed to the repeated attacks of the enemy's horse. At this place he was fortunate enough to meet a thousand Brinjarrie bullocks, which had been sent from Agra with grain for the use of his detachment, and which, fortunately, Holkar had just missed. Scindia's detachment, however, which he expected would aid him, showed a decidedly hostile disposition. Great as had been Colonel Monson's troubles up to this period, they now became infinitely greater. During that night and the following day, the enemy came up in large numbers and surrounded the town, our troops retiring within it, and manning the walls to keep off attack. As the place, however, was not at all capable of defence, Colonel Monson determined to avail himself of the darkness to retire,—whither he scarcely knew. At 8 P.M. of the 26th the attempt was made, our troops forming a square, and moving off in that formation. The retreat, however, was soon discovered, and 20,000 cavalry were immediately on their track. But the steadiness of the 2nd battalion 21st regiment, who formed the rear-face of the square, caused all their attacks, though they continued up to noon of the following day, to fail. The last remaining gun of the force, a howitzer, was, however, spiked and abandoned.

The attacks of the enemy ceasing about noon of the next day, our troops hurried on, living on the hard grain which they had no time to cook, and came about sunset within sight of Hindown. But, to their disappointment, they found it partly occupied by the enemy. Unwilling to risk a contest for its possession with a demoralised army, and an enemy following in his rear, Colonel Monson moved to the ruins of an old fort in the neighbourhood, and gave his men a few hours of repose. They were but a few, however. At one o'clock in the morning, silently and stealthily, they marched on again in the same formation, this time without attracting much attention from the enemy. At daylight, however, the Mahratta horse was seen swarming in their track, accompanied by camels carrying small guns, which, together with rockets, they occasionally discharged. At seven o'clock the force, on emerging from some intricate ravines in very straggling order, perceived that the enemy had formed up in front and on either side of them. Almost before they could realise their position the famed Mahratta cavalry was upon them. But in this terrible extremity, the sepoys showed themselves worthy of their training. Forgetting their long marches, the harassing disquietudes of the previous two months, they formed up steadily, reserved their fire till the enemy were within fifty yards, and then poured in a continuous file-firing. First on the right, then, in lesser numbers, on the front and left faces, did the daring horsemen of Jeswunt Rao make charge after charge. In vain, however. They were as powerless against those brave sepoys as were the chivalry of France against the solid squares of British infantry at Waterloo.

Finding all their attempts to break the square by means of cavalry ineffectual, the enemy commenced the more sure method of pouring in a steady fire from their matchlockmen and camel pieces. In this our troops suffered terribly. Colonel Monson, therefore, moved on, still in square, the enemy hovering about him, and keeping up a desultory fire. Our troops experienced great difficulty in crossing a nullah in their way, and having halted in the ravines beyond it, they again suffered terribly from the matchlock fire which was poured on them from the high banks of the nullah. Many of their wounded fell during the day into the enemy's hands.

Under such circumstances, to halt was certain destruction. Although night was fast coming on, it was, therefore, determined still to move forward. Exposed to a fire from the enemy in the rear, and from the Menahs who lined the high grounds on their left, they straggled into the Biana Pass, one of the most difficult, from its narrowness and steep ravines, in the country. Here the semblance of discipline almost entirely ceased.* Detachments, even individuals, separated from one another. It was impossible to keep any order. *Sauve qui peut* was all that remained for the boldest to dream of. One officer,† who had been overcome by sleep, awoke only to find himself alone. Nor was his a solitary exception. The force which four months before had marched through

* The one corps, however, that did keep some kind of formation to the very last, was the 1st battalion 14th Native Infantry, commanded by Colonel Ashe.

† Colonel Don.

this very pass, full of the highest hopes, had become a disorganised rabble, without discipline or power of cohesion.

No further attempt was made to rally. The next day some stragglers found themselves at Futtehpore Sikree; but even here there was no rest for them, the very townspeople treating them as outcasts, and firing upon them. It only remained for them, as best they could, to push on to Agra. With the poor remnant of strength yet remaining to them, this was attempted by all who possessed the power of motion, and that day and the following the ingress of wretched, footsore, half-starved fugitives, dispirited in mind as much as battered in body, conveyed to the garrison of Agra some idea of the humiliation that is ever in store for the general who retreats before a barbarian enemy.* Would the effect have been worse, would it have been half so bad, if Colonel Monson had attacked Holkar at Rampoora, and been destroyed?

It is easy to imagine the impression which these straggling messengers of defeat produced on the mind of General Lake. For his brilliant achievements in the campaign against Scindia he had received the thanks of Parliament, and had been created, on the 1st of September, Baron Lake of Delhi and Laswarrie, and of Ashton Clinton, in the county of Buckingham. Although he did not receive intimation of these honours till after the siege of Bhurtpore, yet the consciousness of having deserved, the knowledge of the reputation he had ac-

* Our loss in officers during this retreat was fourteen killed; three taken prisoners (of whom one was murdered and one died); one drowned; nine wounded: total, twenty-seven. The loss of the men was never accurately ascertained.

quired, constituted inducements, which, had his own inclinations been wanting,—a contingency of all others most unlikely,—would have impelled him to the same prompt action which formed the foundation of his fame.

Colonel Monson's misfortune had been in no respect owing to Lord Lake. That officer had, in the first place, advanced considerably beyond the limit which the Commander-in-Chief had considered necessary or safe. Having, in the second place, moved on from Peeplah with the declared intention of attacking Holkar on the Chumbul,—an attack in which success would not have been at all improbable,—he had first hesitated, and then retreated, drawing the enemy after him. Thirdly, he had abandoned the pass of Mokundra,—the one place where he might have made a successful stand before his army had become disorganised. And fourthly, after reaching Tonk Rampoora, he had first resolved to halt and defend it, but after five days' hesitation had abandoned it in despair, telling his army to make the best of their way to Agra. For none of these vacillations, of these erratic movements, had the Commander-in-Chief been responsible. None wondered at them more than he, and in his despatch to Marquess Wellesley he had expressed his surprise that a man, "brave as a lion, should have no judgment or reflection."

But Colonel Monson was wanting in something besides judgment and reflection. He himself alleged that he decided to retreat, because he had no experience of, and no confidence in, the native soldiers.* In this respect

* In noticing this avowal on the part of Colonel Monson, and the consequences resulting from it, the Court of Directors issued an order that no purely native force should ever again be placed under the command of an officer of the Royal Army. This order was never deviated from until the period of the Affghanistan war, and then with

he again contrasts unfavourably with Lord Lake, who, by showing confidence in those native soldiers, made them accomplish seeming impossibilities. But if Colonel Monson possessed not sufficient confidence in his men to lead them on to an attack, they at least showed by their courage, their fortitude, their constancy, their wonderful endurance, during the retreat in which his incapacity involved them, some of the best qualities of disciplined soldiers. These "military proletarians," fighting for an alien flag, and an alien people, for a nation differing from them in manners and professing a proselytising faith, displayed from the first to the last hour of that terrible trial, a fidelity to their engagements that has been never surpassed, a devotion to duty which might serve as an example to many Western armies. Though exposed to munificent offers from the emissaries of Holkar, they remained true to their colours, and the scattered remains of that retreating army, though severed for a moment from the main force, hastened to rally under the walls of Agra.

But great as was the misfortune, and though it was in no way attributable to him, Lord Lake did not the less display a resolution to repair it with alacrity. He was not the man, indeed, to whine over disasters, however severe, after they had been accomplished. If his lieutenant had failed, it was for him to obliterate the effects of that lieutenant's error. Upon this principle he acted with the promptitude natural to him. He sent instructions to all the troops he could spare from the

results which were not very favourable. We have not space to refer here, as we could have wished, to the magnanimity shown by Marquess Wellesley towards Colonel Monson. It is paralleled by the generous conduct of Napoleon to Marmont after Salamanca.

several stations under his command to concentrate at Agra, and he himself, hastily fitting out the force immediately about him, marched with it, on the 3rd September, for that place.

Meanwhile, Jeswunt Rao Holkar had not been idle. His pursuit of Colonel Monson's force had not, indeed, been conducted with all the vigour and energy that might have been expected from a man of his undaunted and enterprising character, for, even in defeat, the prestige gained at Cöel, at Delhi, and at Laswarrie, was, to a certain point, a safeguard. In the novel position in which he found himself, Jeswunt Rao, after one or two vain attempts, had abstained from coming to too close quarters even with a retreating and disorganised sepoy army, led by European officers. He pursued them incessantly, as we have seen, from the banks of the Chumbul to the Biana Pass, and even to Futtehpore Sikri. Hence he advanced on the 16th September to Muttra, of which, as it had been evacuated by our troops on the 15th, he took possession, together with much grain and baggage that had been stored there. But though at the head of 60,000 horse and 15,000 infantry, he did not venture to move upon Agra, contenting himself with sending flying parties into the Doab, which were easily repulsed.

Such was the state of affairs when Lord Lake, at the head of the 8th, 27th, and 29th regiments of dragoons, the flank companies 22nd regiment, the 76th regiment, with some artillery, reached Agra on the 27th of the month. He moved at once to Secundra, joined the native troops already arrived there, and, on the 1st October, marched in the direction of Muttra. On the 3rd he arrived close to this place. Holkar, however, had no wish to risk an action. His plans were conceived in a far abler spirit. He wished to delay as much as possible the advance of Lord Lake, by means of his numerous cavalry, whilst his infantry, hurrying on to Delhi, should endeavour to take that place and gain possession of the person of the emperor, by a *coup-de-main.* He had already despatched his infantry for that purpose, whilst with his cavalry he took up a position at the village of Aurung, four miles from Muttra.

Unsuspicious of this device on the part of Holkar, Lord Lake moved from Muttra early on the morning of the 7th to attack him at Aurung. Holkar, however, was true to his tactics. He at once evacuated his position without an action, and retreated more quickly than he could be pursued. On the 10th, a second attempt ended in a similar manner.* On the following evening, Lord Lake received intelligence of the movement of the enemy's infantry upon Delhi. Early on the morning of the 12th, therefore, he took the road to that place, the enemy giving way before him.

Meanwhile, in pursuance of his plan, Holkar's infantry and some cavalry appeared before Delhi on the 7th. The defences of that city were in a very dilapidated condition. The walls were shattered, the ram-

* The Mahratta tactics on these occasions are thus described by Major Thorn:—"Our cavalry, formed in two lines, moved in columns of half regiments at regular intervals. In this order, we swept clear the whole plain where the enemy were encamped at full gallop; but could not succeed in our endeavours to charge them, for they scampered off in all directions, dispersing as usual. When we halted, they did the same, rallied and stood gazing at us; and when we turned our backs to return home, they dashed on, attacking our rear and flanks, firing long shots with their matchlocks, while those who were armed with spears and *tulwars*, flourished their weapons, making at the same time, a noise like jackals by way of bravado."

parts mostly fallen in, and the bastions in a state of decay. The garrison consisted of two regular native regiments, the 2nd battalion 4th, 2nd battalion 14th Native Infantry, four companies of the 17th Native Infantry, and about 1100 matchlockmen. The deficiency of the troops and the weak state of the defences were, however, more than compensated for by the fact that he who wielded the authority of the Governor-General within those walls, was no other than Colonel David Ochterlony. Under this distinguished officer, as military commandant, was Lieutenant-Colonel William Burn.

It is impossible, and indeed unnecessary, to enter in this place into the history of the gallant defence of that important city. For seven days the forces of Holkar, consisting of 10,000 infantry, 8000 cavalry, 160 guns, commanded by Bapoojee Scindia, used all the means in their power to master the place. They hazarded several assaults, but in all they were repulsed. On the 14th they made a grand attempt to escalade it at various points, but not in one single quarter did they make any impression. The vigilance of Colonel Ochterlony, and the gallant conduct of Colonel Burn and his native troops, completely baffled the besiegers. They retreated that night, leaving the scaling-ladders standing.

On the 18th Lord Lake arrived. He had pushed on with all practicable speed from Muttra, leaving on the route, unattacked and even unmasked, three or four strong places which defied his authority. In thus acting, he showed that disregard of rule, the correct application of which is the best test of a true general. He would neither be put off his main object of relieving Delhi, nor weaken the force by which that relief was to be effected. The intelligence of his rapid approach materially influenced the enemy in their retreat on the 14th. Anxious as he was to improve that occasion by an immediate pursuit of the baffled battalions of Jeswunt Rao, he was yet forced to a few days' inaction by that most urgent of all necessities,—the necessity of providing food for his troops. On the 25th he was able to despatch a small force, under Colonel Burn, to relieve a Mr. Guthrie, who was besieged by the Sikhs at Saharunpore, and on the 30th, having meanwhile received intelligence that Holkar had crossed the Jumna at Paniput, and had poured with his whole force into the Doab, he started himself in pursuit at the head of three regiments of dragoons, three of native cavalry, a troop of horse artillery, and Colonel Don's reserve brigade of infantry. The main body of infantry and two regiments of native cavalry he left at Delhi, under the command of Major-General Fraser, with instructions to observe the movements of the enemy in that quarter, and, under certain conditions, to attack him.

Meanwhile Holkar, whose army had been reinforced by levies from Scindia's territory, and by the troops of the Rajah of Bhurtpore, having crossed the Jumna, proceeded in the direction of Saharunpore, hoping to overtake and destroy the detachment which, under the command of Lieutenant-Colonel Burn, had been sent to that place. His advanced parties came up with our sepoys on the afternoon of the 28th at Bagonrah, and succeeded in carrying off some camels. Alarmed at their increasing numbers, Colonel Burn moved off the same afternoon, and marching all night, reached Shamlie at sunrise, having been harassed all the way by the enemy. He intended thence to advance to

Saharunpore, but whilst his men were taking some slight refreshment, Jeswunt Rao came up with his whole force, and took possession of the only road by which an advance was possible. Colonel Burn, therefore, had no resource but to stay where he was, to await the assistance he had asked from Lord Lake. He moved his men, therefore, on the 30th into a small mud fort, and in that, though with but a small stock of provisions, took his stand.

Here, for three days, he was attacked by the whole force of Holkar. At the end of that time the consumption of his provisions, and the impossibility of procuring fresh supplies, caused matters to look serious, and he was seriously debating the expediency of attempting to cut his way back to Delhi, when the retreat of the Mahrattas announced the approach of the Commander-in-Chief.

It was true. On the 3rd Lord Lake's army arrived, having marched eleven and a half hours the previous day, and at once Jeswunt Rao was in retreat. He retired through the Doab, pillaging the villages in his route. Lord Lake halted on the 4th, and resumed the pursuit on the 5th. He followed the enemy by forced marches to Meerut, where he left Colonel Burn and a detachment, thence through Haupper, Mallargurh, and Sheerpore to Allygunje, which village he found burning on his arrival.* Here he learnt that Jeswunt Rao was at Furruckabad, thirty-six miles ahead. He resolved on pursuit that very night with the cavalry. At 9 P.M., the troopers were mounting for the purpose, when he received intelligence of a great victory gained over the main body of the enemy's infantry by General Fraser

* *Thorn.*

at Deeg, not far from the scene of his own triumph at Laswarrie. To the movements that brought about that action we must now revert.

General Fraser had been left at Delhi, with a force consisting of the 76th regiment, the Company's European regiment, and six native battalions. Knowing that his infantry and heavy artillery had not accompanied Holkar in his raid into the Doab, General Fraser, in pursuance of instructions received from Lord Lake, left Delhi in search of them on the 6th, and sighted them at a distance of six miles, from the heights of Goverdon, on the 12th November. They had chosen a very strong position. Their left flank was resting on the fort of Deeg, bristling with cannon; their left and centre were covered by a morass; and their right by a village which they had carefully fortified. General Fraser's plan was soon made. He resolved to turn the morass, and penetrating between it and a large tank that lay behind it, either to destroy the enemy or drive them within the fort. Leaving two native battalions to protect the baggage, he moved with the remainder of his force along the face of the morass, and, passing the village on which the enemy's right rested, formed up his troops at right angles to their line. Having effected this movement without opposition, he directed the 76th to take the village. This they easily did, then charging down the declivity they attacked, and with the aid of the European and native regiments by whom they were supported, carried the first range of guns. Here, however, they were exposed to a tremendous fire from the second range, a shot from which took off the General's leg. The command then devolved upon Colonel Monson. He instantly ordered a fresh advance upon the guns, and, under his gallant direction, battery after battery was abandoned, and the enemy forced to take refuge under the guns of the fort.* But whilst engaged in this advance, the enemy's horse, making a détour, came upon the rear of our army, re-took the first range, and turned the guns against our men. But Captain Norford, of the 76th, taking with him only twenty-eight men of that regiment, drove off this new enemy, though he lost his life in accomplishing the feat. There still remained a body of the enemy who had been posted at the lower end of the morass, watched by the native infantry under Captain Hammond. Upon these Colonel Monson now moved, and taking them in flank with some six-pounder guns, drove those who escaped that fire into the morass. Colonel Monson then encamped on the field of battle, advancing his pickets just beyond cannon-shot of the fort, to watch the enemy's garrison.†

This was the intelligence brought to Lord Lake at nine o'clock on the evening of the 15th November, two days after the battle, just as he was starting to surprise Holkar at Furruckabad. Inspirited by the news, which was at once communicated to them, the troopers moved on, eagerly desirous to emulate the deeds of their comrades. Marching all night, lighted up by the soft rays

* The fort of Deeg belonged to the Rajah of Bhurtpore, who was nominally our ally; but from the time of Monson's retreat or even earlier, he had been in secret communication with Holkar.

† The loss of the Anglo-Indian army in this action amounted to 5 officers killed, and 17 wounded; 621 men were killed and wounded. The loss of the enemy was computed at nearly 2000. General Fraser died a few days after the action from his wound. Amongst the 87 pieces of ordnance captured by Colonel Monson, were eleven 6-pounders, two 12-pounders, and one howitzer taken from Colonel Monson in his retreat.—*Thorn.*

of the moon, the advanced guard of the force reached at daybreak the enemy's encampment. Holkar was entirely unsuspicious of their vicinity. He had been enjoying a *nautch* the night before,* when in the midst of it he too received intimation of the disaster at Deeg. Troubled in spirit, he quitted the entertainment without communicating with his chiefs. Nor was he the more re-assured when the fire of artillery convinced him that the adversary he most dreaded in the world was upon him. Forgetting in a moment the fame he had acquired, the boasts he had indulged in, his visions of empire and dominion, taking counsel only from his own fears, he mounted his steed, and followed by those horsemen who were ready, fled with all speed towards Mainpore, not drawing rein till he had placed eighteen miles of road and the river Kalini between himself and the battle-field. It was just as well that he did flee. On reaching the Mahratta camp at daybreak, Lord Lake had found a grave-like quiescence, the very sentries asleep at their post. Instantly he brought up his horse artillery, and awoke the startled Mahrattas with the roar of his cannon. Then, as they rose up in their hurry and confusion, he dashed amongst them with his cavalry, sabring them in numbers. Those that had the opportunity fled, and for ten miles these were followed up with all the energy that success inspires.†

The vigour of the pursuit which thus met its crowning fortune at Furruckabad, has never been surpassed in military history. The force which left Delhi on the

* *Thorn.*

† Our loss amounted to 2 men killed, 20 wounded; that of the enemy was computed at 3000. The desertions from Holkar after the action were very numerous.—*Thorn.*

31st October had, in the interval between that and the morning of the 17th November, marched 350 miles, rescuing in its course a beleaguered garrison from the clutches of the enemy. In the twenty-four hours immediately preceding the battle, it had marched upwards of seventy miles. It added not a little to the powers of endurance of both officers and men to see that every fatigue, every hardship, were cheerfully shared by their revered chief; to behold him ever prompt to lead them on, ever foremost in the battle or the charge, anxious only to get at the enemy, to bring him to close quarters. What could they not have done, in any part of the world, against any enemy in the world, those troops, under that leader?

Those who have followed the career of Lord Lake thus far, will have noticed how much an essential part of his military system it was to follow up a victory. A victory, in fact, he regarded as nothing without results. Although, therefore, he had driven Holkar with great loss from Furruckabad, he regarded him as not the less an enemy to be pursued and annihilated. He pushed on, therefore, rapidly in pursuit, and finding that he had made for the fort of Deeg, he moved in the direction of that place, and joined the infantry under Colonel Monson on the 28th November, encamped between Muttra and Deeg. Waiting some days for a siege-train from Agra, the army, after moving to within sight of Deeg, took up, on the 13th, a position before that fortress, and opened fire on the following morning. On the 22nd, a practicable breach was effected in one of the outworks, at one of the angles of the city, and a storming party was detached to assault in the dark hours just preceding midnight.

This storming party consisted of three columns,* under the command of Lieutenant-Colonel Macrae. These reached the points of attack indicated a little before twelve o'clock, and at that hour made the assault. The night was extremely dark, and the enemy were taken by surprise. Their resistance, nevertheless, was of a very obstinate nature, as their guns had been laid to sweep the ground immediately in front of their defences. They could not, however, resist the determined valour of our troops, and though their artillery-men stood to be bayonetted at their guns, and their infantry, under cover of the darkness, even attempted to re-take them, it was in vain. By two o'clock in the morning our troops were in possession of the outwork.† This capture so dispirited the enemy that they abandoned the citadel and town on the following day, leaving all their guns behind them, and retiring to Bhurtpore. Our troops entered the citadel on Christmas morning, 1804.

But satisfactory as was the capture of this strong fortress, Lord Lake felt strongly that his work would be incomplete so long as its late master, Runjeet Singh, Rajah of Bhurtpore, was enabled to bid defiance to us from, and to afford protection to the troops of the

* The right column composed of four companies 1st Europeans, and five companies 1st battalion 12th Native Infantry, under Captain Kelly; the left of four companies 1st Europeans, and five 1st battalion 12th Native Infantry, under Major Radcliffe; and the centre, of the flank companies 22nd, 76th, and 1st Europeans, and 1st battalion 8th Native Infantry, under Colonel Macrea.

† In this attack we lost 43 men killed, and 184 wounded. Among the former were two officers, and among the latter thirteen. One of these, Lieutenant Forrest, received upwards of twenty wounds, and was left for dead upon the field; however, he ultimately recovered. One hundred guns were-taken.—*Thorn.*

Holkar within the walls of his capital. Accordingly, after repairing the defences of Deeg, he moved on the 28th December to meet the 75th regiment, which was bringing up stores for the army. This done, he marched on the 1st, and on the 2nd took up his ground in front of Bhurtpore.

The fortress of Bhurtpore was strong, not only in its bastions and artillery, but in the numerous garrison, formed of the débris of the Mahratta infantry and of the hitherto unsubdued Jâts, by which it was defended. It stood in a plain covered with jungle, and abounding with several pieces of water. The town itself was eight miles in circumference, having thick mud walls, and a wide and deep ditch, capable of being rendered unfordable. In addition to the garrison within its walls, a considerable body of infantry had intrenched themselves outside and close to them, whilst the still numerous cavalry of Jeswunt Rao and his associate Ameer Khán moved about the neighbourhood, ready to take advantage of any favourable conjuncture.

Lord Lake, on the contrary, though at the head of an infantry and cavalry tried in many a battle, was but ill supplied with the artillery requisite for the attack of such a place. He had not, at the opening of the siege, more than three or four mortars of a useful calibre, and eight or ten battering-guns. When these, as was the case with some of them, became inefficient from excessive firing, he had none others to supply their place, but was compelled to use guns captured from Holkar, hurriedly furnished with bouches at Muttra. Knowing this deficiency, he had been strongly in favour of repeating the course followed at Allygurh, but had allowed himself to be persuaded, against his better judgment, to try the effect of a siege. He accordingly, though labouring under the disadvantages we have noticed, opened his attack with his wonted energy on the 7th January, dislodged with great slaughter the infantry intrenched beneath the walls, effected a breach on the 9th, and ordered a storming party for the same evening. This party,* headed by Colonel Maitland, moved out of camp at 8 o'clock in the evening, its advance being covered by a tremendous fire from the trenches. But the ground was so broken and swampy that it was found impossible to keep much order, and the party arrived at the ditch in some disarray. Twenty-three men of the 22nd, who were the first to arrive there, waded through it breast high, and even mounted the breach; but being unsupported they could effect nothing. The delay in bringing up supports was fatal. Losing two officers, and the third having left to bring up reinforcements, the few men of the 22nd fell back, and before the assault could be renewed, the enemy had concentrated a tremendous fire upon the approaches to it. The progress of the right and left columns to support the centre was also checked by defences which had not been foreseen. At length the centre column, having, after much difficulty found its way across the ditch, dashed at the breach led on by Colonel Maitland. But all the efforts of that gallant officer were vain. When near the summit of the

* It consisted of three columns; the left composed of 150 of the 1st Europeans, and a battalion of sepoys, under Lieutenant-Colonel Ryan; the right, of two companies of the 75th, and a battalion of sepoys, under Major Hawkes; and the centre, of the flank companies of the 22nd, 75th, 76th, and 1st Europeans, and a battalion of sepoys under Colonel Maitland.—*Thorn.*

breach he was shot dead. Other officers followed him, but to no purpose. The slaughter amongst them was terrible. At last, baffled but not humiliated, they were forced to retreat to the trenches, exposed, as they retired, to a tremendous fire from the enemy.*

Undaunted by this failure, which he justly attributed to the accident of the second column losing its way, Lord Lake at once re-commenced his fire on the place, and, on the 21st, had succeeded in effecting another breach a little to the right of the former one. This time it was determined to attempt the assault in the daytime, and having accurately ascertained the length and breadth of the ditch opposite the breach, little doubt was felt as to the result. At 3 o'clock in the afternoon the storming-party,† having been supplied with portable bridges‡ for surmounting the ditch, advanced to the assault. On reaching the ditch, which had been described the previous day as neither very broad nor deep in that particular part, it was found that the enemy had dammed it up below, and so that the water had accumulated to such a degree as to make even the ladders useless. Some of the men, however, headed by Lieutenant Morris, swam across and clambered up the breach. But the enemy had taken the precaution to withdraw the guns behind the parapet pointing them at the breach, and these opened a

* In this attempt we lost five officers and eighty-five men killed; twenty-four officers and three hundred and seventy-one wounded.

† Consisting of 150 men of the 76th; 120 of the 75th; 50 of the 22nd, supported by the remainder of those regiments, and the 2nd battalions of the 9th, 15th, and 22nd Native Infantry, the whole commanded by Colonel Macrae.—*Thorn.*

‡ These were three broad ladders covered with laths, and easily raised and depressed by levers at the bank of the ditch.—*Thorn.*

tremendous fire on the daring leaders of the assault. Seeing them thus exposed to certain death if they remained, and being unable to convey to them any aid, Colonel Macrae wisely sounded the recall, and hastened back to the trenches, not, however, without the very considerable loss of eighteen officers, and five hundred and seventy-three men, killed and wounded.

The failure of this second attack only rendered the Commander-in-Chief more resolute to persevere. In the spirit which animated the Roman senate when they thanked Terentius Varro after the loss of the battle of Cannæ, he issued to his troops a general order, acknowledging the gallantry and steadiness they had displayed in the attack, and expressing a confident hope that in a very few days the obstacles which had till then rendered all attempts fruitless would be surmounted. This order produced the very best effect,—an effect which was heightened by the repulse and subsequent pursuit of Ameer Khan after an attempt to intercept one of our convoys. That chieftain was himself intercepted, just as his attack on the convoy had failed, by Colonel Need and the 27th Dragoons, and in his bitter extremity only saved his life by stripping himself of his gaudy apparel, and fleeing with his own troopers. A second attempt made in greater force three days later, upon another detachment coming from Agra, was frustrated by the Commander-in-Chief in person, numbers of the enemy's infantry being cut up on the occasion.

From this date there was a lull in the siege operations, reinforcements being expected from Bombay. The interval, however, was employed in the preparation of fascines, pontoons, and rafts. On the 10th February, the reinforcements arrived.* Measures were at once taken more in unison with the scientific character of siege operations, and regular approaches were made, bringing our batteries much nearer to the walls of the city. These having been carried to the brink of the ditch, and a mine having been laid for the purpose of blowing up the counterscarp, it was determined to give the assault at 4 o'clock on the afternoon of the 20th February. This time the storming party† was entrusted to Lieutenant-Colonel Don, a very gallant officer, who had particularly distinguished himself at the capture of Rampoora, in command of the rear guard during Monson's retreat, and during the pursuit of Holkar in the Doab. The night before the assault was ordered the enemy made a sally which was for a time successful, and was only repulsed with loss. The sally was repeated in the morning, but the besieged were driven in, though not until they had cut up several of our men. The storming party then, at 3 P.M., started on its perilous errand, preceded by fifty men carrying fascines which were to be thrown into the ditch.

Again, however, a fatality attended the attack. Whether they were disheartened by previous failures, or were dispirited by the sight of the bodies of their comrades killed in the sally of the morning, or feared that the approach was mined, it is certain that the men

* Under Major-General Jones, consisting of the 86th regiment, eight companies 65th regiment, four battalions of sepoys, and 500 irregular horse.—*Thorn.*

† Consisting of one column composed of 200 of the 86th regiment, and the first battalion, 8th Native Infantry, under Captain Grant; of a second of 300 of the 65th regiment, and two battalions of Bombay sepoys, under Colonel Taylor, the centre column of details from the 75th and 76th regiments and 1st Europeans, and three battalions of sepoys.

composing the storming party stood hesitating at the exit of the approach unwilling to go on. In vain did Colonel Don entreat and exhort, they would not move. That officer, then, turning from the Europeans in front, called upon the men in rear to advance through them. Instantly there came forward a few men constituting the remnant of the detail of the 22nd Foot, and the 12th Native Infantry, supported by two guns. One sepoy at once ran at the breach, but it was impassable; the regiment then attempted a bastion on the right, which many of them succeeded in climbing, and on the top of which the colours of the 12th Native Infantry were planted. Just at this moment the enemy sprung their mine, without injury to our troops, and had the Europeans then taken advantage of the confusion, the place would assuredly have been stormed. But no exertion of the officers could rouse the men to action, and though fourteen of the former dashed to the front to encourage them, they were not followed, and Colonel Don had no resource but to draw off his men. Captain Grant's column succeeded in capturing and carrying off eleven guns, but owing to the failure of the centre column their success could not be followed up.*

Attributing this repulse to exceptional causes, Lord Lake resolved to renew the attack on the following day, prefacing it by a very heavy fire. In selecting the storming party, he thought it right, however, to address himself to the Europeans whose backwardness on the preceding day had led to the disaster. He spoke to them, however, in terms savouring more of regret than

* Our loss in this attack amounted to three officers and one hundred and sixty-two men killed; and twenty-five officers and 732 wounded.—*Thorn.*

of anger, at the same time offering as many of them as should be willing, an opportunity of retrieving their laurels by volunteering. They at once came forward to a man, and Lieutenant Templeton, of the 76th regiment, offered to lead the forlorn hope.

At 3 o'clock in the afternoon, therefore, the storming party,* under the leadership of Brigadier Monson, moved on to the assault. Again was the bastion selected as the point of attack, again were the British colours planted on its summit, though the action was fatal to Lieutenant Templeton who bore them. But few, however, could climb that rugged surface, the approaches to which, moreover, were commanded by a tremendous cross fire. In vain was every opening tried, were every means resorted to, to effect an entrance, for, after two hours' fruitless but heroic efforts, Brigadier Monson was compelled to give the order to retire.†

These four assaults had thus cost our army 103 officers and 3100 men in killed and wounded, and at the conclusion of the last failure, Lord Lake was in a worse position than when he commenced the siege. Not, indeed, that he had lost one iota of his indomitable resolution, but his siege-guns had become useless, his supply of ammunition had diminished, and whilst the confidence of the enemy had increased, that of his own men had been considerably shaken. He determined, therefore, to convert the siege into a blockade.

Those critics who judge by results have been very

* It consisted of the 1st Europeans, two battalions Bengal Native Infantry, the greater part of the 65th and 86th regiments, the grenadier battalion, and the flank companies of the 3rd Bengal Native Infantry.—*Thorn.*

† We lost on this occasion six officers and 125 men killed; twenty-eight officers and 862 wounded.

free in casting upon Lord Lake the entire blame of the enormous loss of life which occurred at the siege of Bhurtpore. We are willing to admit that the system of Lord Lake's warfare was adapted for anything rather than the slow process of a siege. And it is, we think, under those circumstances, to be regretted that he did not obey the prompting of his own inclinations, and attempt to follow the capture of Deeg by a *coup-de-main* on Bhurtpore. Such an attack, in the panic-stricken state of the enemy, would have, in all probability, been successful. It was the confidence gained by the besiegers from our first abortive efforts that contributed to the success of their defence. Once, however, having decided upon a siege, the Commander-in-Chief fell naturally into the hands of his engineers. It was for them to conduct those operations which form the preliminary to the final attack of the infantry on a place. Now nothing is clearer than that up to the time of the last assault, the engineers were utterly ignorant of the defences of Bhurtpore, or of the peculiarities of the ground immediately under its walls. To their incapacity in this respect Lord Lake frequently refers in his dispatches, and there can be little doubt that, no engineer himself, and depending much on his communications with officers of that service for his decisions, he felt, and felt deeply, that he had been led more than once to hazard the lives of his soldiers on impossible enterprises.

Inapplicable then to his case is that criticism which would transfer to Lord Lake the entire blame of these failures. It may be a question, indeed, whether with the inadequate means at his disposal he was justified in undertaking the siege of such a place. But here again experience was in favour of prompt action. Allygurh and Deeg had fallen without difficulty, and Bhurtpore had not, at the moment he sat down before it, any extraordinary means of defence. But for the accident occurring at the first assault, it would assuredly have fallen. But, even as it was, he did not fail in the main result he proposed to himself. It is true he did not take Bhurtpore by assault, but he compelled its Rajah to humble himself before the British power, to recede from the alliance with Holkar, to indemnify the Company for their expenses. Though he was repulsed, his policy was not the less successful. Those terrible assaults, though they resulted immediately in the retreat of our storming parties, led with no less certainty to the accomplishment of the object of the campaign. Had Lord Lake, on the other hand, hesitated to attack Bhurtpore, he would have been unable, having that strong position within thirty miles of our frontier, to venture far in pursuit of the indefatigable Holkar.

We cannot, then, altogether sympathize with these critics after the event. In the siege of Bhurtpore, fortune was against Lord Lake, and he failed. But at the commencement of it nine chances out of ten were in his favour, and his failure is more fairly attributable to the accident which caused the first repulse, than to any defect in his own arrangements. But though the fickle goddess for the moment abandoned him, he possessed, as we shall see, the iron will to force her to become again, as she had been before, his submissive and willing votary.

It will be recollected that after the second failure at the assault, Ameer Khan, a famous partisan Rohilla, had attempted to cut off our convoys, but had been signally repulsed. He had then left Bhurtpore, and made an incursion into Rohilcund. Thither, however, he had been followed by a portion of our cavalry under General Smith, who reached Moradabad just in time to save it from the clutches of Ameer Khan. That chieftain then attempted to return, but on his way was attacked and defeated at Afzulgurh on the 2nd March. He, however, contrived to escape with a few followers and rejoined Holkar at Bhurtpore on the 23rd, having in the interim received some accessions to his party. His arrival so increased the forces at the disposal of Jeswunt Rao, that Lord Lake considered the moment opportune for endeavouring to bring the enemy to action in the open plain, or at all events to drive them from the vicinity of Bhurtpore. At two o'clock in the morning of the 29th March therefore, taking with him the whole of his cavalry, and sending Colonel Don with some infantry to attack his right, Lord Lake moved upon the position occupied by the allies. But though he came in sight of it at daybreak, the enemy had had notice of his approach, for he found them in readiness to run away. They moved off at once, and though pursued for several miles, they lost only two hundred men and some cattle. On the 1st April, the attempt was renewed with more success, our troops coming upon the enemy before they had time to mount their horses, sabring numbers of them, and pursuing the remainder for fifty miles. This successful affair completed the discomfiture of Jeswunt Rao. But before this occurred, the Rajah of Bhurtpore had opened out negotiations for peace. Weary of his allies, disliking the enormous expenses imposed upon him, and above all, having a just dread of the pertinacity of the English general, he had taken advantage of the intimation he had received of the elevation of Lord Lake to the peerage to offer him his congratulations, accompanying it by a profession of his desire for peace, and of his readiness to proceed in person to the English camp. This frank offer met with a corresponding return on the part of Lord Lake. Formal negociations were opened on the 10th March, the conclusion of which was rather hastened by the defeat of Holkar, on the first April, and by the overthrow of the last remnant of his infantry by Captain Royal on the 7th April, at Ahmednuggur. On the 10th of that month, the army having meanwhile taken up a position with a view to renew the siege, the conditions of a treaty were agreed to. The Rajah bound himself to renounce his alliances with the Mahratta chieftains, to restore the territory which we had made over to him from that yielded to us by Scindia, and to pay a sum of twenty lakhs of rupees towards the expenses of the war. We should scarcely have demanded more, had the place been taken by assault.

Free now to follow up Holkar, who had thrown himself on the protection of Scindia, Lord Lake broke up from Bhurtpore on the 21st. The doubtful conduct of the latter chieftain made it more especially necessary that the movements of his army should have no uncertain character. He, accordingly, marched to Dholpore on the Chumbul, threatening the territories of both Mahratta rulers. Alarmed at this, Scindia, detaining Mr. Jenkins, the English resident, precipitately retreated in conjunction with Jeswunt Rao in the direction of Kotah. This conduct on the part of Scindia led to negotiations being entered into with the Supreme

Government, pending the issue of which Lord Lake, with the bulk of his force, returned to Agra for the rainy season, keeping it, however, in a state ready to move at a moment's warning.

Whilst the negotiations we have referred to were still going on, and the army was in daily expectation of a declaration of a war against Scindia, the great ruler who had so long and so successfully directed the fortunes of his countrymen in India, and who, if Clive deserves to be styled the first, is as surely entitled to the designation of the second founder of the Anglo-Indian empire, —the illustrious Marquis Wellesley,—ceased to govern. His successor, the Marquess Cornwallis, had arrived with peaceful instructions, and with a pre-conceived determination to undo as far as possible the policy of his predecessor. He resolved, therefore, not only to overlook the conduct of Scindia as evinced in his detention of the resident, but to restore to him the fortress of Gwalior, and the province of Gohud, which had been taken from him in the last war. With reference to Holkar, the Governor General announced his intention to restore to him all the possessions which he had held at the commencement of the war.

It can easily be believed that such resolutions would be regarded by Lord Lake as extremely detrimental to British interests,—even fraught with danger to the security of our possessions. To throw away the advantages which we had gained with so much glory, and at the cost of so many lives,—to replace in their former position men who had shown themselves the determined and formidable enemies of the British, appeared to him to indicate a feebleness little short of insanity. He accordingly, took upon himself to detain the letter containing the offers alluded to, until he could receive a reply to a remonstrance he at once addressed on the subject to the Governor General.

But before Lord Cornwallis received that remonstrance, the stroke of death was upon him. On the 5th October he died, and the Government devolved *ad interim* upon the senior member of Council, Sir George Barlow.

It has been well observed* that the sole object by which this gentleman appeared to be animated in his administration, "was to get quit of present difficulties at any cost, even at the sacrifice of the national power and credit. This was cutting, not disentangling the Gordian knot, and evinced little prudence or judgment in the operators." Sir George Barlow not only confirmed the arrangements entered into by Lord Cornwallis, even adding a pension to Scindia of four lakhs annually, but, agreeing on his part not to enter into separate treaties with any of the independent chiefs, styled by Scindia his tributaries, in Meywar or Malwa, he went so far as deliberately to sacrifice to the vengeance of the Mahratta chieftains, the Rajas of Boondee and Jyepore, whose stedfast alliance throughout the war, more especially at the time of Monson's retreat, had been of incalculable service to us. The earnest and repeated remonstrances of Lord Lake on this point, he treated with utter disregard. It is scarcely to be wondered at that it should have become necessary before many years to pour out blood and treasure again to reduce these puffed up chieftains to the position in which Lord Lake had brought, but was not allowed to keep, them, nor that the task should have devolved upon another

* *Professor H. H. Wilson.*

Governor General, the most brilliant successor* of Marquess Wellesley, to place the most powerful of them in a position in which it should become his interest to support the predominance of the British power in India.

Meanwhile, Lord Lake, disgusted at the too self-denying policy of the acting Governor General, was not the less determined to perform the part of Commander-in-chief so long as the war continued. By a threatening letter to Scindia he procured, in July, the release of the British resident, and as soon as the season permitted, having learned that Holkar had eluded all the columns sent to intercept him, and was moving on the Panjab at the head of a numerous rabble and sixty guns, he set out in pursuit. Marching to Delhi, thence, *viâ* Paniput and Pattealah, he arrived on the 2nd December at Loodhiana, the first British general, and leading the first British army, that had ever beheld the waters of the Sutlej. They crossed this river on the 5th, and marching through the country without meeting any opposition from the people,—the supplies being carefully paid for,—reached, after passing through Jullunder, the banks of the Beas on the 9th. Here intelligence was received that Jeswunt Rao was at Umritsur, in very great straits, the chiefs of the Sikh nation, alarmed by the prompt pursuit of Lord Lake, having resolved to withhold from him all material aid. Thus abandoned, Jeswunt Rao, hopeless of aught but his life, threw himself on the mercy of the conqueror, admitting that his whole country lay upon his saddle's bow. To his surprise this chieftain, who had waged war with us with an unrivalled animosity, who had murdered in cold blood the Eng-

* We need scarcely say that we allude to Lord Ellenborough.

lishmen in his employ, because they refused to fight against their countrymen, who had treated the prisoners he had taken with unparalleled atrocity, found himself, according to the instructions of the Supreme Government "reinstated in dominions to which he never had any right, and which, even if he had, he deserved to have forfeited."*

This treaty being concluded, Lord Lake after reviewing his army for the benefit of the Sikh chieftains, began, on the 9th January, to return to our own provinces. He had previously transmitted a proposal to make the Sutlej the boundary of British India, but such a plan was not at all consonant to the ideas then prevailing in high places.† He accordingly moved on leisurely to Delhi, where he halted for two months to make the necessary arrangements for the occupation of the country. He then proceeded to Cawnpore, thence at the end of the year to Calcutta, and there, in February, 1807, amid addresses from all classes, from natives and from Europeans, from soldiers and from civilians, he embarked for Europe. Never before had such a general ovation been given to any public man on his departure from the country, and never has that ovation been repeated. It was as true and genuine from all classes, as was the testimonial offered in 1844 to Lord Ellenborough by the army alone.

Had he deserved it? Was he, in sober truth, the great general his soldiers believed him? Did he, in reality, possess those great military qualities for which the enemies he defeated gave him credit? We at least,

* *Major Thorn.*

† It was nevertheless carried out four years later, under the administration of Lord Minto.

do not doubt it. We believe that he had completely mastered, before he had fired a shot in this country, the one principle which in India, at all events, makes victory to an English army a matter of certainty. That principle is never to fear moving forward, never to care for strong positions or numerical superiority, but to dash onwards to the attack. This is the rule that has been adopted, and adopted successfully, by all our great Indian commanders. It was the rule of Robert Clive and of John Adams; of Forde and of Coote; of Goddard; of Wellesley; of Hastings; of Napier and of Gough; of Havelock; of Rose; and of Nicholson. It was because we had men possessing the spirit and sagacity to carry out this rule, who did not wait to count the numbers or to reconnoitre too closely the position of the enemy, that we won India. "Show me where the enemy are," said the greatest of Russian generals, Suwaroff, "and I will attack them; I want no reconnoitring." Suwaroff drove the French out of Italy. It is not, it is true, every man who is capable of attacking. To attack with effect requires the possession of a cool head, a brain that becomes more energetic, more compressed, under the influence of fire, a resolute and imperturbable nature. Success in attack depends mainly on the capacity of being able to see as clearly amid the whistling of bullets as when sitting at a chess-board. It requires a man to possess the faculties attributed by Napoleon to Massena, of whom he said that he was dull in conversation, but that when under fire his mental energy redoubled and his thoughts were then clear and forcible. It was because Lord Lake possessed this faculty to an eminent degree, accompanying it by unlimited confidence in his men and the power of winning their affections, that he was right to attack under all circumstances, and that he always was successful when attacking in the field.

But he possessed in addition another great quality, scarcely if at all less important for a general. It was a quality he possessed in common with Napoleon, and may, therefore, be described in the same language. "The battle of Napoleon," writes Sir William Napier, "was the swell and dash of a mighty wave, before which the barrier yielded, and the roaring flood poured onwards covering all things." That, too, was the battle of Lord Lake. He was never content with merely beating an enemy in the field; with the possession of the field of battle; he was not satisfied till he had utterly annihilated and destroyed him. Thus, in the war with Scindia, he was not content even with the capture of two fortresses and one imperial city; he hastened from them in pursuit of the broken remnants of the enemy, and was only satisfied when he had annihilated their last disciplined battalion at Laswarrie. Again, in the contest with Holkar, he pursued that chieftain from Muttra to Delhi; from Delhi to Furruckabad; then, surprising him and beating him there, drove him to take refuge under the walls of Bhurtpore; assaulting that city, and though repulsed four times, yet gaining it over from Holkar at the last, he followed him through regions untrodden by a British army; crossed the Sutlej in such array, as to prevent the fugitive chieftain from finding new alliances among a warlike people; and finally forced him to surrender himself and the "kingdom on his saddle's bow," at Umritsur. Who will deny that in this instance "the roaring flood poured onwards, covering all things"?

There is yet a third point of view in which the

arrangements of Lord Lake as a general were admirable, worthy even of imitation in the present day. We allude to the facility which he so happily exercised of moving his troops and their baggage. "The march of our army," writes Major Thorn, "had the appearance of a moving town or citadel in the form of an oblong square, whose sides were defended by ramparts of glittering swords and bayonets. On the one side moved the line of infantry, on the opposite that of the cavalry, parallel to, and preserving its encamping distance as near as possible from the infantry, and keeping the head of the column in a line with the former. The front face was protected by the advance guard, composed of all the pickets coming on duty, and the rear by all the pickets returning from duty, and then forming the rear guard. The parks and columns of artillery moved inside the square, always keeping the high road, and next to the infantry, which moved at a short distance from it. The remainder of the space within the square was occupied by the baggage, cattle, and followers of the camp. Notwithstanding the immense magnitude of this moving mass, and the multifarious elements of which it consisted, nothing could exceed the regularity observed by the troops in maintaining their respective distances, and adhering closely to the order of formation on the march." This was the case in an ordinary march against an enemy, but we find from the same authority how advantage was always taken of local circumstances to alter it. Thus, in advancing from Muttra, in face of the entire cavalry of Holkar,—the cavalry led, followed by the infantry; between them and the river Jumna, the course of which was followed, were placed the baggage and camp followers,—a mode of advance which effectually prevented depredations, and gave free scope to the action of the army. To enable him to make those unsurpassed marches, the rapidity of which contributed as much as any other cause to the defeat of the enemy, it was the practice of Lord Lake to serve out gratuitously to each fighting man and public follower six pounds of flour. This quantity lasted six days, and being carried by the men, reduced the carriage. The diminution in that respect more than defrayed its cost.

In other respects Lord Lake fulfilled all the requirements of a great general. A strict disciplinarian, he carefully consulted the comforts of the soldier. Their toils, their privations, their fatigues, their exposure, he shared with them. It needed only that an officer or soldier should show himself zealous and active to ensure notice from the Commander-in-Chief. He knew no distinction of service. That man was rewarded who best knew, and who best did his duty. No man ever possessed a greater power of attaching others to himself. In private life, he was equally to be esteemed. Generous, unselfish, and open-hearted, he was a favourite everywhere. If his temper was quick, he never hoarded up an enmity. His anger often cooled down before the cause of it had been removed. No man had a larger or more attached circle of friends.

He left India, as we have stated, in February, 1807, and reached England in the following September. He received the most flattering welcome from his countrymen, and, on the 31st October following, was created by his sovereign a viscount, and was appointed governor of Plymouth. He did not, however, live long to enjoy these dignities and honours. In the month of February following, he was attacked by an illness, which on the 21st terminated fatally. He died, as he had lived, in the performance of his duty.

With no more appropriate sentence could we conclude our necessarily imperfect outline of the life of this famous warrior. It forms alike an epitome of his career, and a justification to us for having undertaken it. It is possible that to some this long record of battles fought and won; of sieges undertaken; of pursuits followed up; of advances and pursuits; coloured only by details of slaughter, and an account of the sufferings of the wounded, may appear tedious and purposeless. But we do not hesitate to avow that to our minds there are few stories more instructive, none more interesting, than that of the career of a noble and successful soldier, fighting the battles of his country. There is something inspiriting even in the idea of men giving themselves up to a career of this nature,—a career in which everything is to be risked, and little that is material to be gained,—a career promising great toil, exposure of the most trying kind, and an ever recurring chance of loss of life or limb. There must at least be much that is unselfish in the yearning that prompts a young man to undergo all this labour for so little profit. For, the real soldier, be it always remembered, fights not that he himself may gain, but that his country may benefit by his exertions. To that country he gives the best years of his life, his best energies of body and mind, often too those prospects of a peaceful life which will not always be banished even from his imagination. He gives all these, careless of the consequences, not only careless of, but rejoicing in, the fatigues, difficulties, and dangers he may encounter; doubly happy if fortune will but give him the chance that may connect his name with the scene of the triumph of his country's arms. But to the general reader the contemplation of the career of a great soldier, such as Lord Lake was, presents a lesson of a character more practical and instructive. Does not the story of his constant advances, his eagerness to close with the enemy, his grappling with him till he had overcome him,—does not that indicate a state of things which comes within the life-experience of most men? Do we not realise the fact that the military career of a soldier is but the type of the every-day life of an ordinary man? If the soldier is cowardly, indifferent, and careless, he will assuredly be beaten by his enemy, just in the same way as the man who is cowardly, indifferent, and careless in every-day life, is overcome by the temptations which are to him a formidable foe. When, on the other hand, we read of Lord Lake ever advancing, caring for no obstacle, riding at the long grass which he knew covered the guns behind them, do we not at once recognise the type of the man of every-day life, who, conscious of his own dignity, confident of the rectitude of his motives, advances in the path marked out to him, thrusting down every temptation, careless of the sneers of the world, scorning to compromise with evil, resisting the seductions which are disguised under some plausible title? Well would it be for men in general, if they would not disdain to take a lesson from this simple-minded warrior, if they would treat the sins that beset them as Lord Lake treated his enemies, taking no breath until they were utterly and for ever subdued. In that view of the question, the study of his life may not be quite valueless to all.

We cannot conclude without expressing the opinion

we entertain of Major Thorn's contribution to the military history of that period. It must ever be the text book of the campaigns against Scindia and Holkar, more especially of that portion of them conducted by Lord Lake in person, throughout which the Major bore a part. We have followed his account in all important particulars, excepting, indeed, when he speaks of the numbers of the Mahrattas. On that question Major L. F. Smith, who was himself in the service of Dowlut Rao Scindia, is a far more safe and trustworthy authority. The exaggeration, however unintentional, of the number of troops brought into the field by a defeated enemy, is no compliment to the conquering army, for it induces doubts as to the real merit of the victories achieved.

LECTURE ON THE CAREER OF

COUNT LALLY.

[Delivered in the Dalhousie Institute, Calcutta, 16th January, 1865.]

The career of Count Lally must always have special charms for the student of individual character. It is a career bristling with incidents, and not only with incidents of a private or ordinary nature, but with incidents affecting some of the most important events in European and Anglo-Indian history. It is a career full of instruction, for it shows how varying circumstances, and varying scenes, may affect the conduct of a man of great resources and real ability. It shows us a human character in innumerable phases, now buoyant under prosperity, now struggling with the animosity of secret and avowed enemies; a character single-minded yet passionate, resolute and self-reliant, and whilst perhaps limited in the scope of its intellectual vision, yet regarding difficulties as obstacles to be overcome, as obstacles which every man was bound, as part of his heritage from his Maker, to grapple with and trample upon. Such a character has ever appeared to me well worthy of study.

I have styled this lecture "The Career of Count Lally;" but it might, I think, somewhat more correctly be entitled the 'Careers' of that eminent man. For, undoubtedly,—and herein lies the great interest of his life,—Lally had two careers,—two careers so distinct from one another that it would seem, to the casual reader, quite impossible that the same man had been the chief actor in both; two careers,—the one eminently successful, the second a crushing failure,—the one in Europe, the other in Asia;—both alike interesting, both alike instructive, and containing, when fairly looked at, a moral which we, to whom, in different spheres and under different circumstances, careers in Europe and Asia have also been assigned, cannot fail to understand and to apply.

Lally was the son of a very distinguished Irish Officer. His father, Sir Gerard O'Lally, descended from a race of Chieftains,—whose lineage might be traced back to the period when Ireland stood alone, unconnected with the sister isle,—had inherited the religion, and had remained loyal to the cause, of the House of Stuart. When the events of 1690 and 91 had shattered the fortunes of that house in Ireland, Sir Gerard and twelve thousand of his countrymen still faithful to it, took advantage of the clause in the capitulation of Limerick which permitted the garrison to march out with all the honours of war, and to take service under the French King. Arriving in France, Sir Gerard was made colonel of one of the regiments of the new Irish Brigade—a Brigade that soon gained for itself the reputation of being the flower of the French army,—ever most forward in fight, ever entrusted with duties that were considered of all others most arduous. Some few years later, Sir Gerard married a French lady of noble family, and to them, in the month of January, 1702, a son was born. This son was Thomas Arthur, Count de Lally, Baron de Tallendal, the hero of this lecture.

Lally was literally a soldier from the hour of his birth. According to the custom then prevalent in the French army, he was entered, as soon as he was born, as a private in his father's regiment. Nor did his service continue long merely nominal. At a very early age he began the practice of spending his holidays with his father in the French camp. He was barely nine years old when he was present at the siege and capture of Gerona (25th January, 1711). Three years later, he mounted his first guard in the trenches before Barcelona. In such a school, and amid such scenes, under the direct tutorage of his father, Lally continued till he attained the age of fifteen years. His opportunities were great. His father's experience gave him knowledge of his profession, whilst his mother's relationship to some of the most illustrious families of France caused his introduction to the higher circles of society, and imparted to his manners that tone and polish so characteristic of the old French aristocracy. The manners thus acquired were set off by a handsome person.

Amongst other lessons impressed upon the mind of Lally at this early and most impressive period of his life, was a bitter and unrelenting hatred of the English, —or rather of the family which then sat on the throne of England. Sir Gerard O'Lally could never forget that he was an exile, and, not content with hating with all the bitterness of an exile's hatred, he imparted all his feelings, with all their bitterness, to his son. He trained that son, as Hamilcar trained Hannibal, to a fierce detestation of his great enemy. He taught him to consider the humiliation of the House of Hanover, as the one great end and object of his life. The young Lally never forgot that teaching. By it every important event in his career was influenced, and he counted no toil too great, no sacrifice too heavy, if, by making it, he could inflict injury on those whom he regarded alike as the enemies of his God, and rebels against his King.

In consequence partly of his great attention to his duties, and partly, perhaps, to the influence he had acquired through his mother at the French Court, Lally obtained, at the age of nineteen, the command of a company in his father's regiment. Two years later, his principal patron, the Regent Orleans, died (1723). Lally, however, was not the man to need the services of a patron; he required only the opportunity to develope his abilities; and like all sterling men so situated, he felt that, sooner or later, that opportunity would come; that meanwhile, it was only necessary for him to be patient, and to prepare himself for all eventualities. This, at least, is a maxim that must always commend itself to any man who is at once able and ambitious, and to whom the immediate future may appear overshadowed. The opportunity, we may depend upon it, will come, and it is for the man, who is at once strong-willed and daring, capable and resolute, to seize it.

Certainly, Lally, when his opportunity came, showed no lack of these qualities. When, twelve years after his promotion to captain, war broke out, he was still only aide-major in his regiment, a rank almost equivalent to that of adjutant. But then his opportunity came. His regiment formed part of the French army sent to besiege Kehl, on the Rhine. Kehl was reduced, and Philipsburg, the strongest fortress on the Rhine, was invested and taken, in the face of an Imperial army under the famous Prince Eugene. Rollin, the French historian of ancient history, describes this capture as an achievement worthy of the Roman legions in their palmiest day. To us, it has this interest, that it gave Lally his first opportunity of showing the stuff that was in him. He not only greatly distinguished himself, but he was fortunate enough to save the life of his father by a deed of unsurpassed gallantry. For his conduct in this campaign Lally was promoted to the rank of major.

The taking of Philipsburg was the last event of the war, and further opportunities for promotion seemed to have ceased with the peace (1735). But Lally was a man who could not be idle. Shut out from military employment, he devoted himself to the accomplishment, by other means, of the great dream of his life. To this end he made a journey to England, and sounded the sentiments of the Jacobites in the southern portion of the kingdom. But this convinced him that an insurrection in England could only be successful, if supported by the intervention of a foreign power. Hopeless of France, he turned his thoughts to Russia, and as that country was then engaged in war with Turkey, he applied to be permitted to serve with the Russian army, then commanded by his uncle, General Lascy, in that war. His real object was to interest the Czarina, Anne of Courland, in his projects against England. His leave was granted, but before he could set out, the French Minister, Cardinal Fleury, knowing his sympathies, conferred upon his mission an official character, and directed him to use all his efforts to bring about a coalition of France and the Northern powers against England. Lally went direct to St. Petersburg, and by his skill and address, found great favour at the Court of the Czarina. But he had scarcely left France, when Cardinal Fleury, already frightened at the possible results of his mission, resolved that it should have no important consequences. He therefore left Lally himself without instructions, and his despatches without definite reply. Lally, therefore, unable to come to any understanding with the Northern Courts, and feeling himself compromised, resolved to quit St. Petersburg. He returned, irritated to Paris, and vented his reproaches on the Cardinal. "I entered Russia," he said to him, "like a lion, and thanks to you, I consider myself fortunate to have quitted it like a fox." The Cardinal was much disconcerted, but could give no satisfactory reply. He promised, however, to examine two memoranda transmitted to him by Lally on the subject of a concert of the northern powers and France against England, but death struck him down before any notice of the question had been taken (29 January, 1743).

But, though thus unsuccessful as a negotiator, the attempt had greatly increased Lally's reputation. He had gained the admiration of the Czarina by his address, and of the French Ministry by his loyalty. He was thus regarded as something more than a mere soldier, and, from the time of his return from the Russian mission, was looked upon as one of the most rising characters at the French Court. Indeed, opportunity alone seemed wanting to enable him to rise to the highest pinnacle of success.

That opportunity soon came. The death of the Emperor Charles VI. (1740) threw Europe in a blaze, and the year 1741, Lally being then thirty-nine years of age, saw France and Austria again in hostile array against one another.

Of the campaigns that followed it is impossible that I should speak here in detail, or even give a cursory outline. The occasion does not demand it, nor does time admit of it. On the breaking out of the war, Lally's regiment was sent into Flanders under the Marshal de Noailles. In this campaign Lally gave so many instances of ability, that the French marshal applied for his services as adjutant-general on his staff. In this capacity he accompanied the French army into Germany, in the famous march in which the French general succeeded in cutting off the allied army, under the personal command of King George II., from Frankfort on the Maine. The battle of Dettingen which followed, terminated disastrously to the French arms, although, had ordinary prudence been displayed by the Duc de Grammont, who had been left in command at the village of Dettingen, the capture of the King of England, and the defeat or capture of his entire army, would have been assured. Lally took an active part in this engagement, and in the subsequent movements consequent upon it. In the following year (1744) he was present at the capture of Menin (5 June), of Ypres (25 June), and of Furnes (11 July). In this campaign, the French army, 120,000 strong, was commanded by Louis XV. in person, having under him the Marshals de Saxe and de Noailles. It was under these two generals, the most distinguished of that period, that Lally enjoyed the opportunity of displaying his abilities, and so highly were those abilities estimated, and so favourable was the impression he made, that after the taking of Furnes, he was commissioned to raise a new regiment of Irish, to be called by his name, and of which he was to have the command.

Lally set about this task with his wonted energy. In four months after the regiment had been raised, he had brought it, by his own efforts, into a high state of discipline. So high indeed was the opinion formed of it, that the most important position in the trenches before Tournay, then besieged by the French army (1745) under Marshal Saxe, was assigned to it. From this position it was removed to one of even greater importance in the field, on the receipt of intelligence that an English army, commanded by the son of the King of England, was marching to the relief of Tournay.

Then ensued the famous battle of Fontenoy, a battle glorious alike to the vanquished and the victors;—glorious to that ever memorable column of stout Englishmen which, uncovered by its allies, pierced the very centre of the French army, threatening even its King with capture;—glorious to Marshal Saxe, who, though carried on a litter, declared, when the battle to all but him appeared lost, that notwithstanding all unfavourable appearances, the day was his own;—glorious to the renowned chivalry of France, who refusing, in a spirit of romantic courtesy to be the first to fire, then, after their foremost ranks had fallen, repeated charge after charge on that dense column that would not be broken; —glorious even,—perhaps his last deed of heroism,—to the French King, who, though entreated by all his *entourage*, when the day seemed absolutely lost, to quit the field, declared he would remain to share the fortunes of his army;—glorious, finally, to that famous Irish Brigade, and especially to that Irish Regiment de Lally, whose last charge decided the victory, and drove back that nearly victorious column, already shaken by the artillery brought to bear on its front, reeling, though not disordered to its reserves. Yes, reeling, though not disordered, beaten back by those who may be termed their countrymen, this renowned column, to use the words of the French historian, "quitted the field of battle without tumult, without confusion, and was covered with honour."

Lally's conduct on this occasion may be estimated by the fact that Louis XV. made him colonel on the field of battle, and that he was personally thanked by Marshal Saxe for the gallantry that had mainly contributed to the victory.

The battle of Fontenoy decided that campaign. Not only Tournay, but almost all the towns of the Netherlands fell into French hands, and Lally, finding further opportunities of distinction disappearing from that scene, transferred his services to another sphere.

The success of the French arms on the Continent had again revived the idea of making an armed intervention in favour of the House of Stuart. The youthful heir of that house had shown himself ready and able to seize the opportunity, for, less than two months after Fontenoy had been fought, he had made a descent with a handful of followers on the coast of Scotland. Lally was eager to support him, and he impressed his views with so much force and energy on the French Court, that all his plans were adopted. A force of ten thousand men, under the Duc de Richelieu, with Lally himself as Quarter-Master-General, was organised. Eager for action, Lally set out himself, as soon as the orders for the force had been issued, and, accompanied by a few friends, joined Charles Edward during his retreat from Derby. He was at once appointed aide-de-camp to that prince, and served in that capacity at the battle of Falkirk. After that battle he was sent to the south of England to encourage a rising amongst the partisans of the House of Stuart.

In one sense, Lally's journey into England had been unfortunate. He had been the soul of the expedition at that time being organised in France. Voltaire, who knew him personally, says of his efforts at that period, "He was the soul of the enterprise. I have never seen a man more zealous; it needed only that success should be possible for him to succeed." Thus, when Lally left, the soul indeed departed, and the body languished and died. The expedition never left the French shores. The battle of Culloden added to his misfortunes, and these seemed at their climax when the object of his mission to London was discovered. The Duke of Cumberland, thirsty for the blood of the Jacobites, caused a price to be put upon his head. But by means of some influence Lally possessed with the Prince of Wales, he was enabled to elude his pursuers, and, in the disguise of a sailor, crossed the channel and landed in safety at Dunkirk. He immediately rejoined the French army under Marshal Saxe, and reached it in time to take part in the conquest of the most important places in Flanders in 1746.

The following year we find Lally still serving under that great master of the art of war. He commanded his regiment with great credit at the battle of Laffeldt (2nd July), in which the Duke of Cumberland, at the head of a combined army of English, Austrians, and Dutch, was again beaten by Marshal Saxe. Louis XV., who witnessed this battle, and who noticed the contrast between the valour of the English and the apathy of their allies, gave expression on this occasion to that famous *mot*, destined to be verified so often: "The English fight for all and pay for all." At Laffeldt the Irish Brigade again bore the brunt of the action, and suffered terribly in men,—and irreparably, in the death of its famous leader, Count Dillon, who had brought the materials of it from Ireland, and who had shown himself one of the most distinguished soldiers even of that eventful period. He was Lally's great uncle.

Whilst the French Marshal amused the Allies after Laffeldt, he despatched General Lowendal to attack Bergen-op-Zoom, a fortress commanding the navigation of the Scheldt, and then reputed impregnable. But in spite of its reputation, Lowendal assaulted it after three weeks' open trenches, and to the surprise of Europe, and to the dismay of England and Holland, he took it. Just before the assault Lally had been taken prisoner in a sortie.

He was, however, soon exchanged, and rejoined his command. He was present with the army when, early in the following year, Saxe invested Maestricht. In the siege which followed he was severely wounded, and had not recovered when the treaty of Aix-la-Chapelle restored peace to Europe,—Maestricht being surrendered to the French as a matter of form. Lally, immediately afterwards, in consideration of his services during this campaign, received the rank of Major-General.

Thus had Lally fought his way up from the lowest grade in the army to the rank of General Officer. We have followed him in every step of his career. We have seen how his energy, his gallantry, and his abilities, constantly called forth the special notice of those under whom he served. We have seen this evidenced in the trenches before Philipsburg, in the early campaigns in Flanders, on the glorious field of Fontenoy, and in the final siege of Maestricht. We have seen how he moulded his soldiers, as one man, to his will. We have proof of this in the ease with which, in four months, he organised the regiment which bore his name, by the devotion shown and the success achieved by that regiment at Fontenoy. We have seen him, a trusted subaltern, knowing how to obey; an efficient staff-officer, knowing how to impress his general's orders upon others; an unsurpassed regimental commander, receiving on two occasions his promotion on the field of battle; a zealous and skilful diplomatist, retaining the confidence of his own Sovereign at the same time that he won the esteem of the Monarch to whose court he was deputed. We have seen him patient, though never idle, in times of inaction; and while rather seeking than waiting for opportunities, eager and prompt to seize those opportunities when they came in his way, and not only to seize them, but to use them, to press and squeeze out their very marrow, till nought but the dry hide of them remained. We have seen him, all this time, rising in the estimation of men, gaining the goodwill of all, till, made a major-general before Maestricht, he found himself, at the conclusion of the war, universally regarded as the rising genius of France, as the general who, to all appearance, would have to occupy, in the next war, the places about to be vacated by the Saxes and the Noailles, by the Belleisles and the Lowendalls. Ah! if such indeed had happened, how different might have been his destiny! He knew Europe, her statesmen, her soldiers, her modes of warfare, her habits of thought; he had acquired his knowledge in an European school; and in those days it was seriously believed, as in these it is sometimes even seriously argued, that knowledge thus acquired was certain to command success in every part of the world. Let us see how all his experience, all his knowledge of the men and nations of Europe, availed Lally in the new and distant land to which he was about to be transported.

For seven years after the treaty of Aix-la-Chapelle Europe remained at peace. In 1754, however, England and France came in contact in Canada, and it was not long before the animosities thus caused involved the two nations in war.

Whilst, however, they were yet nominally at peace, the news of the capture of two French men-of-war by the English fleet, off Newfoundland, caused immense excitement in France. Lally was at once summoned to the ministerial counsels, and his advice was asked as to the course the French Government might pursue in the event of their determining to reply to this infraction of the common right of nations by a declaration of war. Lally suggested three courses, any one of which, he insisted, might be advantageously followed. His first plan,—in forming which he was doubtless influenced by the leading idea of his life,—was to fit out a fleet and army sufficient for the purpose, and, taking Charles Edward on board, to make a descent upon England; his second proposal was, to send a sufficient force to the East Indies, to chase the English from all their possessions in that country; and the third, to drive them out of America; but, he added, "whatever course you adopt, it is primarily necessary that you should think and act at the same time." This prudent counsel,—prudent because, at such a conjuncture, as in many that occur to us in our lives, boldness was prudence,—was not accepted by the French Ministry. Desirous to avoid war, they mistook timidity for wisdom, and it was only a year after, when three-fourths of their merchant marine had been swept from the seas, that they could make up their minds to act boldly. An alliance was then formed with Austria, Russia, and Sweden, and it was resolved to act simultaneously in Germany, Canada, and in the East Indies. On the 17th May, 1756, war was formally declared.

No sooner was it known that the French Government had resolved to send a force to the East, than the East India Company pressed upon them the nomination of Lally to its command. His great reputation, his experience in war, his wonderful energy, seemed indeed to point him out as the fittest man for the task. That task was no light one. Not only were foreign enemies to be subdued, but there was an administration to be purged. At that time the reports of the corruption of the French administrators in the East were universally rife, and were all but universally believed. This was an additional reason which influenced the Directors in their choice of Lally. They felt sure, not only that his unsullied honour would be proof against corruption, but that he would scorn and loathe that vice in others, and would spare no means to extirpate it. They felt confident, likewise, that he, of all others, was a man to make himself obeyed, and obedience to their orders had been, up to that time, a virtue "conspicuous by its absence." They repeatedly, therefore, urged upon the Minister of War the appointment of Lally.

The minister was not very willing. He liked Lally personally, but he feared that his stern and unbending character, made still more stern by a long course of prosperity, was not exactly suited to encounter such a state of affairs as were believed to exist in Pondichery. He dreaded lest such a nature, passionate and energetic, would become unreasonably wild in the presence of a resistance that did not openly resist, a corruption which, though existing, might not be tangible. For a long time, therefore, he opposed the nomination, but the importunities of the Directors, backed by the voice of public opinion, at length prevailed, and on the 19th November, 1756, Lally was appointed Lieutenant General and Commander-in-Chief of the expedition to the East.

Never did the Crown confer on any of its officers a fuller commission than on this occasion. On the 31st December, Lally was appointed Commander-in-Chief and Commissary of the King for the French possessions in the East, including the Isles of France, Bourbon and Madagascar: he was to preside in Council, and to make all the inhabitants, the governors, and the commanders of the land and sea forces of the Company take the oath of obedience, "without any contravention whatever." He was only not permitted to alter the mode of collecting votes in Council, and he had no absolute control over the movements of the ships of the Royal Navy.

It was intended that the Military portion of the expedition should consist of about 3000 men; that it should be supplied with specie to the amount of six millions of livres; and that it should leave France in three detachments. The first of these, consisting of nearly one thousand men of the Regiment de Lorraine, fifty Artillerymen, with twenty siege guns, and its proportion of treasure, under the orders of the Chevalier de Soupire, second in command of the expedition, sailed from the port of Lorient on the 30th December, 1756, and reached Pondichery on the 9th September of the following year.

The second detachment, consisting of the regiment de Lally, with a due proportion of artillerymen and guns, was to leave in the February following, escorted by a squadron under Rear-Admiral Count d'Aché. A superstitious man would have done well to mark the hour on which Lally first met his naval colleague, for most certainly the new Governor then came into contact with his Evil Genius. It is a great, though not an irreparable, misfortune for a man to be born with barren brains. The absence of conceptive power may be atoned for by the possession of a strong character, a brave heart, a hand to carry out, in all their fulness, the ideas of a master mind. But that man is surely most miserable, who, to an unproductive brain adds infirmity of purpose; who, when the path he cannot see is pointed out to him by others, has neither the spirit nor the manliness to tread it; to whom, fear of responsibility and doubt, supplying the place of the imagination in which he is deficient, double difficulties and halve resources. Such a man is, of all others, to be avoided as a colleague in an important expedition, and yet such a man was d'Aché.

The effects of this man's nerveless vitality were soon apparent. The fleet sailed on the 20th February, but, in clearing Brest Harbour, two of the vessels belonging to it were slightly damaged. The injury was so unimportant that all the principal naval officers of the expedition were in favour of continuing the voyage, and making the necessary repairs at sea. The wind was favourable, and nothing imperatively demanded their return. But d'Aché doubted; the inevitable "if" paralysed the action of his shadow of a heart, and he put back.

The squadron had scarcely re-anchored in Brest Harbour, when one of the results of d'Aché's timidity became manifest. An order arrived from the Court to transfer two of his men of war to the squadron fitting out for Canada, their places to be supplied by vessels belonging to the Company. Lally was also informed that the remaining third of the force originally destined for him, could no longer be supplied.

In the face of these difficulties d'Aché remonstrated, and resigned. Lally remonstrated, but expressed his willingness to carry out his master's orders at all hazards. The reply from the Court of Versailles was an order to d'Aché to put to sea as soon as the ships destined for him should arrive, and a promise to Lally that the remaining third of his force should be sent after him six months later. It never was sent.

More than two months were spent at Brest in idleness waiting for the promised ships, and it was only on the 2nd May, 1757, that the squadron made its final start for its Eastern destination.

How slowly it sailed; how it pursued a course which, the English historian states, ought to be known in order to be avoided; how two months were lost by every night lying by a little merchant ship that d'Aché had picked up; how six weeks more were wasted in an obscure port in trying to dispose of her cargo; six weeks more, from the fear of rounding the Cape during the Equinox; how the course was constantly altered at night to avoid the sail descried in the day time; how a capful of wind was always a signal for taking in the sails; how all these things occurred, need not be described. They did occur, however, and as we read the heart-breaking account, we wonder, not that d'Aché took twelve months to accomplish his voyage, but that he ever accomplished it at all. Had he only continued his voyage on the 20th February, and pursued it with ordinary speed, he would have arrived in the Indian seas five or six months before the English fleet; or had he sailed as the English did, he would still have been three months before them, and three months at that time might have been fatal to English domination in India. As it was, the two fleets arrived about the same time; the French on the 28th April, 1758, the English a day or two later.

But before describing the scenes that followed their landing, it is necessary to take a short retrospect of French policy in India.

The French settlement of Pondichery, established in 1674, attained, in the course of a few years, to a state of great prosperity. The place itself was fortified, and the surrounding country was by degrees brought into subjection. Other factories, too, were established at Mahé on the Malabar, at Karikal, on the Coromandel coast, and at Chandernagore in Bengal, all subject to the parent settlement.

Nothing occurred to interrupt the rising prosperity of these settlements till the year 1744, when war broke out between France and England. Even then, the French, sensible of the advantage of peace for the consolidation of their power, were anxious that India should be regarded as a neutral ground, and they made proposals to that effect. But the English had sent a squadron to the Eastern seas, and they were unwilling to forego the opportunities which seemed to present themselves of destroying the commerce of their rivals. War thus became inevitable.

At this juncture, La Bourdonnais, a self-made man, one of the most energetic characters that ever lived, and whose career well merits on every account a separate notice, was Governor of the Isles of France and Bourbon. Resolving to make a counter stroke against the English, this man, full of energy and fertile in resources, fitted out a fleet, trained the crews, and trampling over the opposition of the Company, and the opposition of those around him, brought his squadron in safety to Pondichery.

The Governor of Pondichery at that time was Dupleix. This extraordinary man had then perhaps only half confessed even to himself the idea, which almost immediately afterwards became the leading idea of his being —the formation of a French Empire in India. He it was, who, at the outbreak of the war, had proposed that India should be neutral ground for both belligerents, but on the rejection of this proposal he set to work to aid with all his energies the efforts of La Bourdonnais. On the arrival of this latter at the head of a squadron which, in its course, had beaten off the English squadron, the soaring spirit of Dupleix aspired not only to the rooting out of the English from the Coast of Coromandel, but to their entire expulsion from Indian soil. He hastened to endeavour to impress these ideas upon La Bourdonnais, urging him, as the first step, to attack and destroy Madras. But, unhappily for French interests, La Bourdonnais was not formed to act under superior authority. Sailing, after some hesitation, to Madras, and taking it without the loss of a man, he professed to regard himself, in virtue of that conquest, as independent of the controlling authority of the Governor of Pondichery. Far, then, from carrying out the views of Dupleix regarding the destruction of Madras, he consented to ransom it on easy terms, receiving from the English, as the price of his concurrence, a considerable present for himself. But the capture of Madras had only rendered Dupleix more fixed in his idea, more resolved to carry it out. The insubordinate conduct of La Bourdonnais for a time, indeed, paralysed him, and lost him moments which no one better than La Bourdonnais himself could have used to the advantage of France. But Dupleix was well aware that on the setting in of the monsoon it would be necessary for La Bourdonnais to return to the Isle of France. He therefore refused to ratify his convention with the English, and when La Bourdonnais, forced to depart, made over to him his conquest, he boldly kept possession of it, refusing to restore it to the English.

Time will not allow me to do more than glance at the system then put in force by the fertile genius of Dupleix. The main principle of that system was to make himself and his French absolutely necessary to the native rulers of India,—to make himself so necessary, that the native princes should be ready, not only to comply with his demands, but to offer him such extension of territory as they thought he would covet;—to make himself so necessary, that he should really pull the wires which should move his puppets into action; and that thus, insensibly and by degrees, by skill rather than by force, India would become French,—French not only by inclination, and by policy, but finally also in fact. But with this view he regarded it of primary importance to rid himself of the English. Free from their observation, he felt he could carry out his scheme without hinderance or control. So long as they remained on the coast, he had to use all his resources in endeavouring to counteract their rivalry. He wished to be face to face with the Native Powers, so as by balancing one against the other, to use them for the purposes of France; by making himself essential to the strongest, to use the power of the strongest to forward, gradually but surely, the dream he had formed of a French Empire in India.

To carry out this system, it was requisite that its originator should possess a cool brain, a fertile imagination, an unscrupulous conscience, a readiness that never was at fault, and resources in himself that were incapable of exhaustion. And Dupleix was such a man. He was a match for the natives at their own weapons. He was, in fact, everything but a soldier. Had he been that also, he would have realised all his visions. As it was, his scheme failed; but how near it was to success! When the year 1752 opened, the system of Dupleix had been six years at work, and what was the result? Dupleix had made the Subadar of the Deccan; he had made the Nawab of the Carnatic; the limits of the French possessions had increased enormously; the English candidate for the Nawabship of the Carnatic had been driven to his last stronghold in Trichinoply, and this he was hopelessly defending. The English themselves had little beyond Madras (restored to them after the Treaty of Aix-la-Chapelle) and Fort St. David, and it appeared that the fall of Trichinopoly would be the signal for their expulsion from India. Mahommed Ali, whom they recognised as Nawab, had even offered to make his submission to Chanda Sahib, the Nawab appointed by the French.

But the scheme, when just on the point of accomplishment, tottered to its fall. Dupleix, no soldier himself, had sent Bussy, the only general he possessed, far away to the North; and just at that moment, when on the eve apparently of the accomplishment of all his plans, the genius of Clive delivered at them a blow which shook the very foundations of French dominion in India.

But it was when reverses came that Dupleix showed how boundless and inexhaustible were his resources. The English Company received supplies of men and money from England. Dupleix received nothing, or next to nothing. Still for two years he maintained the unequal struggle; and when recalled, in 1754, he still showed a bold front to his enemy, and had not even then despaired of the realization of his dream.

Peace followed the departure of Dupleix only nominally. In reality hostilities continued with almost unabated rancour, and with varying fortune; and when, in 1756, war broke out again in Europe, it seemed that that power would gain the supremacy in India which should first send a well-appointed fleet and army to the scene of action. It was a conviction of this nature that had inspired Lally's advice to the French Minister, "to think and act at the same time." So favourable an opportunity indeed had never before presented itself, for at that time the English could scarcely bring 200 Europeans into the field.

It is now full time that we should return to the movements of the force commanded by Lally. It has been seen that the first detachment of that force, under the Chevalier de Soupire, left France on the 31st December, 1756, and reached Pondichery on the 9th September following. It had been intended that De Soupire's force, and the squadron which escorted it, should make a combined attack on Fort St. David, then garrisoned by only sixty invalids; but the accidental interception of a letter from the Governor of Fort St. David to the Admiral of the English squadron, expected from Europe, affording as it did the first intimation of the anticipated arrival of such a squadron, produced so great an alarm amongst the French, that they hurried back to the Isle of France, without even landing the heavy artillery and ammunition they had brought with them for the purpose. De Soupire, thus left alone, allowed himself to be controlled by the Civil Governor of Pondichery, M. de Leyrit. As the career of this official is henceforth intimately connected with that of Lally, it is fit that we should inquire who and what manner of man he was.

Before Lally set sail from France, a description of the members of the Council of Pondichery was given to him by the Directors of the French Company. In this De Leyrit is spoken of as a man "fit for trade, but weak, phlegmatic, and silent; one who suffered others to get the start of him; and who did not know how to maintain proper subordination." But this was a very loose and incomplete portraiture of the man. In reality,

De Leyrit was one of that class of men, not very uncommon even now, who, placed in a position in which they are called upon to act, are yet so afraid of acting wrongly, that they prefer not to act at all; who think they have decided a question if only they can get the consideration of it postponed; who persuade themselves that affairs left to themselves will surely right themselves in the end. He was the sort of man, in fact, who in these days would have sent even the most urgent and pressing question to a department "for report;" and who then, regarding that question as disposed of because reported upon, would have consigned it, report and all, to the Charybdis of the Record Room. If his advice were asked, "the oracle was always dark."

It was characteristic of the man, therefore, that when the Chevalier de Soupire, having landed with his thousand men, and having found another thousand ready to his hand in Pondichery, naturally wished to do something with them; that although Fort St. David, not many miles distant, was garrisoned at that moment by only sixty invalids, and might easily have been taken; De Leyrit, fearful of sanctioning an enterprise that might fail, held him back from the enterprise, and forced him to content himself with the capture of a few forts in the vicinity of Arcot. On these slight expeditions were wasted the eight months that intervened between the landing in India of De Soupire and the landing of Lally.

At last, on the 2nd May, 1758, Lally arrived. The main portion of the squadron had anchored before Cuddalore, near Fort St. David, and Lally had come on in a 60-gun ship, attended by a frigate, to Pondichery. He received an ominous greeting. The guns which fired off a salute in his honour happened to be loaded, and their fire took effect on the ship on board of which was the new Governor, three shots hitting the sides, and two going through the rigging. However, he landed. The first news that greeted him was the loss of Chandernagore and Mahé to the English. Nevertheless, prompt as he ever had been in Europe, he ordered out 800 men, and three hours after his landing, he marched to Cuddalore, fifteen miles distant. The place, invested by sea and land, fell on the third day. He then marched to Fort St. David; and though the garrison had been increased, and the place much strengthened since the arrival of De Soupire, he took it after seventeen days' open trenches: he then sent a detachment against Devi-cottah, which was abandoned at its approach, and, thus successful, returned, on the 10th June, in triumph to Pondichery.

But in this first expedition, successful though it was, the seeds of subsequent failure had been plentifully sown. Accustomed only to Europe and to European habits, Lally was unable to comprehend the existence of a state of things such as forced itself upon his attention immediately after he had landed in India. To his mind he and the few thousand Europeans at Pondichery represented the dominant race, and he was surprised that the millions of native inhabitants objected to be regarded as slaves. The institution of caste appeared to him to be simply an excuse of which men availed themselves to escape toilsome occupation. He regarded it, and was resolved to regard it, in no other light. He at once reversed the policy of Dupleix. That able administrator had been careful to respect native prejudices; his whole policy, in fact, had been a policy of conciliation. But Lally, confident in his strength, tried to ignore the existence as a nation of the dusky millions of Hindustan. In his eyes France and England were fighting for the possession of India; and his policy was expressed in his own words, that he had come to drive the English from India. He went directly, far too directly, to this purpose. He acted as he would have acted in Europe. When men, whose caste forbade them to labour, refused to act as coolies, they were at once impressed, and driven to their tasks. The native inhabitants of Pondichery were in this way condemned without distinction to all sorts of labour. Brahmins were compelled to carry the loads their caste forbade them to touch, and were yoked with Pariahs and Soodras to draw carts. The result was an universal panic in Pondichery. When De Leyrit and the Council remonstrated, they were treated as accomplices who had been bribed. It was another mistake thus to insult those whose co-operation was so necessary. Poor De Leyrit was not corrupt, he was only incapable. But Lally was inexorable. He redoubled his exactions, and stormed at and derided the Indian experience of men whose duty it was to advise him. The consequences were fatal; and when he returned from the conquest of Fort St. David, he returned to a city, the European and Native inhabitants of which were alike struck by a paralysis of terror, and imbued with a feeling of savage hatred. Of these two feelings he himself was at once the cause and the object.

It was Lally's intention, after his return to Pondichery, to march upon Madras; but he had neither money nor carriage; he was at feud with his Council, and had lost the confidence of the natives. In despair he determined to claim the payment of a bond given by the Rajah of Tanjore for five crores and a half of rupees, and then in the possession of the Government of Pondichery. The Rajah refused, and the siege of Tanjore was resolved upon.

Then were seen, in all their completeness, the difficulties, the insuperable obstacles, which a man,—even a man endowed with great abilities and immense energy, —must face should he determine to run counter to the cherished convictions of an entire nation. It was a struggle between the determination and obstinacy of the man on one side, and a feeling stronger than armies, stronger than force, stronger than time, on the other! Can we doubt the result? Means of transport were wanting, provisions even failed. When the army at length reached Tanjore, it had neither money, nor food, nor ammunition. A pagoda which, to the horror of the natives, they attacked and plundered, was found to contain only rice in the husk. At last the unfortunate Lally was reduced to the device of selling the plunder of the place for two hundred thousand rupees; but the place did not choose to be plundered. The resistance was obstinate,—so much so that Lally, furious at the idea of being thus thwarted by one of the children of the soil, sent to the Rajah and threatened that, unless he chose to surrender, he would send him and all his family as slaves to Bourbon; but the spirit of the Tanjorean revolted at this indignity, and he resolved to perish rather than submit. Just then there came a report of the defeat of the French fleet; and this, combined with the exhaustion of his ammunition, determined Lally to retreat. But that retreat was nearly fatal. The French camp was attacked; and Lally himself, signalled out especially as an object of assault, escaped death only by something short of a miracle. The enemy were finally repulsed, but the retreat was conducted in the midst of the most terrible embarrassments of all sorts. (18 August, 1759.)

On his return to Pondichery, Lally, nothing daunted, resolved to prepare to attack Madras. But here d'Aché failed him. This officer had encountered the English fleet on the 29th April, and had been worsted in an indecisive combat; he had met the English a second time on the 2nd August, and had again sheered off after an hour's fighting. He now expressed his determination to proceed at once to the Isle of France; and, in spite of the earnest entreaties of Lally, he sailed on the 2nd September.

Thus left to himself, Lally resolved, nevertheless, to persevere in his designs against Madras. He was confirmed in this determination by the departure of the English fleet for Bombay. For the immediate expenses of the army he advanced from his own funds thirteen thousand rupees, and induced some of his officers to follow his example. He stayed only twenty-five days at Pondichery, and then moved upon Arcot, with the garrison of which place he had contrived to come to an understanding. Arcot was entered in triumph the 4th of October, 1758.

At Arcot Lally was joined by Bussy, whom he had recalled from the Court of the Subadar, where Bussy had succeeded, ever since the departure of Dupleix, in maintaining with a handful of Europeans the power and authority of the French name. Lally, who could not understand Bussy's plans, who regarded the system of native alliances with contempt, and who saw no enemy in India but the English, treated Bussy himself with marked "hauteur," and his proceedings at the Court of the Subadar as a means of personal aggrandisement. He looked upon him as a Company's officer; a man destitute of European, and therefore of useful experience; in a word, as a mere Indian general. But Bussy,—a man who united to much of the political subtlety of Dupleix the fighting power of Clive,—made a far different impression upon the unprejudiced officers of the French army. Six of them,—men bearing the most illustrious names in France,—joined in a request that Bussy might be made brigadier-general over their heads. To this request Lally had no course but to accede.

He refused, however, to allow Bussy to return to the Subadar, notwithstanding the most pressing letters on the subject from that viceroy. He even regarded the very idea of his return as something akin to madness.

Had Lally, instead of taking Arcot, marched directly upon Chingleput,—whence the English drew their supplies,—he would, probably, have been able not only to provision his army, but to force Madras to surrender. At Arcot he found nothing in the way of resources, and, even before he could take it, the English had thrown a garrison of 850 men into Chingleput. Lally, therefore, returned full of anger to Pondichery, to seek there the sinews of war.

He obtained but few, except those which he himself and his officers advanced, amounting in all to 94,000 rupees, and with this sum he was forced to put his army in motion,—an army of 2700 Europeans, 300 cavalry, and 5000 native infantry, against the stronghold of the English. He arrived before Madras on the

14th December, and at once occupied the Black Town almost without striking a blow.

It is impossible to conceive a more heart-breaking time than that spent by Lally before Madras. He had supplies but for fifteen days when he sat before it, and, on their consumption, he and his troops literally lived from hand to mouth. Now they were supported by a supply of rice captured from an English vessel, now by some chance arrival from Pondichery. Meanwhile the troops were not paid, the officers were discontented, and worse than all, Lally,—this Lally whose personal influence used to carry all before it in Europe,—was here regarded as the cause of every failure, and the originator of all the privations.

There is no need to recount every particular of the sad tale, to shew why this attack failed, and that sortie was no tcut off:—everything went wrong,—and everything went wrong because the man at the head of the troops, though a most gallant soldier, and distinguished for his abilities as an officer, had destroyed confidence by trampling on the cherished feelings of others.

There could be but one termination to a siege so carried on. When, at last, a breach had been made, the officers and men showed a disinclination to storm; and before the day arrived on which Lally had resolved to attempt it at all hazards, the appearance of an English fleet, with considerable reinforcements on board, compelled him to forego his schemes, and to raise the siege. He returned with rage in his heart to Pondichery, 17th February, 1759.

Such was the hatred entertained against Lally in Pondichery that the news of his failure before Madras caused the greatest rejoicing in that town. It must have been a strong feeling that could make French hearts rejoice at the uprising of the Star of England; that could inspire them with a sense of relief when they heard that a French army was in full retreat from before an English fortress. Yet such a feeling Lally had caused. He was not sensible of it himself. He knew that the feeling existed, but he persisted in attributing it to the treachery, the corruption, the want of patriotism of his enemies. Even in the trenches before Madras he could not restrain his invectives against the mode of managing matters in Pondichery. He declared that "fire from Heaven, in default of the fire of English, would, sooner or later, inevitably destroy that new Sodom."

Time will not allow me to follow, step by step, the proceedings of Lally after his retreat from Madras. That retreat was a death-blow to his hopes of conquest. The possibility of having to defend Pondichery seemed rather now to loom in the future. It was, however, yet in the power of d'Aché to avert this calamity. But d'Aché was the reed that invariably pierced the hand that leaned upon it. This officer had received a reinforcement of three ships, and had again sailed for the Indian Seas. Here, on the 10th September, 1759, he had again met the English squadron, again had fought it, and had again been beaten, this time receiving a severe wound in his thigh. He managed, however, to reach Pondichery, and to land there a small amount of treasure, and 180 troops. But, once at Pondichery, nothing could induce him to remain. In vain did Lally and the Council point out to him that Pondichery, left by him, would be in imminent danger; in vain did they appeal to honour, to sense of duty, even to his interest; in vain did they protest against his departure. D'Aché would not have been himself had he listened to these appeals. The utmost that he could do was to land 450 of his crews, and of these Lally writes, in his memoirs, that they were "the scum of the squadron; that 200 deserted to the English; many ended their lives by the executioner; 50, who garrisoned Wandewash, let the enemy into it, and the rest abandoned their post in front of the enemy at Pondichery." Such was the characteristic termination to the Indian career of Count d'Aché:—he abandoned his countrymen to their fate.

But this was not the only blow to Lally's hopes. Though he himself had, after his retreat from Madras, maintained his army with fair fortune in the field, yet the total defeat and capitulation of Conflans, the officer by whom he had replaced Bussy in the north, had caused even a greater injury to the French policy by alienating the Subadar of the Deccan, and compelling him to seek an English alliance. These losses forced Lally at last to have recourse to the one general under him on whose talents he could rely, and he resolved to detach Bussy to the north. But Bussy had scarcely left his camp, when the army, deprived of pay, clothing, and provisions, and hearing reports of the large fortunes made by private individuals, broke out into open mutiny. The effect of this was to cause Bussy to return, and the delay which thus ensued proved fatal to the French cause in the north. The mutiny was quelled by the payment of six months' arrears, and the promise of an amnesty, and Lally prepared again to take the field.

But whilst he himself, with one division of his army,

had obtained some slight advantage in the neighbourhood of Trichinopoly, the other had allowed the English to surprise Wandewash, and to threaten Arcot. To recover the one and save the other Lally massed his forces and marched against Wandewash, rejecting the advice of Bussy to compel the retirement of the English by acting with his superior number of cavalry on their communications. Rather than do this, Lally resolved to have recourse to the dangerous expedient of fighting a decisive battle, the result of which, if disastrous, would be fatal.

He had attacked and carried, sword in hand, the town of Wandewash, on the 10th of January, 1760, and had sat down the day following before the fort, but his chief engineer was so dilatory that it was not till the 20th that the fire opened upon it. On the 21st a breach was reported practicable. Then it was that the English, under Colonel Coote, advanced to its relief. Lally went out to meet him. He had only 1350 Europeans, and 800 sepoys. The English had 1900 Europeans and 2100 sepoys. In the action that follows, Lally himself behaved with his usual gallantry, but his sepoys ran away at the first onset. The Regiment de Lorraine which then advanced, succeeded, under a murderous fire, in breaking the English line, but it was immediately taken in both flanks and beaten back. It was then that Lally, eager to redeem the fortunes of the day, put himself at the head of his cavalry, and ordered them to charge. But scarcely a man would follow him. Just about this time considerable confusion had been caused in the left wing by the explosion of a tumbril, and the English took advantage of the opportunity to advance on that side. Bussy, who commanded here, brought up the Regiment de Lally to recover the day, but in leading them to the charge his horse was shot under him, and he was taken prisoner. The rout was now general, and would have been fatal had not the European cavalry, recovering from their panic, shewed a firm front to the enemy, and prevented any pursuit.

Lally, after the battle, recalled the part of the army he had left before Wandewash, and retreated on Chettapet, and gradually thence, step by step, on Pondichery, the English occupying the fortified places from which he was forced to retire. By the 1st May, 1760, the French army was confined almost to the limits of Pondichery, and the place was virtually invested by sea and land. Even then, Lally never for a moment shewed the slightest sign of despair. For the nine months that followed, though thwarted by intrigues and opposition within the walls, by the discontent of some of his troops and the faithlessness of others, he still maintained a lofty mind in difficult circumstances. All that could be done to repel the attack he did. But in everything a fatality attended him. No longer despising native assistance, he entered into negotiations with Hyder Ali, then rising into power, but that astute chief, though promising much, declined to commit himself to fortunes so absolutely desperate: he projected a night attack (2nd September) on the English, but his left wing failed him at the critical moment. All this time he was surrounded by those whom he had made his enemies, he was ill, harassed, and opposed. The Regiment of Lorraine had been reduced to 327 men, that of Lally to 230; whilst the enemy had received large reinforcements. Finally, all resources having been exhausted, and having but four ounces of rice left for distribution to each soldier, he agreed on the 14th January to capitulate; but the English refused to grant him terms, and he was compelled to surrender at discretion (16th January, 1761). The following extract from the letter of an English officer who was present at the siege will shew the straits to which Lally was reduced before he gave in. "Our artillery," he says, "performed wonders, but the want of every necessary within was what chiefly wrought in our favour. The inhabitants had subsisted for a long time upon their elephants, horses, camels, &c. I can assure you for a truth that a dog sold for 24 rupees; of this miserable provision there did not remain enough for one day longer when the English took possession of the place." Again referring to Lally, he says: "It is a convincing proof of his abilities, the managing so long and vigorous a defence, in a place where he was held in universal detestation."

This detestation indeed was so great that, as he marched out of the citadel of Pondichery, he was saluted with a loud and general hiss, and was loaded with the most abusive and opprobrious epithets. The Intendant of his army, who followed him, an old man half blind, and upwards of seventy years old, was killed on the spot. Lally himself would have shared the same fate but for the opportune appearance of some English hussars.

With the surrender of Pondichery closes the Indian career of Count Lally. But little more remains to be told, and that little is perhaps the saddest of all. He was detained after his surrender for nearly two months at Madras, and, he states, was treated in a most unworthy manner by the English Governor and Council. At last he was sent to England as prisoner of war in a small merchant ship. Arriving in London, he learned for the first time that his enemies had preceded him to Paris, and that he had been charged with treason, incompetency, correspondence with the English, peculation, and tyrannical administration. More jealous of his honour than careful for his safety, he applied to be allowed to return to France on his parole. The application was granted, and he returned, "carrying with him," he said, "his head and his innocence." But he found that all France had been stirred to its very depths by the news of the loss of the French Indies, and that the ministry were determined to have a victim. Who was this victim to be? On the one side Lally stood alone, without a friend, not desirous to have a friend, himself accusing all; on the other, were the Council of India and their friends, and allied with them, because equally accused by Lally, were two such opposite characters as d'Aché and Bussy. In vain did the two latter offer him terms of accommodation. Lally scorned and spurned them; in vain did the minister, the Duc de Choiseul, advise him to save himself by flight, as the tide was too strong: Lally rejected the advice with disdain. He stood upon his innocence, the purity of his motives, the justice of his cause,—strong supports in the abstract, but utterly powerless to save, in the presence of a despotic Government thirsting for a victim.

For twelve months Lally was engaged in soliciting an enquiry into his own conduct, and that of his accusers, but learning at the end of that time that he was to be placed under arrest, he voluntarily surrendered himself, and was confined in the Bastille.

In the course of the long months that followed, a circumstance occurred which proved decisive of his fate. It so happened that amongst the many intriguers in Pondichery, one Father Lavaur, a Jesuit Priest, had made himself especially active. This man was one of those plausible sycophants who are found occasionally in all countries and in all societies: a man of that class of which King Solomon wrote that "a whisperer separateth very friends:" a man who paid his court alternately to contending parties, according as the barometer of their fortunes appeared to be rising; who abused Lally to Bussy, and Bussy to Lally; who repeated remarks not intended to be told, and who insinuated even more than he repeated. This man had latterly rather inclined to the party against Lally, but with the low cunning and habitual baseness of the sycophant race, he had contrived a method by which he might stand well with either party, whichever might succeed. For this purpose he had prepared two memoirs of the events in the East, in one of which he had lauded the administration of Lally, and in the other had condemned it. He kept these carefully by him, waiting for some sign of the action of the ministry to use one or other of them. But death struck him down when still wallowing in his baseness. His papers were then searched, and the two memoirs were found; but they were found by the enemies of Lally. One of them only was consequently given to the world. It was that in which Lally was condemned.

This decided the fate of Lally. Proceedings against him had been commenced at the Châtelet on the 16th July, 1763, they were transferred to the Parlement of Paris in January, 1764. Lally was not allowed an advocate. The trial lasted more than two years and a half. At length on the 3rd May, 1766, a decision was arrived at. On the following day Lally was removed to the Conciergerie, and on the 5th at seven in the morning he was brought before his judges. On appearing before them he was required to give up his red riband and cross, and was then placed in the dock in order to be interrogated. On finding himself in this situation, he clasped his hands and exclaimed, "Is this then the reward of fifty-five years' service?" He was interrogated that day from seven o'clock to one, and again from three to nine P.M., after which he was taken back to the Bastille. The next day the Parliament delivered judgment, and pronounced "Lally attainted and convicted of having betrayed the interest of the King and of the India Company, of abuse of authority and exactions against the subjects of the King and the foreign residents of Pondichery." For reparation of this, it deprived him of all titles, honours, and dignities, and condemned him to have his head severed from his body, and declared his property confiscated.

When this sentence was read to Lally, he listened very quietly as far as the expression that "he had betrayed the interests of the King." The moment he heard those words he exclaimed, "that is not true, never, never;" and snatching up a pair of compasses, with which he had been tracing a chart of the coast of Coromandel, he endeavoured to strike them into his heart. But the wound, though severe, was not mortal. His enemies, however, deeming that he might thus escape the full measure of their vengeance, caused the execution to be advanced six hours. His confessor had promised him that he should go to the place of execution in a carriage, followed by a hearse. But even this slight favour was denied him. He was hurried into a dung-cart, which had been put into requisition for the purpose; a gag was thrust into his mouth by the executioner to prevent him from addressing the populace; and thus ignominiously was the man who had fought for France since his boyhood, who had given her his best years, his best energies, the first-fruits of all he had inherited, led to the scaffold Yes, to the scaffold, gagged, and in a dung-cart, sent thither by his King: —by that King who had witnessed his prowess at Fontenoy and Laffeldt; who, when some germs of grace yet remained to him, had named this same Lally Colonel on the field of battle; but who now, sunk in vice, wallowing in debauchery, the slave, and by his being the slave, making France the slave, of the vilest of women, could forget all past services, and when Lally's pardon was solicited by the Marshal de Soubise in the name of the army, could only reply: "It is too late, he is condemned." Yes, he was thus led to the scaffold:—the gag was then taken from his mouth, and he was blindfolded. During the operation he turned to the Commissaries of the Parliament and said: "Tell my judges that God has given me grace to pardon them; if I were to see them again, I might no longer have the forbearance to do it." He then knelt down and placed his head upon the block. The executioner severed it from his body in two blows; he then threw them both into a common hackney coach, and buried them in the churchyard nearest the place of execution.

Many years later repentant France annulled the unjust sentence which had thus sent to his doom one of the most gallant and devoted of her sons.

I have now brought to a conclusion the two careers of Count Lally. It has necessarily been only an outline, for time would not allow more,—and I have been compelled to omit many details that would have been interesting. I trust, however, I have succeeded in conveying to the minds of all who have heard me, a clear conception of the object of this lecture. It was not only that we might obtain a knowledge of Count Lally's career, but that we might derive from a glance at that career some ideas that might be advantageous to ourselves. I have shown him to you as a zealous, active, energetic officer in Europe, working his own way up to the top of his profession, till chosen by his sovereign to command in India. But here we find him at once face to face with a new set of difficulties,—difficulties which had never occurred to him before, which, in fact, were not incidental to European life. How did he meet those difficulties? Did he have recourse to those whose experience might have pointed out a mode of surmounting them? Did he even take them calmly into consideration? He did neither. He acted as if he argued that because there were no such obstacles in Europe, therefore none should exist for him in Asia, and that the plea of Indian experience was but an excuse for the non-performance of duties. He paid no regard to institutions which were stronger than time, or to the experience of men who were as anxious to serve France as himself, but he rode roughshod over all. The consequence was he failed, as those who attempt to govern by brute force must in the end always fail. The absence from his composition of sympathy with his kind was sufficient to neutralise his great talents, his daring energy, his invincible perseverance. It is this sympathy, which in any undertaking involving association with different classes of men, is one great element of success; its absence the certain prelude of failure. Unfortunately, Lally had it not.

Then, again, to look at another feature of his conduct. A military man himself, trained up in the army, he cared only for the opinions of men who belonged to his own profession. An English officer, writing of him at the time he was a prisoner at Madras, says, "Monsieur Lally is arrived amongst us; notwithstanding his fallen condition, he is now as proud and haughty as ever. A great share of wit, sense, and martial abilities, obscured by a savage ferocity, and an undisguised contempt for every person that moves in a sphere below that of a general, characterise this odd compound of a man." It was probably the demonstration of this contempt, the undisguised intimation that he considered it impossible that virtue, or public spirit, or talent, could exist out of the pale of his own service, that made him so many enemies at Pondichery. Men, even when undistinguished by abilities, can feel little heart in a system under which they are treated as inferior animals because of the difference in the colour of the coat that they wear; still less will those submit to it who feel within themselves the proud consciousness of deserving.

But if we admit his faults, we must not refrain from doing justice to the many virtues of Count Lally. Energy, perseverance, and determination, were concentrated in him to an extent never surpassed in man. "It needed only," as Voltaire said, "that success should be possible for him to succeed." Putting out of sight the fact that he himself was the cause of many of the obstacles against which he contended in India, it must yet be admitted that it would have been impossible for any one to have shown more firmness, more energy, more resolution than Lally showed. His perseverance was never more apparent than when all hope of success seemed vanished. He knew not what it was to despair. His mind rose buoyant from disasters which would have overwhelmed any ordinary man. He acted ever in accordance with the golden motto: "Whatsoever thy hand findeth to do, do it with all thy might." He did not succeed, simply because success under the circumstances was impossible. He was a gallant soldier, a loyal subject, and was imbued with the loftiest sense of honour. The eloquent language applied to an English general may truly be used with reference to Lally, that "he not only shunned, but scorned and spurned the base." We at least must recognise and admire these great qualities. If they had been united with patience, forbearance, and sympathy, they would have procured for him a place on the highest pedestal of Fame, and in that case it is probable that neither would I have been here to recount, nor you to listen to this imperfect lecture on "the career of Count Lally."

SIR HENRY HAVELOCK.

[From the 'Calcutta Review,' November, 1860.]

As, gliding down the stream of the tranquil present, w look back upon the tumultuous past; as we recall th excitements, the terrors, the atrocities of 1857, it impossible to feel insensible to that wonderful dispens tion of Providence which, when the danger was highes when the career of triumphant rebellion was as yet u checked, at least in the central provinces, when ou own resources were at the lowest, brought to the scen of action from another and a distant part of Asia, a ma suited to the hour, whose strong character, pitted again hordes of conscienceless traitors, sufficed to restore victo to our standards, and to re-establish the prestige, n lost in fair fight, but stolen after foul murder, of th British arms. How this was accomplished, how by th determined energy of this man the tide of rebellion w first turned, must be fresh in the memory of all. If w allude now to the subject, it is because we would wish t dwell for a moment on the character of the chief act in that part of the great drama, and to ascertain by wh mental training, through what amount of practical e perience his natural powers had been moulded to attai so brilliant a development.

A shy, contemplative, but strong-willed boy, Hen Havelock had been educated for the bar. Circumstance however, which he could not control, but which in their immediate result were opposed to his wishes, changed his destination, and at the age of twenty years he entered the army. He entered it at a period when England had had but five years' experience of that peace which was destined to remain unbroken till 1853. The signs of its probable continuance, however, were even then plenteous, and Havelock, dreading the career the most fatal of all others to genuine aspirations,—that of being a soldier merely in name,—turned his thoughts to a country which held out certain promise of becoming at no distant period the theatre of great events. Of all the possessions and dependencies of England, India at that time alone offered the inducement of a chance of active service. To noble ambitions, to high hopes, to lofty aspirations, she was the land of promise. What wonder then that Havelock, who had mastered the theories of his profession with all the ardour of an enthusiast, who had even then brooded over the achievements of the great captains of ancient and modern epochs, what wonder that he, left free to choose for himself, should have selected a career in a country in which, if there were many candidates for honour, there appeared to be at least many chances for the aspirant. The studies to which he had devoted the initiatory years of his military life, the complete theoretical knowledge which he had obtained regarding the actual science of war, his perfect acquaintance with the details of all the famous battles of history, had inspired him with a hope, near akin to confidence, that he too would be able to seize and employ rightly that golden moment, which occurs once always in the lifetime of all who seek it, but which, once missed, in most cases vanishes for ever.

To India then he made up his mind to proceed, and having so resolved, with a just appreciation of the first difficulties which would meet him in that country, he devoted himself, whilst yet in England, to the acquirement of the native languages. To a mind organised as was his, the sudden transition from Jomini to Gilchrist presented no insurmountable obstacles. The ardour which had prompted him to acquire a complete knowledge of the principles of the one, enabled him to master the peculiarities set before him by the other. His progress, therefore, was rapid, and the gain real and solid. So much in fact had he advanced in his Oriental studies during the few months that preceded his embarkation, that he was able during the voyage out to become a teacher in his turn, and to impart to others some of the advantages which he had acquired for himself.

Havelock embarked in the 'General Kyd,' in January, 1823, a lieutenant in the 13th Light Infantry. The country to which he was proceeding was at that time under the temporary sway of Mr. John Adams, a gentleman who unconsciously, and in spite of himself, did more to upset the monopoly of the East India Company than any previous or subsequent ruler. The same month that witnessed Havelock's embarkation, witnessed also the departure from India of the great marquess who, in the course of a domination extending over nine years, had raised the glory of our arms to the highest pitch, and had placed upon the firmest basis the material prosperity of the empire. Like others who succeeded him, he sailed from India in the full belief that he had left to his successor a legacy of peace; unlike those others, he did leave to that successor an elastic revenue, and a treasury full even to overflowing,

—a source of strength and power to the strong,—an irresistible temptation to the weak.

Havelock reached Calcutta in May of the same year. Within two months of his arrival Mr. Adams, whose tenure of office had resulted from the purely accidental circumstance of his being at the time of Lord Hastings' departure senior member of Council, was succeeded by Earl Amherst,—not however before the occurrence on our eastern frontier of certain manifestations, which laid the foundations of future warfare.

It is not necessary to refer here to the particular causes which brought about actual hostilities with the Burman empire. From the moment that barbarism, till then victorious and uncontrolled, came into contact with European civilisation, the result was inevitable. Commencing in the first instance with an actual attack on our possessions, the court of Ava regarded the gentle remonstrances of the Indian Government as sure signs of conscious weakness. To such an extent did their conceit increase, that it became absolutely necessary for the security of our own territories to give to their monarch a convincing proof that, however great might be his superiority to the rude tribes that surrounded him, he was yet unequal to the task of dictating terms to an English Government. In consequence of this necessity, and in pursuance of that wise principle of warfare, of which Hannibal may be considered the most brilliant exemplar, Lord Amherst resolved, in the early part of 1824, to transport a sufficient force under an experienced general to a part of the enemy's coast, which was at once the most vulnerable, and which at the same time might possess the advantage of communicating most easily with the capital. It was confidently believed that a march on Ava, entailing, as it necessarily must, more than one encounter between the hostile forces, would suffice to bring the enemy to reason, and to lower the arrogant spirit which had tempted him to invade our possessions. Two divisions from Madras and Calcutta were accordingly organised, and these leaving their presidencies in the months of April and May, 1824, united at the Andamans on the 5th of the last named month, and proceeded at once under the command of Sir Archibald Campbell to Rangoon.

At the time that the Bengal division of this force was organised, Havelock had not completed twelve months' service in India. Occupying the position during this period of a subaltern of the corps which garrisoned Fort William, no work beyond the mere routine of regimental duty had been assigned him. He had, however, distinguished himself in a manner which does not always commend the performer to the favourable notice of the authorities. With all the fervour of his nature he had devoted himself to the study and practice of religion, and not content with that, he had endeavoured to extend among his own soldiers the knowledge of the truths which he had found so precious. He became known in the regiment as a pious, earnest, and at the same time a most zealous and devoted officer. Fortunately for his worldly prospects this knowledge was not confined to his regiment. Thus it happened that at the time when the Burmese expedition was being organised, and when inquiries were being made regarding smart, intelligent officers to fill the more subordinate positions on the general staff, the name of Havelock was brought to the notice of those in whose hands lay the dispensation of patronage, and he was appointed Deputy Assistant-Adjutant-General of the expedition.

The war which was at that period undertaken proved, in a military and scientific point of view, the least interesting of all in which the Indian Government has been engaged. Combating in swamps, opposed to an enemy who never fought but behind stockades, and then generally fought badly, a prey to the ravages of a pestilential atmosphere, our troops were merely called upon to display that courage and that endurance which are so peculiarly their own. There was no call for the manifestation of the manœuvring capabilities of our commanders. To move straight on, to attack the enemy wherever he could be found, and to follow up with promptitude every advantage gained in the field,—these were the conditions on which to bring the war to a successful issue. To a soldier, nevertheless, thoroughly acquainted with the details of European conflicts, versed in that strategic science which prompted the operations of Marlborough and Eugene in their campaigns against the tried Marshals of Louis XIV., of Gustavus against Tilly and Wallenstein, of Frederic against Daun, and of General Bonaparte in 1796, this expedition to Burmah opened a new field. It was here that Havelock first learned that the success of Europeans combating against Asiatics must depend less upon science than upon dash; that with one good blow, dealt energetically and followed up rapidly, the fate of an empire might be decided. The Burmese campaign it was, that taught him that no troops were more liable to depression, none less inclined to struggle against hostile fortune, none who possessed to an inferior degree the power of rallying *en masse* than Asiatics. To him then, destined as he was to an Indian career, the experience thus gained was invaluable. Grafting it upon his theoretical knowledge, he was able thereafter to plan, devise and execute schemes calculated for every emergency. The fact that he himself had borne no light part in a campaign that terminated only at the gates of the enemy's capital, that he had been able thus practically to test his theoretical knowledge, and to compare it with the actual measures of his own commander, gave him a confidence in his own judgment, and a proud self-reliance that never after deserted him. In Burmah were sown the seeds of that strategy that afterwards triumphed at Cawnpore.

The Burmese campaign lasted twenty-one months. Havelock, who arrived just too late for the storming of Rangoon, was yet able to take a prominent part in the operations which succeeded the occupation of that important town. As the year advanced, however, it was found that sickness was our most dangerous foe. By the end of July more than half the force had become non-effective. Havelock himself was amongst the latter, and to save his life he was compelled to proceed to Calcutta, and thence by the sea route to Bombay. After an absence of eleven months, during which our army had advanced no higher than Prome, Havelock returned to his duty. He was in time to take a share in the advance which resulted in the defeat of the enemy in three pitched battles, and in the acceptance by the King of the conditions of peace which our Commander-in-Chief had imposed. In these actions his was naturally a subordinate part; but to a subordinate on the staff, great opportunities of observation are often granted, and Havelock showed, not very long afterwards, that he had allowed none of these to pass unnoticed.

For nearly thirteen years after the treaty of Yandaboo, India remained at peace, and not a single opportunity was afforded Havelock of practically testing his acquirements in the field. With an ill-fortune, which in the present days of high pressure and quick promotion would be accounted marvellous, he was doomed throughout this period to remain a lieutenant. He was not, however, altogether unemployed. As interpreter to Colonel, afterwards Sir Willoughby Cotton, one of the brigadier-generals of the Burman expedition, and then commanding at Cawnpore; as adjutant of the depôt of royal troops at Chinsurah; as interpreter to the 16th Foot, and, finally, as adjutant of his own regiment, he found ample opportunities for increasing his own experience, and perfecting himself in that knowledge, the most valuable of all to the soldier and the statesman,—the knowledge of human nature. In his two appointments as adjutant, first to the depôt and afterwards to his regiment, the moving springs of human action were constantly open to his inspection. It was probably during this period of probation that he acquired that experience in the art of managing men's minds, of appealing to their hearts, of directing their instincts to a particular point, which he afterwards put in practice with so much effect. Religious as he was, and ever anxious to increase the number of those who cared for their eternal welfare, he could not but have perceived, that even on the scoffer and the profane it was possible to exercise a strong moral influence. There is probably no class of men more quick-witted, more imbued with a sense of their own rights, or more jealous of maintaining them than the private soldiers: no men, at the same time, oftener subject themselves to the sway of passions incidental to fallen man. To manage such men, to direct their energies to a useful and a noble end, mere theories are valueless. It is necessary that each move in the lower organisation should be checked, and, if possible, exalted, by a corresponding and answering movement on the part of a more commanding mind. For this purpose, knowledge acquired by actual experience, imbibed, as it were, by mixing heartily with the men, by seeing their natures open before one, is the first requisite. None are more sensitive on this point than the men themselves. Their spirits spurn the control which is measured out by rule, and which, applied therefore without any consideration of the varying attributes of humanity, must often act unjustly. It is when their natures are in the presence of another nature, not only superior to theirs, but intimately acquainted with its component parts, yet partaking of the higher and the better portion of those parts, and, at the same time, sympathising with the whole, that their minds swayed by the magnetic influence, yield themselves entirely to its control. That Havelock penetrated to the very depths of this great mystery may perhaps be doubted. There have been warriors, famous in history, who have acquired a greater insight into the secret springs of human actions, and who have gained consequently a greater influence and control over their men. But his after career proved, nevertheless, that his knowledge of mankind, and his power of directing the instincts of the soldier, were very great indeed. The manner in which he showed this knowledge will be spoken of in its proper place: it is alluded to here, because it was at the period of which we are now treating that that experience must have been acquired.

But there were seasons during those thirteen years of peace when Havelock was not brought into such close contact with his men. There were years when he was forced to be content with the mere performance of the duties of a subaltern with his regiment. Then it was that his active mind went in search of other occupations, and, searching earnestly, soon lighted upon a congenial theme. We have before alluded to the opportunities which presented themselves to him during his campaign in Burmah of criticising the manœuvres of his commanders. These had appeared to him to be, in many instances, opposed to those principles of war on which the greatest generals of ancient and modern times had invariably sought to act. Their erratic courses, as he supposed them to be, he had noted down at the time; and it appeared to him, in his moments of leisure, that it might be useful to his profession, and profitable to himself, to give to the world a critical history of the entire campaign. He had scarcely, however, entered upon his work when the idea occurred to him that it might possibly be considered presumption, and more than presumption on his part, thus to criticise his superiors. Yet only a subaltern, his right to pass in review, and to animadvert upon the movements of full-blown generals, would almost certainly be called in question. Writing at all, he would be compelled to write the whole truth, and would that be palatable? These were startling questions; especially startling were they to a soldier dependent on his profession for support, and looking to it as the sole ladder by which he could advance to distinction. We know, from the memoirs published of him by his brother-in-law, that he debated the matter long and carefully with himself. "I am half afraid," he says in one of his letters to Serampore, "of the storm of hostility which the free discussion of recent events might draw upon a subordinate officer. Men of years and rank are so unwilling ever to be proved in the wrong; and I cannot, in common honesty, attempt to show that in 1824-25, and '26 they were always in the right." Again, "were the manuscript carried in *statu quo* to the press, it is not impossible that I might find my name omitted in the army list of some subsequent month for having presumed to think that a Brigadier-General can do wrong." These extracts prove that even when sending his manuscript to the press, Havelock was not free from doubt as to the manner in which the publication might affect his own prospects. With the knowledge which we possess of his conscientiousness, of his rigid morality, of his strong views regarding right and wrong, of the manner in which he would have clung to the one and spurned the other, we have a right to believe that in deciding to publish, Havelock pursued the course which after deep and earnest consideration he felt himself called upon to undertake. Possessing a knowledge not shared in by the world at large, enabled by his reading, by his practical ability, to point out errors, which to be avoided in future it was necessary to illustrate with peculiar reference to this particular expedition, was he, on account of purely personal considerations, for fear of injuring his own prospects, to be absolutely dumb? To be silent, he must have felt, was to be criminal. Balancing then the criminality of silence against the "imprudence" of publication, Havelock felt it impossible to falter. Not careless then of consequences, but confident in the purity of his motives, believing that his criticism was just, that his conclusions would bear the strictest examination, he published. Written in a manly and classical style, outspoken in its remarks on the execution of the campaign, awarding with an impartial hand blame and praise, the work appeared at the Serampore press in 1828, two years after the conclusion of the war of which it treated. It was most unfortunate that it had not been published in England. An Indian work never has a fair chance. It may be a prejudice, but it is a fact, that even the Indian public look upon the name of the English publisher as a guarantee, to a certain extent, of the value of the work. They look forward also before they buy, unless they are by chance acquainted with the author, to the criticisms of the English press. Deprived of these advantages, printed too on inferior paper, and with inferior type, an Indian book scarcely makes a fair start. It has happened that when subsequent events have recalled public interest to the subject on which it treated, a work originally published in India has reappeared in an English dress. But this is a rare occurrence; it almost always happens that the work published in India is discredited on account of its Indian imprint, and enjoys consequently but a limited circulation.

It is on no other grounds that we can account for the failure, as a literary speculation, of Havelock's 'Campaigns in Ava.' The style in which it was written, the professional acumen displayed in the criticisms, and the general interest of the narrative, were sufficient under ordinary circumstances to attract to it a large amount of public support. Published in England, it must have commanded attention, but an offspring of Serampore it never surmounted the ineradicable blot of its nativity. In India, therefore, its circulation was limited, whilst in England it became known to but a select few. It did happen, however, to find its way to the Horse Guards, and in that hallowed region its boldness, as might have been expected, found no favour. "Is he tired of his commission?" was the question asked of the elder brother of the author, when he presented himself within those sacred precincts. No active persecution, however, followed this remark, although we are informed by his brother-in-law that the book made him many enemies.

We might pause here for an instant to enquire with his biographer how it happened that with the evidence of professional knowledge displayed in this work before them, the Government of India left the subaltern author to pine in neglect. Was it because they thought that soldiers ought to remain mere instruments, without feelings and without passions, debarred from the exercise of every intellectual faculty, and that they regarded as little less than a crime, this effort on the part of Havelock to vindicate his claim to a position in the world of responsible humanity? Did they consider that the duties of an officer should be confined to a punctual attendance at drills and parades, and to the necessity never to appear drunk on duty, and did they wish to repress every effort on his part to exercise his brain for the performance of the higher duties of his profession,—an exercise which in times of peace can best be promoted by a critical study of past campaigns? These are no light questions, for they affect the present even more than the past. Let us examine for a moment the circumstances of Havelock's case. Here was a man, who had instructed himself thoroughly in the science of war, who enjoyed the highest character as an officer, and in whom there lay, dormant at that time, and waiting for an occasion, very high military powers. Impelled by an imperative sense of duty, by a conscientious resolve to do what was right in spite of consequences, he publishes a work, to the excellence of which, he subsequently recorded, three Commanders-in-Chief bore their testimony. Yet although that book was rich in military lore, although it contained instruction of the most valuable nature, because, in the course of its truthful narrative, it trenched upon the vanity of a few high officials, the writer was allowed to linger in obscurity. The abilities which were conspicuous in every page of the book, the talents which the Government might themselves have directed to some great purpose, were restricted to the performance of trifling duties, and for nine years afterwards the Havelock of 1828, who possessed within himself all the powers and more than the vigour of the Havelock of 1857, was deemed doubly rewarded in being allowed to remain, unmolested on account of his opinions, a hardworking subaltern. One of the most touching pictures in the history of France immediately prior to the Revolution, presents to our eyes Dumouriez pacing the streets of Paris, conscious of his abilities for command, but conscious also that his plebeian birth deprived him of every chance of the attainment of his desires. But how infinitely more affecting were the circumstances of Havelock's position! He, too, was conscious of the possession of great abilities, and yet he had the mortification to find that he was restricted to the duties of a subaltern, because, in the only manner in which as a conscientious officer he could perform the task, he had written a work in which those abilities were made known to the Government he served.

After long delays, however, and three failures to obtain his company by purchase, promotion came at last. In 1838 Havelock was able to write Captain before his name, and by a strange coincidence the same year witnessed also the abandonment of that peaceful policy which, without interruption, had been fostered by the Indian Government ever since the peace of Yandaboo. It was in December of that year that the expedition to Affghanistan, which had formed the great theme of discussion in every station in India for twelve months preceding, was actually entered upon. On the 10th of that month the Bengal division of the British forces, under the command of Sir Willoughby Cotton, commenced its march for an object, which, for disregard of all moral obligation, as well as for political unsoundness, is unequalled by any recorded in the history of the British nation. Decided upon originally for the purpose of compelling the Persian army to raise the siege of Herat, it might have been supposed that with the accomplishment of that design, all necessity for the further progress of the expedition would have ceased. The Persian army, thanks to the gallantry of an English officer who accidentally found himself in the place, had been forced to retire from before Herat on the 9th September, 1838, three months before a single British soldier had left our territories. The original object of the expedition had thus been accomplished, without the expenditure of a single drop of English blood, or an ounce of English treasure. Nevertheless, so bent were those who directed the counsels of the Indian Government on making a grand demonstration in Central Asia, so terrified were they at the bugbear of Russian aggrandisement, then distantly looming in the future, that losing sight of those greater dangers nearer their own possessions,—dangers which in a cooler moment would have been obvious to none more than to themselves,—they resolved, at the cost of an immense expenditure of money, in defiance of right, and at great military risk, still to send on an army for the purpose of expelling the energetic sovereign who was all the time well disposed to fall in with our views regarding Persia, and to replace him by an imbecile *fainéant* whose weakness had rendered him contemptible in Affghan eyes. So extraordinary was the excitement that reigned amongst the governing classes at the time, that they did not perceive either the foolishness or the immorality of the course which they had resolved to pursue. The advance into Affghanistan was heralded by those high-sounding phrases and lofty professions which those who have at their disposal numerous battalions know so well how to employ. These phrases and these professions produced an effect at which men of the present day, with their experience of thirty subsequent years, may well be surprised. In 1838, however, belief in the character of public men was not wholly extinguished, and certainly the greater number of those who started from Ferozepore on that 10th December, started in the belief that they were about to restore a legitimate sovereign to his throne, and to give an effectual check to the ambition and to the encroachments of Russia. It would appear that Havelock entertained some such opinion at the outset. Certain it is that he hailed the prospect of service which the offer of the appointment of Aide-de-camp on Sir Willoughby Cotton's staff opened out to him. It was a position most favourable for one whose active mind would not permit him to be a mere instrument of authority, but who judged every movement by the standard set up by those great captains, the history of whose achievements was stored in his mind. Throughout that long march from Ferozepore through the Bolan Pass to Candahar, he must often have mused on the fact that on the fidelity to his engagements of the ruler of the Punjab, depended the safety of our force. We had no base of operations; our army was separated from its resources; on our right and our right rear lay the army of Runjeet Singh, splendidly organised, flushed with victory over the Affghans, and ready to obey his nod. The further we proceeded, the more isolated, the more dangerous became our position, and to the chances arising from that position were added the barren nature of the country, and the necessity which existed of carrying our supplies with us. As we read the account of that campaign, every page increases our astonishment that a British army should ever have been sent on such an expedition, and for such a purpose.

It is not our design to follow the expedition step by step on its onward course. Its details are well-known to all readers of Indian history. The part played by Havelock, as aide-de-camp on the staff of a general of division, was necessarily limited. He was able nevertheless to improve his experience in matters which it is beyond the power of mere book-learning to impart. He it was who, after the junction at Candahar by the

Bombay division, and the assumption by Sir John Keane of the chief command, strongly urged that the siege train, which had been conveyed thus far at the cost of much trouble, should be taken on to be used against Ghuznee. His advice was, on the representations of the "politicals," disregarded, and in consequence, the army found itself some weeks later in front of a fortress, the defences of which could only be breached by heavy artillery. It is true that the combined daring and ingenuity of Captains Thomson and Durand of the Bengal Engineers rescued Sir John Keane from his false position, but the circumstance made an ineradicable impression on the mind of Havelock, and materially influenced his own operations at a later period. Never to attack fortified places without artillery, and to be himself "political" as well as general, ranked thereafter amongst his best conned maxims. It was in this campaign also that the impressions which he had imbibed in Burmah, as to the advisability of losing no opportunity of attacking an Asiatic enemy in the field, with but small regard to his superior numbers, and his convictions likewise as to the enormous advantages to be derived from following up rapidly even the most trifling victory, received fresh confirmation. Havelock accompanied the force in its triumphant progress to Cabool, but finding, shortly after his arrival there, that the puppet king whom we had placed on the throne by our bayonets, could only be supported by the same means, and that our occupation of Affghanistan might be prolonged indefinitely, he resisted all the offers of Sir Willoughby Cotton, and resolved to return speedily to India. He was prompted to this determination chiefly by a wish to publish an account of the campaign, before the interest excited by it had entirely evaporated. For a task of this nature he was peculiarly well qualified. He had not only taken notes of his own, but he had possessed the entire confidence of Sir Willoughby Cotton, and had obtained from the Commander-in-Chief free access to all the records in his office. He naturally imagined that a work at once accurate, interesting, and professional, could not fail to find many readers, and although he wrote at the time that he considered himself "too old for fame," he might nevertheless have pictured to himself that such a work, if well performed, would convince those in whose hands lay the power of advancing deserving officers, that he at least had mastered the higher branches of his profession. He was doomed however, on this occasion, as on the former, to bitter disappointment. The work, although lucid in arrangement, forcible in style, and vivid in description, although too it had the advantage of an English publisher, fell still-born from the press. This result may perhaps be partly attributable to the intense excitement which prevailed in England at that time (1839-40), on account of the movements of the Chartists. The "battle of Newport," so fatal to the pretensions of Messrs. Frost, Williams, and Jones, presented a problem of far deeper moment to the politicians of England than the history of the taking of Ghuznee. Then again the march to Cabool, though teeming with hardships to the soldiers, was, for a campaign, singularly barren of fighting results. The successful assault on Ghuznee, was, in a military point of view, its solitary triumph. It is probable therefore, that the general public, unacquainted with the locality, ignorant of the dangers *in posse* and the privations *in esse*, saw only that we had reached Cabool without a battle, and imagined that it was almost unnecessary to acquaint themselves with the details of such an expedition to a greater extent than could be ascertained from the despatches. Had there been a few more casualties, and a fair proportion of stirring adventures, the history would probably have been more favourably received.

It may not be out of place here to state the matured opinion of Havelock, written in after years, on the subject of the publication by an officer of his own experiences on service and elsewhere. Even in the year 1860 the opinion on this subject of one of the most real and practical soldiers that ever lived, may not be altogether unworthy of consideration. The passage, as recorded by his biographer, is too long to be extracted in its entirety. We cull, however, that portion of it which may be considered general in its application. "Our institutions and public opinion secure to us the liberty of printing; and common sense unawed by a few who have not kept pace with their age, recognises in the nineteenth century the perfect compatibility of the most implicit obedience in the ranks and in the field, with thorough independence of spirit in the republic of letters. Contemporary memoirs are the means of which the future historian gladly avails himself, or of which he bitterly laments the want, when he comes to trace with an impartial hand the picture of events which have influenced the happiness of large portions of the human race."

Although Havelock was naturally mortified by the ill-success of a work on which he had bestowed no ordinary labour, his was not a spirit to be cast down by any disappointment. Its first result was to determine him to bend his mind more closely to his profession. It happened that, after he had rid himself of the labour of revising and despatching his work, he was directed to proceed to Cabool with recruits. Arriving in the course of his journey at Ferozepore, he fell in with General Elphinstone, then lately appointed to the command of our troops in Affghanistan. By him he was offered the post of Persian interpreter on his staff. This he accepted, and it was in that capacity that in February, 1841, after an absence of fifteen months, he found himself once more in Cabool.

It was on the occasion of this, his second residence in Affghanistan, that the nature of Havelock's qualities was destined to the severest trial. The weakness of our political agent, and the incapacity of our military commander, contributed even more than the treachery of the oligarchy of Cabool, to bring about the greatest disaster that has ever befallen British arms. It was not so much, as Havelock remarked with astonishment on his arrival, that the position which should have been occupied as a fort had been given up to the purposes of a seraglio; it was a vicious but not a fatal arrangement that located our soldiers in a cantonment commanded by neighbouring heights, and that placed all the supplies of the army in a detached fort. These evils, great as they were, would have been remedied by the valour of our troops, if they had had but a commander. But with an old gentleman at the head of the army enfeebled by disease, with an envoy who had trained his intellect to believe that to be true which he wished to be true, and who persisted, in spite of the most glaring evidence of bad faith, in giving credence to the assurances of the natives,—with division everywhere, and self-reliance nowhere, it was impossible to effect anything great.

There was in fact no command. The measures that had been resolved upon one moment, were cancelled an hour later, and this indecision, commencing in the tent of the general, could not but have a most lamentable effect upon the army. As if, too, to add to the difficulties of our situation, the most open marks of hostility on the part of the Affghans served but to induce our leaders to pretend a greater confidence in their good faith. It seems at this distant period almost incredible, that after the slaughter of Sir Alexander Burnes, after the murder of the envoy in cold blood, after manifestations of hostility too striking to be misconceived, the leaders of that force,—a force numbering 5000 men,—should still have preferred to trust to Affghan honour rather than to the bayonets of their soldiers. Once having resolved to retire, they should have regarded every Affghan as an enemy, and have trusted to their own energies alone. Instead of this, to use the emphatic language of Havelock, "they credulously confided in Affghan faith, moved in the power and at the dictation of Akbar Khan, took up the positions which he pointed out, forbore to fire on the partisans whom he had arrayed to destroy them; and as much to the last the dupes of intrigue and treachery as the victims of the sword, cold, hunger and fatigue, were engulfed in the eastern Gilzye mountains." Surely, if history be indeed philosophy teaching by example, the details of this terrible disaster ought to have served as a warning to the men that were to come after. The tale told by it, of the folly, the incredible folly, of trusting to the oaths of Asiatics, of placing ourselves with respect to them in a suppliant and inferior position, ought to have rendered impossible any similar infatuation in future. Yet only sixteen years later, the events of the mutiny too clearly shewed, that in many instances the warning of Asiatic duplicity had been vouchsafed in vain, though, unfortunately for us, the recollections of European credulity had been eagerly treasured up and remembered.

In the movements of the Cabool force Havelock was not a sharer. Although on the staff of the general, he had obtained permission to join his regiment, the 13th Light Infantry. This regiment, under the command of the gallant Sale, had been ordered in the month of October, 1841, to the assistance of the 35th Native Infantry, upon which an attack had been made in the passes near Cabool. The nature of the conflict in which the two corps were engaged on the following day made it clear to those who took part in it that the whole country was in arms against the British. General Sale indeed found that it would be impossible for him to move forward to Gundamuck,—the destination assigned him by the general in command,—unless reinforcements were promptly furnished. He selected Havelock to carry the despatches in which he stated his necessities on this head, and it was probably owing in a great measure to his influence that within a week not only were reinforcements provided, but plentiful supplies were sent with them. Havelock again obtained permission to rejoin General Sale's brigade, which the authorities at Cabool, lulled by their reliance on Affghan promises, considered at that time the post of danger.

For the eighteen days that followed the force was in continual conflict. Harassed on all sides, attacked sometimes in front, oftener on the flanks and rear, the brigade, encumbered as it was with baggage, could only with difficulty push forward. It had been Havelock's wish after the second march, when it had been resolved, in accordance with instructions from Cabool, to send back one of the native regiments, to return with it in order to resume his appointment on the staff of General Elphinstone. This he considered to be his post of duty, and he was, at the moment, the less tempted to swerve from it, because the Gilzyes had but just before agreed to an accommodation, for the due performance of which they had furnished hostages. General Sale, however, could not patiently endure the idea of allowing Havelock to leave him. He had himself been wounded on the previous day, and he felt, therefore, more than ever all the responsibilities of his position. With Havelock he had been associated for many years, and he had had opportunities of witnessing how fitted he was to cope with a crisis. He therefore pointed out to him that in his opinion it was his duty to continue with the force, and finally took all the responsibility of his compliance on his own shoulders. Havelock obeyed, and from that moment became one of the most confidential advisers of the general. He it was who, in conjunction with Captains Macgregor, Backhouse, Broadfoot, and Davies,—four names famous in the history of that eventful period,—persuaded the general to attack the fort of Mamookhail, the possession of which secured the safety of the advance from Gundamuck to Jellalabad. He it was who, when a council of war was held at Gundamuck to debate as to the nature of the movements that ought to follow the receipt of the first disastrous accounts from Cabool, threw all the weight of his influence in support of the march on Jellalabad, on the solid ground, that there, at all events, they would occupy a position that could be held until reinforcements should reach them from India. He it was who, after the arrival of the force at that place, resisted with all his energy the proposal to give up the town and to retire within the citadel. He it was who, by the influence inspired by his character, by his sound judgment, far-seeing sagacity, and knowledge of soldiers, contributed as much as any single individual could contribute, to the successful defence of the illustrious garrison. If his labours were not so "pronounced" as those of George Broadfoot, it was because he occupied a far less prominent position than that most distinguished officer. It is yet a striking fact that it was to Havelock that Broadfoot ever looked for moral support during the sittings of those councils of war, in which he advocated, often alone, a determined policy, and it was owing to that support, always accorded, that the resolution to resist to the last was finally decided upon. It was due to these two men that when the hopes of the garrison were most gloomy,—when the government of India expressed only a desire to withdraw as much as possible from the affairs of Affghanistan, and when the news of the destruction of the Cabool force had caused unusual depression in the minds of all,—it was due, we say, to these two men that another treaty was not entered into with the Affghans, the expressed object of which was the withdrawal of the British troops from Jellalabad. The council of war had, in fact, decided in favour of the measure, and had noticed their acceptance of the propositions to the ruler of Cabool. Fortunately for the garrison the Affghans would not credit their good fortune, and sent to propose fresh stipulations. But before these could arrive the exertions of Broadfoot and Havelock had worked an immense change in the minds of the garrison, and it was then finally resolved to dismiss diplomacy to the winds, and if necessary to perish where they stood.

It would be foreign to the purpose of this article to enter into a detail of the daily events of that illustrious defence. Entering Jellalabad on the 12th November, the force under the command of General Sale, in spite of the original want of defences to the place,—in spite of deficiencies of supplies,—in spite of enemies without and traitors within its walls,—maintained their position until the arrival of the relieving army of General Pollock on the 13th April following. Throughout this period Havelock served on the staff of the general in command, and he enjoyed, therefore, the peculiar advantage of being acquainted with the reasons which guided the decisions of his chief. Of the influence which he was able to bring to bear on those decisions we have already spoken. His views were directed not only to the maintenance of our position at Jellalabad to the last extremity, but to impressing on the minds of others the vital importance of seizing every opportunity to meet the enemy in the field. His experience of men combined with his knowledge of the art of war to make his opinion especially valuable on this point. It was not only that he was animated by the conviction that under no circumstances could Asiatic troops resist a charge of Europeans in the open field, but he was profoundly impressed with a sense of the effect which constant inaction must produce on the minds of the garrison. These feelings reached their full intensity when, on the final repulse of the Affghan force under Akbar Khan from the walls of Jellalabad on the 10th March, that prince took up a position within two miles of the town, and commanding all the approaches to it. Then it was that Havelock scented the opportunity of making an attempt warranted by every rule of war, and conformable to sound policy. The defeat of the Affghans, the benefit to the "*morale*" of the soldier, and the raising of the blockade,—these were the points for which, the immediate prospect of relief being even then uncertain, it was surely desirable to strike a blow. When, after some discussion, General Sale determined to make the attempt, with a confidence which testified to his opinion he gave the command of one of the divisions to his most importunate adviser. On this the first occasion of his holding a responsible command in the field, Havelock gave proof of the possession of high military ability. The right wing under his orders had been directed to lead the attack, and penetrating if possible between the enemy's advanced position and the river on which it rested to drive away his skirmishers, and then combining with the two other divisions to pierce his centre. Havelock performed his part to admiration; seizing the line of the river, he drove the enemy's skirmishers before him, and pushed on in the preconcerted direction. All at once, however, the centre column under Colonel Dennie was diverted to another part of the field, and Havelock found himself exposed without warning to the brunt of the enemy's attack. Having received instructions from the general at the same time to halt, he drew up his men partly behind a wall and partly in square, and awaited the attack of the enemy's cavalry. These came on with great determination, and Havelock's horse rearing at the moment, he lost his seat and was only saved from death by a sapper and two men of the 13th who rushed forward to rescue him. The enemy in the interval failing to make an impression on the square, and being exposed to a galling fire from the men posted behind the wall, drew off in some confusion, and Havelock, observing almost immediately that the other columns were proceeding to his support, gave the signal to advance. Scarcely, however, had his men got well away from the protection of the wall, than the Affghan horse wheeling round came down upon them like an avalanche. Attacked this time in the open, Havelock formed his men into a square, and directing them to reserve their fire, he awaited the charge. Made more feebly than on the first occasion, it was even more unsuccessful, and Havelock instantly re-forming his men, completed the confusion of the enemy by pursuing him into his camp and capturing two guns. At this point the other columns came up, the camp was stormed on all sides, and the victory was complete.

How, nine days after this well won fight,—a fight which left the garrison of Jellalabad without an enemy within their reach,—the avenging army of General Pollock arrived; how for four months longer the united forces remained in the valley of Jellalabad, waiting for the co-operation of General Nott on the other side of Cabool,—how then, owing to the wise resolution of Lord Ellenborough, the army advanced, and triumphing on its route at Jugdulluk and Tezeen, entered Cabool flushed with the glow of victory; how our countrywomen were rescued from captivity, how that portion of Cabool which witnessed the treacherous murder of our envoy was destroyed, and how the enemy were utterly dispersed at Istaliff,—an action planned by Havelock in the capacity of Deputy Adjutant-General to General McCaskill; how finally the united armies of Nott and

Pollock, satiated with victory and sustained by the ennobling idea that they had restored the *prestige* of England in those distant regions, returned in the cold weather of 1842 to Hindoostan, and were met at Ferozepore by the grandest of India's Governors-General,—one who possessed in its greatest perfection the power of influencing men's minds,—and how finally the troops,—their leaders rewarded,—were dispersed to their peaceful cantonments, are matters which history has recorded. Hitherto however, history, in dealing with one of the subjects above alluded to,—the rewards dealt out to those who most greatly distinguished themselves,—has omitted all allusion to Havelock. Had she spoken, it would have been but to record that he was left unnoticed in the ruck. In the heat of popular enthusiasm, the merit of the great deeds accomplished was awarded to those under whose authority they had been carried out. Thus it was that Havelock, conscious of deserving, and yet too modest to claim that which was his due, was allowed, as a reward for his meritorious services, to proceed once more to the dull routine of regimental duty. He was informed confidentially by a friend,—his tried comrade Major Broadfoot,—that there existed *prejudices* against him. So true is it that even in these more liberal days, a man of really independent spirit finds in the very qualities which constitute his greatness, the most stubborn obstacle to his fortune!

Such merits as his, however, could not long remain unnoticed. In the course of time those who had been prejudiced against him disappeared from the scene, and in 1843 he found himself simultaneously major of his regiment and Persian interpreter to the new Commander-in-Chief, Sir Hugh Gough. He did not long enjoy this new appointment in peace. Recent and constantly recurring *émeutes* in the Punjab had warned Lord Ellenborough that the time was approaching, when he would be compelled to gather together all the resources of the empire over which he so wisely ruled, for an encounter with the trained and disciplined soldiers of Runjeet Singh. Whilst too he beheld the cloud, as yet scarcely bigger than a man's hand, that was rising steadily in the horizon before him, he was aware also of another tempest, not so dangerous, though more quick in its action, brewing within fifty miles of the capital of the North-West Provinces. Both these demonstrations were met by that noble man with the prescience and the spirit of a great statesman. Deeming the Gwalior danger the more pressing, knowing that it would be in the highest degree dangerous to march towards the Sutlej, whilst the hosts of Scindia lay armed and watchful on his flank and rear, he forced that Durbar to an explanation. Finding this unsatisfactory, and penetrating the hostile intentions of the Court, he marched in his army under Sir Hugh Gough, defeated the enemy in two pitched battles, and then, abstaining with a rare magnanimity from annexation, restored the country to its legitimate sovereign, having first reorganized its government upon principles which, fifteen years later, produced results which contributed greatly, in the dark hour of our calamity, to the safety of the Anglo-Indian Empire.

In the battle fought at Maharajpore, Havelock, as one of Lord Gough's staff officers, bore a part as prominent as one in such a position could hope for. In the heat of the action he rallied and inspired with enthusiam a native regiment—the 56th—against which he was afterwards destined to combat at Cawnpore. He found then that it was as feasible to inspire Asiatics to great deeds of courage, as to induce them, as in Affghanistan, to acts of rare and generous devotion. The appeal that he made to them in the heat of the action, riding in their front, and reminding them that they fought under the eye of their Commander-in-Chief, carried all hearts before it. He remarked afterwards that "whereas it had been difficult to get them forward before, the difficulty now was to restrain their impetuosity." It is an occasion like this that marks the really great soldier,—the man that to perfect acquaintance with his profession adds that still more necessary knowledge,—the knowledge how to exert a moving and animating influence over the minds of others.

It is recorded that after the action, standing over the grave of General Churchill, Havelock expressed his regret to Lord Ellenborough that the war had not been a war of subjugation. The same opinion was expressed pretty generally at the time, and the Governor-General was blamed for maintaining a rallying point for disaffected spirits. Subsequent events, however, showed that had Havelock's ideas on this point been carried out, his victorious career in 1857 would have been impossible, and in all probability the Central and Lower Provinces of India would have been, during that year, overrun by the mutineers. It was the inaction of the troops stationed in Gwalior, that enabled Havelock at a critical moment to maintain his position at Cawnpore; and that inaction, forced upon these troops by their Maharaja, was the offspring of Lord Ellenborough's policy. Two years after the Gwalior episode, the other and greater storm foreseen by Lord Ellenborough, burst with unprecedented fury upon the land. Unfortunately when the crisis came, the steady hand of that great nobleman no longer guided the helm of the state-vessel. He was recalled by men to whom his prescience was a reproach, in spite of the protests of the Duke of Wellington and Sir Robert Peel,—both of whom appreciated to the highest degree the great qualities which had been evinced throughout Lord Ellenborough's tenure of power. Combined ignorance and nepotism, however, shrink from the service of unsullied genius; they prefer employing as their agents men whom they can use to their own purposes. Thus it was that when the Sikh war broke out, Lord Ellenborough, who had foreseen it, and who had busied himself in preparations to meet it, was no longer Governor-General. One of the first acts of his successor, Sir H. Hardinge, was to countermand all his preparations, thereby committing the error, then almost fatal, but which notwithstanding has in later years been repeated, of endeavouring to disarm Asiatics by showing them that we were disarming ourselves. This conduct on our part naturally hurried on the catastrophe it was intended to avert. Without note or warning, taking advantage of our want of preparation, an enormous Sikh army crossed the Sutlej in the early part of December, 1845, and threatened to destroy our troops in detail in their cantonments.

Fortunately for us, the Sikh army, vast as it was in point of numbers and arrogant in its spirit, able too from the perfection of its equipments and the strength and valour of its soldiery to have carried all before it, was yet a body without a head. There was not a man amongst its commanders able to conceive or to appreciate the immense advantages within its grasp. It is possible that had the inroad of 1845 been made upon a purely Asiatic power, the chiefs of the Sikh army would have acted with that confident boldness which had distinguished them in their contests with the Affghans. But this aggression was made upon British territory, and the British arms had still a great reputation. It was this reputation that gave us breathing time; which induced timidity into the Sikh councils, and made them first hesitate and then decline to strike that blow, which would have been of all others most fatal to our prestige. This indecision was further confirmed by the resolute bearing and the heroic determination of the general who commanded at Ferozepore. Although he had only five thousand troops under his orders, of whom less than one-fourth were British, yet no sooner had the Sikh army, 60,000 strong, crossed the Sutlej and threatened Ferozepore, than Sir John Littler, taking counsel only from his own brave heart, marched out and offered them battle. It was a prudent, wise, and heroic resolve. Ferozepore was not defensible, it was crowded with women and children; to remain in it was to confess weakness, and at the same time to invite attack; to go forth and face the foe was, on the other hand, to intimate to them that a British general feared no odds, and considered himself with his handful a match for the thousands opposed to him. It was a movement, in fact, inspired by high military genius, and by a consummate knowledge of the Asiatic character. It was as successful as it deserved to be. The Sikh general, scared by the boldness of the British, declined the proffered combat and marched forward in the direction of Delhi. Meanwhile the Commander-in-Chief had not been idle. No sooner did he hear that the enemy had crossed the Sutlej than from Umballa, from the hill stations, from Meerut, and from the lower provinces troops were summoned into the field. The first division of these troops met the enemy, quite accidentally, on the 18th December at Moodkee. A battle without plan or arrangement of any sort ensued, which, without any very decisive issue, resulted in the retirement of the Sikhs to a strong position previously selected at Ferozeshuhur. In this action, Havelock, who acted as a sort of aide-de-camp to the Commander-in-Chief, had two horses shot under him. Two days after, both armies having been reinforced, ensued the great battle of Ferozeshuhur, remarkable for the courage of the British troops, for the determination of the enemy, and for the incapacity of his generals. To use the expression of Havelock, who was by the side of his chief throughout the two days' contest, "India was again saved by a miracle." Six weeks later, a victory having been in the mean time gained by Sir H. Smith at Alliwal, the crowning battle of Sobraon gave the *coup de grâce* to the Sikh army. Then followed the march upon Lahore, and the treaty which, with the loss of a portion of territory, restored vitality and independence to the Sikh Government.

In an article devoted to Havelock it would have been impossible to pass by without notice three battles in which he was hotly engaged. So closely, nevertheless, did these battles follow one another, and so devoid were they of anything approaching to tactics or manœuvres, that it need but be recorded that Havelock was present in them, and that he did his duty, as he ever did, most nobly. His situation on Lord Gough's staff had, however, brought him prominently to the notice of the Governor-General, and he was not suffered to waste his great capacities in uncongenial appointments much longer. In 1846, on the recommendation of Lord Hardinge, he was appointed Deputy Adjutant-General of the Queen's troops at Bombay. By this appointment the certainty of future promotion was secured, at the same time that there was obtained an insight into those paper duties, which are nowhere more onerous, and which nowhere need more to be mastered, than in India.

For nearly three years Havelock continued to perform the duties of the Adjutant-General's office at Bombay. They were years of peace and tranquillity, preshadowing the tempest that was to follow. In the third year of his appointment that storm burst in the Punjab. Commencing with the murder of Messrs. Agnew and Anderson, it was followed almost instantaneously by the revolt of the Dewan Moolraj, by the brilliant achievements of Herbert Edwardes, then more leisurely by the siege of Mooltan, the defection of Shere Singh, the actions at Ramnuggur and Sadoolapore, the day of Chillianwalla, and the "crowning mercy" of Goojrat. Havelock, finding that on the formation of Lord Gough's army, the 53rd Foot, to which he had been removed, had been ordered to the scene of action, obtained permission from the Commander-in-Chief at Bombay to join it. He had not reached Agra, however, *en route* to the Punjab, when he received a peremptory order from Lord Gough to return to Bombay. This disappointment, bitter though it was, he bore with the fortitude and resignation of a true hero. Instead of finding fault with the Commander-in-Chief, or railing at fortune, he probed his own conduct, and concluded by condemning himself for having left Bombay without having previously obtained the sanction of Lord Gough. It was this self-command, this freedom from passion, this ability to judge his own conduct as though it were the conduct of another man, that gave to the actions of Havelock a real consistency, and confirmed in no slight degree his influence over those with whom he was brought into contact.

It was in the autumn of the same year that failing health compelled Havelock to return after an absence of twenty-six years to England. He remained there two years, spending his furlough principally in renewing his acquaintance with old schoolfellows and friends, and subsequently in travelling for his health in Germany. It is a curious fact, that at one period of his leave he was actually contemplating selling out and settling in that country. He dreaded the effect which the Indian climate might have upon his constitution, and he found that a very small income would enable him to educate his family and live even comfortably at one of the large German towns on the Rhine. There was, however, some difficulty about the income, and after reflection he resolved, fortunately for his fame, to return to Bombay. He did so, and, leaving behind him his wife and children, took up his old appointment in December, 1851.

In the course of the three years that followed nothing interfered to mar the tranquillity of Havelock's existence. In the second Burmese war, which broke out in 1852, he was not destined to share, though eager himself to join in it. He felt indeed an uncontrollable desire to revisit as a responsible commander the scenes of his earliest campaigning, and he made application to Lord Dalhousie to be employed. Before, however, his letter could reach that nobleman, the preparations for the campaign had been completed, and the appointments filled up.

Promotion, however, was near at hand to console him for this disappointment. In 1854 he was made Quarter-Master-General of the Queen's troops, and shortly afterwards received the rank of Brevet Colonel. But he was not to rest there: in 1855 General Markham was summoned to the Crimea, and the post of Adjutant-General of the Queen's troops was bestowed upon Havelock, and this appointment, though bestowed by the Horse Guards, was ratified by the tacit approval of every soldier in India.

The manner in which the duties of the Adjutant-General's office were exercised by the new official was eminently characteristic of the man. With all his sympathy with weak and erring humanity, he was yet a stern and strict disciplinarian. It was part of his creed that the discipline of a regiment depended mainly upon the example set by the officers, and that where these were careless in the performance of their duties, the men would be negligent also. Convinced likewise of the importance of impressing a rigid sense of individual responsibility upon all officers, it was his especial care to inform the commandants of royal regiments that he held them personally and individually responsible for every breach of discipline that might be committed under their orders. On this point he insisted with a pertinacity that caused him to be regarded in some quarters as a martinet. He was nothing of the sort. Individual responsibility is the soul of military discipline, and it was by insisting on the carrying out of this principle, that the regiments which were in India when the mutiny broke out, had advanced to that high state of efficiency which enabled them at that period to confront and beat down the countless hosts opposed to them.

Havelock had held this appointment nearly two years when, by direction of the Home Government, war was declared against Persia. An expedition under the command of Sir James Outram was forthwith organized at Bombay, with the design of steaming up the Persian Gulf, occupying the island of Karrack and the town of Busheer, and of carrying out such other ulterior measures as might be deemed necessary. Sir James Outram, when consulted by Lord Elphinstone as to the nomination of his divisional commanders, at once expressed a desire to secure the services of Havelock in that capacity. A telegram was immediately despatched to General Anson with the requisition, and six days later Havelock started for Bombay. But two days before he reached that island, Sir James Outram had embarked, and Havelock did not reach the scene of action until after the first blow had been struck, and the Persian army had been hopelessly discouraged by the loss of their camp at Burayjoon, and of the flower of their forces at Kooshab.

Sir James Outram had conceived the idea of bringing the war to a speedy termination by one of those Napoleonic blows so successful in the Imperial wars—viz. an advance on the enemy's capital. But the experience he had gained of the country, during the march which led to the events just recorded, had demonstrated to him the almost utter impracticability of such a course by land. It appeared, however, quite feasible to act upon the Euphrates, and seizing a stronghold which commanded its communication with the gulf, to send up his troops along its course to Ispahan. For this purpose the strongly fortified town of Mohumra was fixed upon, and a division of the army was despatched under Havelock to take it. This service was performed with equal ability and success. Embarking his force, which consisted of nearly five thousand men, of whom one-third were Europeans, upon steamers and flats, he took up a position abreast the works, which each day was making more formidable, and then poured in continual broadsides from his ships of war. In three hours and a half the defences were abandoned by the enemy, and Havelock, instantly landing his troops, took possession of the town. The enemy suffered considerably from the cannonading, but he had so much the start of our troops in his retreat that it was impossible to follow him up with any effect. Our loss was insignificant. A successful attempt was made three days later to beat up the enemy's quarters at Ahwaz on the Karoon—a place which he evacuated with precipitation on the approach of our troops. All further operations, however, were put a stop to by the intelligence which reached the camp almost simultaneously with the account of that success, that a treaty of peace between the two nations had been signed at Paris on the 4th March.

On the 15th of the same month, with the prospect before him of resuming the peaceful duties of the Adjutant-General's office, Havelock sailed for Bombay. On reaching that place on the 29th, however, he learned what he calls "the astounding intelligence" of the first overt act of the promoters of that great convulsion, which, gathering fresh strength as it poured onwards in its rapid course, went so near to overwhelm India. At such a crisis Havelock's place as Adjutant-General of the Army was with the Commander-in-Chief. General Anson, however, was at the time marching on Delhi, and a land journey to that place across Central India, supposed also to be disaffected, was impossible without such an escort as could not be spared. There remained then but one course, and that was to proceed to Calcutta by water, and to place his services at the disposal of the Indian Government. This course Havelock adopted. He remained but two days in Bombay and on the 1st June embarked on board a steamer, the 'Erin,' bound for Calcutta. But he was not destined to reach that city without adventure. On the night of the 5th, when steaming at the rate of eleven knots, the 'Erin' ran upon the rocks which girt the island of Ceylon. It seemed at first as though all lives must be lost: the forepart of the vessel filled with water, and for four hours she continued to bump heavily on the rocks: at last, however, she was driven right on to the reef, and fortunately remained fast. With the dawn of day assistance was available from the shore. The European officials of Ceylon, ever prompt in deeds of charity, had come down to the shore, and, under their directions, a communication was established with the vessel, which resulted in the safe landing of passengers and crew.

From Caltura, the point on which the 'Erin' was wrecked, Havelock proceeded to Galle, and finding there the steamer 'Fire Queen' ready to start for Calcutta, he hailed the opportunity thus presented of prosecuting his journey. On reaching Madras, however, he learned that an unlooked-for occurrence had made Bombay his head-quarters. General Anson had died on the 26th May, and had been succeeded by the Commander-in-Chief of Bombay, Sir Henry Somerset. Thither it behoved Havelock to repair, and thither he would have proceeded, but for the fact that Sir Patrick Grant, the Commander-in-Chief at Madras, had been summoned to Calcutta, and he, anxious to avail himself of Havelock's experience and abilities, pressed him to waive compliance with the letter of the regulations and to accompany him to Calcutta. To this, after reflection, Havelock acceded, and the two generals proceeding together landed in Calcutta on the 17th June. Before alluding to the important events which followed the arrival of Havelock in Calcutta, it may not be unprofitable to take a retrospective glance at the occurrences which preceded, and which, in the opinion of the general himself, certainly nurtured the development of the mutiny. We are fortunately able to present, not our own view, but the view which Havelock himself entertained on this important subject. Certainly if any man in India were entitled to give a decisive and categorical opinion on the point, that man was General Havelock. He was in India when, in 1824, the very first appearance of mutiny was evinced by the Native army, on the occasion of the refusal by the 47th N. I. to proceed to Burmah. The prompt and energetic measures taken by Sir Edward Paget had on that occasion entirely crushed out all vitality from the spark. It is true that after the event, when the feelings which were then no doubt inherent and ready to burst forth had subsided, feeble natures had denounced the measure as one of unnecessary cruelty. It did not appear so to one who was a real soldier, and at the same time one of the most conscientious of men. In military law, in the articles of war with which every soldier, native or European, is acquainted, it is laid down that the punishment for mutiny is Death. To enforce that punishment with stern and rigid impartiality is not only a necessity, but a mercy. It would be impossible to calculate the number of soldiers who have been made helplessly vicious or incurably bad, who have been led on from weakness to crime by acts of constant and ill-timed lenity on the part of their commanding officer. Among no classes does contagion spread more rapidly. No men have keener instincts regarding the practical ability of those who are placed over them. One offence passed over with a light punishment in a regiment is an absolute invitation to a thousand men to commit crime. No men are better aware as to the lengths to which they may go in this respect. With a weak man at their head they quickly degenerate into becoming an armed mob, but a strong man is invariably their master. An officer who has acquainted himself thoroughly with the workings of human nature can do anything with them. And, if this is the case with minor offences, what must it not be with positive crime? If to condone small acts of indiscipline injures the *morale* of a regiment, what will be the effect, if the highest crimes of which a soldier can be guilty, are suffered to pass by with but a light and inadequate punishment? This was a subject upon which Havelock held a very strong opinion. He felt that in the face of mutinous disposition on the part of soldiers, weakness was synonymous with cruelty. Such a disposition must be crushed in the bud or not at all. He regarded, therefore, the decimation of the 47th N.I.

in 1824, as a merciful and effectual, though a severe, remedy for a crime which, if allowed to run out its course, could only have been suppressed by the outpouring of torrents of human blood. In this view he was confirmed by the events which took place on the occasion of the next ebullition of a mutinous spirit,—in 1844. At that period the events of 1824 had been forgotten, a new generation bore arms under the Company, puffed up with the triumphs of Affghanistan, of Gwalior, and of Sind. In the haughtiness of their hearts, deeming themselves the real conquerors of those before whom, if left to themselves, they could never have stood one hour, some of these men refused to proceed to Bukkur. In an evil hour a policy of pseudo-mercy was resolved upon: the punishment for mutiny, the punishment absolutely necessary to repress mutiny, was sparingly inflicted, and it happened that, whilst the rulers imbibed the notion that an outbreak was amenable to a few fair words, the sepoys regarded the mildness of the punishment inflicted as a confession of their power. Subsequently, again under the government of Lord Dalhousie, a similar spirit was manifested, and, although the vigour and energy displayed by the Commander-in-Chief of the day nipped rebellion in the bud, the general measures of the Government exhibited even a greater tendency to regard mutiny as a crime not dangerous in itself, and reprehensible only when it ran counter to any settled plan.

Havelock was not the man to allow occurrences of the nature we have noticed to pass before his eyes without the keenest scrutiny. Those who knew him can well imagine how each in their turn confirmed him in his original opinion as to the wisdom of the plan adopted in the year 1824. During his voyage from Bombay to Calcutta he had had time to take a dispassionate review of the events which had immediately preceded the latest manifestation of sepoy loyalty. These events had come upon him all in a lump. He heard simultaneously of the simple disbandment of the 19th for mutiny, and of the capture of Delhi by the insurgent sepoys. That he regarded the one event as a necessary corollary of the other is evident from the minute which he recorded upon the occasion. At that dark moment he saw, though others could not, that no native infantry regiment could be trusted, that all were implicated in the treason in heart, if not in act. He then recorded his opinion, as a policy for the future in contradistinction to that which had been adopted in the past: "There must be no more disbandments for mutiny. Mutineers must be attacked and annihilated; and if they are few in any regiment, and not immediately denounced to be shot or hanged, the whole regiment must be deemed guilty and given up to prompt military execution." He added: "Much depends upon prompt action. The time for threats and promises is gone by; the slightest overt act must be followed by the same retribution which, in 1824, Sir Edward Paget dealt out to the 47th N. I., thereby putting back mutiny in Bengal eighteen years."

Such were the opinions formed by this great soldier as to the best mode of dealing with the revolted sepoys. That severity in the commencement was mercy in the end was his conviction: a contrary system pursued for years had, in 1857, reached its climax, and it became necessary to sacrifice the lives of our troops, to spend millions of money, and to entail misery upon thousands, to bring affairs back to the *status quo ante* rebellion.

The state of the Bengal Presidency when Havelock arrived in Calcutta may be described briefly as follows. Kept down by the vigour, no less than by the policy, of Sir John Lawrence, and the able men whom he had selected from the two services for employment under him, the Punjab was not only quiet itself, but it had sent the greater part of its European garrison to join the army before Delhi: it was raising troops from its own bosom to fight against the sepoys; a moveable column had been formed to put down the first appearance of revolt amongst these latter; whilst thanks to the energy of Herbert Edwardes, and to the military spirit which animated Sidney Cotton, Peshawur, till then the most dangerous residence in India, had become the safest; the native allies of the ruler of the province were arming on our behalf, whilst that ruler himself, prescient as to the future, was in turn advising, exhorting, and imploring those whom he deemed to stand in need of his counsel. The country between Ferozepore and Loodianah at one extremity, and Meerut and Delhi on the other, was held by our troops. Below, however, it was different. Central India was in revolt; the Gwalior Contingent in open mutiny, though kept back from open action by the loyalty of the Maharaja. The province of Rohilcund was entirely occupied by insurgents. Oudh, with the exception of its capital Lucknow, was in the same category. The country from Meerut to Allahabad was lost to us for the time, and Allahabad itself, the arsenal of the North-West, had been preserved to us, more in consequence of the incapacity of the enemy than of any forethought on our part. Below Allahabad we had still undisputed possession of the country, although even there, the maintenance of armed sepoy regiments, mutinous at heart, and watching their opportunity, paralyzed the action of those gallant English soldiers whose presence might have averted the catastrophe from other districts.

Of fortified places in the North-West, we possessed Agra, the Residency of Lucknow, two barracks at Cawnpore and Allahabad. The great bulk of our troops were employed in the siege of Delhi. There were, however, a regiment at Agra, another at Lucknow, two hundred men at Cawnpore, whilst the nucleus of a moveable column destined to act in the North-West had just reached Allahabad under Lieut.-Colonel Neill of the Madras Fusiliers. It is to this officer that the credit is due of having first rallied the energies of the handful of men who were maintaining the British authority in the districts that yet remained in our possession. Leaving Calcutta in the month of May with his own regiment, he had, by the influence inspired by his energy, averted catastrophe from Benares, and restored our *prestige* at Allahabad. At the moment of Havelock's arrival in Calcutta he was making superhuman exertions to procure carriage and supplies, to facilitate an advance on Cawnpore. In little more than a week he had managed to evoke order out of disorder, disciplined arrangements out of chaos, and stirred up no less by the promptings of an heroic soul than by the accounts which he received of the condition to which the defenders of Cawnpore were being reduced, he fondly hoped that to himself would be allotted the privilege of completing the work he had so well begun, and of planting the British standard on the battlements of Bithoor. He was destined in this respect to be disappointed. Sir P. Grant who had now assumed temporary command of the Bengal army, had been much struck by a proposition made by Havelock during the passage from Madras to Calcutta to form a moveable column at Allahabad, with which to act in the Central Provinces or in Oudh. Finding then on his arrival, that a nucleus of such a force had been established at Allahabad, Sir Patrick, true to his purpose, pushed up reinforcements to join it, and either ignorant of Neill's merits, or, what is more probable, having unlimited confidence in Havelock, he appointed him to the command of the combined column. It was just the command that Havelock had longed for. For the first time he was entirely his own master, unfettered by orders, and unperplexed by suggestions. He had but one definite object before him,—to relieve the sorely-pressed garrison of Cawnpore. To that object every other consideration must necessarily be subordinated. Promptitude, energy, determination,—these were to be the watchwords of his undertaking, and certainly no man ever entered upon a difficult enterprise more firmly resolved to accomplish, at any cost, the end he had marked out.

Havelock reached Allahabad on the 30th June. The arrangements which Colonel Neill had carried out in the mean time had very much cleared the difficulties in the way of a general advance upon Cawnpore. A column of 400 Europeans, 300 Sikhs, and 120 native cavalry had been despatched under the command of Major Renaud along the grand trunk road towards that station; 100 men with two guns had been placed on board a steamer with instructions to ascend the Ganges and co-operate with the land force, and the country had been heavily indented upon for carriage. These as they came up were instantly pressed into service.

Havelock had, as has already been shewn, felt assured in his own mind, ever since the first great blows struck by the mutineers, that henceforth no reliance could be placed upon native troops; and as in the difficult operations which he felt to be before him, he knew that it would be absolutely necessary to have at his disposal a body of cavalry upon which he could depend, he had, before his arrival at Allahabad, telegraphed to Government to be permitted to avail himself of the services of unemployed officers and volunteers for this duty. The application was acceded to, and his first care after arrival was to provide horses and equipments for the corps. So short a time intervened between the announcement of its formation and his actual march, that it did not at the latter period exceed twenty in number. It received, nevertheless, considerable subsequent additions, and under the command of its gallant leader, Major Barrow, performed the most splendid service. His other preparations for an advance were, if possible, hastened by the authentic intelligence which reached him the third day after his arrival of the fate of the Cawnpore garrison. His mind was instantly made up. To retake Cawnpore and inflict signal vengeance on the murderers was his settled determination. Believing at the same time that the enemy, in the pride of their strength would endeavour to crush Renaud's column, he sent orders to the latter, who was already near Futtehpore, to halt, and to await his arrival with the main body.

On the afternoon of the 7th July Havelock left Allahabad. His force consisted of about a thousand Europeans from the 64th and 84th Foot, the 78th Highlanders, Madras Fusiliers, Royal Artillery, and volunteer cavalry, and nearly two hundred natives. For the first three days he took the ordinary marches to inure the troops gradually to fatigue. On the fourth day, the evening of the 10th, he started from Synee and marched fifteen miles to Khagu, within five miles of Major Renaud's encampment. Though strongly urged to halt here, the news of the advance of the enemy, and the composition of Renaud's force, of whom nearly half were Sikhs whose fidelity had not yet been tried in the field, induced him to resume the advance the same evening. Starting, therefore, at midnight, he reached Renaud about 1 o'clock in the morning of the 12th, and the combined force marched on fifteen miles to Belinda, a small village only five miles distant from Futtehpore.

Meanwhile the enemy, elated with his victory over women and unarmed men, was marching in force, in full hope of overwhelming the small detachment under the command of Renaud. On the morning of the 12th he approached Futtehpore, and, ignorant of the advance made by our troops during the night, came on in a leisurely, disorderly manner, the infantry, artillery, and cavalry being all mixed up together. Intelligence of their movements was quickly conveyed to Havelock, who at once ordered his Quartermaster-General, Colonel Tytler, to proceed to the front to reconnoitre. Colonel Tytler, advancing about two miles with his escort, found the enemy marching through Futtehpore, and preparing to encamp on this side of it. No sooner was he perceived than the enemy's cavalry, thinking they saw

Renaud before them, dashed at him with their whole force, the infantry and artillery following without any attempt at order or method. Colonel Tytler galloped back with the intelligence to the general; but the guns of the enemy, which had meanwhile been brought to the front, gave the first intimation of his movements. The first sound of the cannon served as a signal for our troops to fall in. Though engaged in cooking their breakfasts at the time, and though tired after a march of eighteen miles, they did this with an alacrity which could not be surpassed. The guns, eight in number, were moved to the front, one hundred Enfield riflemen being with them: the infantry were formed in quarter-distance columns at deploying distance behind, whilst the Volunteer Horse and Irregular Cavalry guarded the flanks.

These dispositions were scarcely made before the enemy, still advancing in a determined though disorderly manner, came within range. Their guns had already fired two or three ineffective rounds before the fire on our side opened. No sooner, however, was the order given to our men, than the rapid advance of the enemy changed its character. The long range of the rifles told with murderous effect on the head of their columns; and Captain Maude, enabled to advance his guns under cover of this fire to point-blank range, speedily gave them the *coup de grâce*. They broke at once, and retreated to a position in front of the town, abandoning the guns to our victorious troops.

Havelock was not slow to take advantage of this success. Deploying his infantry, he drove the enemy from his new position, and pursued him helter-skelter through the town. Guns, ammunition, plunder, fell into his possession. Everything was abandoned; and although a last stand was attempted on the other side of the town, the guns and riflemen succeeded in forcing him to take refuge in a flight, which our exhausted troops were unable to follow up. Whilst this was going on in the centre, however, the enemy had almost succeeded in turning our flanks. Their cavalry, outnumbering ours considerably, came down in great force on our right. Our Irregulars justified Havelock's bad opinion by a display which he characterised as "worse than doubtful." But on this occasion the Europeans were not wanting to themselves. Captain Beatson, the Assistant Adjutant-General, who was with the right column of infantry, halted his men, and directing their attention to the enemy's horse, poured in so murderous a volley, that they too hastened to follow their comrades in a precipitate flight.

It was one o'clock before the troops, wearied with thirteen hours' combined marching and fighting, reached their encamping-ground. They were encouraged, however, not alone by their victory, but by the spirit-stirring congratulations which their general addressed to them on the occasion. They recognised in those congratulations a different spirit to that for which such documents are usually celebrated. There was a direct appeal to each man's individual exertions, an acknowledgment of the obligation under which the general felt to all, which went directly to their hearts. Those hearts were touched because it was felt that the general spoke to them from his own. From that moment his influence with them was established. They felt they had one at their head who knew how to lead them, and who thoroughly comprehended them. A mutual confidence became established, so absolutely without limit as to contribute more than anything else to make them, as an army, invincible in the field.

On the following day the troops halted. On the 14th the irregular cavalry, on an alarm of the enemy's approach, made as though they would plunder our baggage; they were therefore disarmed and dismounted, and their horses made over to the volunteer cavalry. On the 15th, after marching six miles, the general found a strong detachment of the enemy intrenched in the village of Aoung. He at once directed Colonel Tytler to move to the front with about six hundred men and the guns to drive the enemy from his position, whilst he himself should protect the baggage against the attacks of the large bodies of cavalry who were threatening him. On this occasion the enemy fought much better than at Futtehpore. He commenced by opening fire upon Colonel Tytler with his guns; and finding that that officer did not at once reply, he moved out of his position to attack him. The colonel, who had been engaged in completing his dispositions, showed no disinclination for the combat. Sending the Madras Fusiliers to engage the infantry, he directed a heavy fire upon the enemy's intrenchment, and in less than two hours had put him completely to flight. The attempts of the cavalry to turn our flanks were equally abortive. On the same day, whilst the troops were refreshing themselves after their encounter, intelligence reached the general that the enemy had crossed the little river Pandoo, and were preparing to blow up the bridge. He at once felt that success in this point would be fatal to the speedy prosecution of his designs, as, with the entire country in the hands of the enemy, it would not be possible for him, without immense difficulty and delay, to achieve the passage of that river in the face of a hostile force. Though the hour was midday, and the month July, the men were summoned to fall in. They showed their appreciation of their leader by obeying with alacrity. After marching little more than an hour they suddenly, by the bend of the road, came in sight of the river, considerably swollen by the rains, and still spanned by a narrow stone bridge. Almost simultaneously the enemy's fire opened, sweeping the road by which our troops must advance. Our dispositions were soon made. The guns were moved to the front, and so arranged as to bring a flanking as well as a direct fire on the enemy's position. Aligned with them again were the Enfield riflemen. Their fire proved most effective. The first discharge from our guns broke the sponge-staffs of their gunners, and, having none in reserve, they could no longer load their pieces. Their fire therefore ceased as if by magic; and the Madras Fusiliers dashing forward with great gallantry, the rebels, after attempting ineffectually to blow up the bridge, gave way at all points, and fled with precipitation towards Cawnpore. The general was unfortunately, from want of cavalry, unable to pursue them.

Intelligence reached the general during the night that the Nana had taken a strong position in front of Cawnpore with his whole force, and he felt that he had got his hardest battle before him. He well knew, however, that, humanly speaking, the victory must be with himself. He had met these rebels flushed with their bloody deeds, and deeming themselves the masters of India: he had beaten them whilst indulging in their boastful dreams of conquest, and he did not fear to beat them in their new attitude of rallied fugitives, oppressed with a sense of their own crimes. He sat down therefore that evening, and wrote instructions to General Neill to send up reinforcements, as he intended to advance to Lucknow from Cawnpore. This was no boastful announcement; it was the calm and deliberately expressed intention of a man who had counted the cost and weighed the consequences of the proceeding on which he had determined,—who felt that he had a right to look upon the possession of Cawnpore on the following evening as a certainty, and who regarded that possession but as the prelude to the performance of greater things. With the foresight of a great master of his art, he planned all his moves so that they should tend, directly or indirectly, to the accomplishment of a great though still distant end.

On the following morning he marched to fight that which may be considered in every respect as his greatest battle. He could not, from sickness, mortality, and other causes, bring into the field more than thirteen hundred men, of whom three hundred were Sikhs. The English portion of the force was animated, however, by the noblest spirit. Combined with the confidence of victory, there was besides a hope that they might arrive in sufficient time to save their countrywomen from death. They had twenty-two miles to march, a great battle to fight, the heat of a terrible sun to endure, yet their cheerfulness was never more apparent. They felt that they could accomplish anything that morning. After marching fifteen miles, they reached Maharajpore, seven miles distant from Cawnpore. Here they took a breakfast of biscuit and porter, and here the general fell in with two sepoys, faithful to their salt, who gave him important and accurate information regarding the strength and position of the enemy. His artillery had been so laid as to sweep the only road by which he thought it possible we could advance; his right rested on the railway embankment; his centre, which was more retired than the flanks, was immensely strong; whilst his left was covered by the Ganges. His troops were strongly intrenched, and were protected moreover by the nature of the ground which was intersected by numerous ravines. Havelock at once felt that to attack in front a position so strong, defended by five thousand men, with only thirteen hundred, would do no credit to the school in which he had been trained to arms: he thought it possible so to manœuvre as to render the defences which the enemy had prepared almost useless, and at the same time to gain the day without any great sacrifice of life. If he could only interpose between the left flank of the enemy and the river, and seize the high ground on the right bank of the Ganges, he would take the enemy completely in flank, render useless his preparations for a front attack, and compel him to fight, on all points except as regarded mere numbers, on disadvantageous terms. On this flank movement, then, he resolved.

It was now two o'clock: the sun glared fiercely overhead, and they were still seven miles distant from Cawnpore, when the order to advance was given. For three miles they moved steadily on, although many men succumbed to the influence of the terrible sun, and fell to rise no more. They marched in order of battle, the volunteer cavalry in advance, the artillery behind them, and the infantry in the rear. At the commencement of the fourth mile, they came in view of the enemy's position; and the fire of their guns at once convinced Havelock of the accuracy of the information on which he had based his plan. Still the volunteer cavalry moved on, drawing upon itself the whole fire, and attracting the sole attention of the enemy. At the same moment the artillery and infantry, under cover of a thick grove of trees, diverged to the right. For about half a mile their movement was unperceived. It could not be so much longer. As the heads of the columns emerged into the open, the enemy, discovering the nature of the movement, endeavoured with all haste to change the direction of his fire. Not a gun replied. The point to be reached was the high ground on the right bank of the Ganges, and to attain that every other consideration was sacrificed. For a quarter of an hour, with sloped arms, exposed to a fire which they did not return, the men marched on till they gained the turning-point of the movement: then wheeling them up into line, with the artillery in the intervals, Havelock led them on to the enemy.

To describe, as they deserve to be described, all the details of the battle that followed would trespass too much on the space allowed to a single article. We must content ourselves by observing that, having such soldiers under his command, the battle was really gained when the flank-movement was accomplished. It is true that even then they were little more than one man to five; but, considering the opponents, such odds were not unfair. That which generalship had so successfully commenced, the most determined courage as successfully carried out. Vying with one another in their eagerness to meet the enemy, the troops pressed on with a fury which was not to be withstood. Position after position was taken, one gun after another was captured. The general, in the language of one of the combatants, "seemed to be gifted with ubiquity;" he was seen everywhere animating and inspiring the soldiers, whose last charge, performed under his eyes and in obedience to orders issued by himself, was given with an ardour and impetuosity which were irresistible. Notwithstanding the great efforts of the enemy,—and they never fought better,—that night beheld the Nana a fugitive from Cawnpore, and the army, which was to have won for him empire, a defeated and disorganized rabble.

The political results of the battle of Cawnpore were immense. It gave the first intimation to the rebels of the Central Provinces that the rebellion against the British was not to have a successful termination. The chief conspirator, who had proclaimed himself the legitimate inheritor of the dignities of the Peshwa, and who had endeavoured to cement his installation by the indiscriminate slaughter of women and children, had been defeated on his chosen battle-field, and been driven by his terror to take refuge in Oudh. On the spot where the British standard had been treacherously struck down, British troops had, in the short space of three weeks, and in spite of unheard-of difficulties, triumphantly re-established it. Every sign of the reign of the usurper, save that of the devastation which he caused, disappeared as if by magic; and Cawnpore, taken by Havelock, and never afterwards lost, was destined to prove the base of many of the most important undertakings for the recovery of British authority. At the moment, its position was strategically most important. Secure of his communications by two routes,—the river and the road,—with Allahabad, and not threatened from the north, Havelock could operate in Oudh, undisturbed as to Cawnpore, so long as the Gwalior Contingent, then fortunately held in check by the Maharaja, should abstain from any movement towards Kalpee. Against isolated attacks he could provide; this alone was like to prove a serious danger.

On the morning of the 17th July he entered Cawnpore. On the 18th he was occupied in making arrangements for the accommodation of the troops, and in deciding the locality of an intrenchment on the Ganges, and commanding the communication with Oudh, of such a nature that a small number of troops might be able to hold against any attack. In this way he proposed to make of Cawnpore a secure base for his operations in Oudh. The plateau which he selected was admirably adapted for the purpose. No time was lost in tracing out the plan; and such was the haste employed, that on the arrival of General Neill, on the 20th, with a reinforcement of upwards of 200 men, the work was sufficiently advanced to be defensible, and Havelock did not hesitate to send the first detachment across the river. Previously to this, on the 19th, he had beaten up Bithoor, and found it empty: the successor of the Peshwas had fled across the river. Rendered more secure by the absence of any immediate apprehension of attack, having, too, in Neill, a man capable of coping with any difficulty, whom he could leave in command of the new intrenchment, and urged on by a consideration of the danger of the Lucknow garrison, Havelock resolved to push on his new enterprise with all possible expedition.

Never perhaps before had it been attempted to

undertake an enterprise so vast, with means so disproportionate. Not Hannibal when he crossed the Alps, not Alexander when he forced the Granicus, not Frederick when he battled against the combined powers of the Continent, were so utterly overmatched in point of numbers as was Havelock in his expedition into Oudh. Hannibal found allies as well as enemies in his path; Alexander commanded nearly all the resources of Greece, and was opposed by an effeminate people; Frederick fought on the defensive, and won battles with his soldiers' legs; but Havelock, with only 1500 men, went to attack the most warlike people in Hindostan,—a province teeming with soldiers, many of them trained by our officers, acquainted with our habits, and drilled after our fashion. He threw himself upon this province relying upon the courage, the discipline, and the powers of endurance of his soldiers; for they had neither tent nor covering, they were exposed to the extremes of heat and wet, their supplies were precarious, and their power of advancing depended entirely upon their ability to cope with difficulties such as seldom fall to the lot of British troops to encounter. It was an enterprise from which, we think, most men would have recoiled. Success could only be accomplished under a combination of circumstances such as no skill could arrange. To advance at the head of fifteen hundred men into a hostile province boasting of its tens of thousands under arms, would seem to partake somewhat of rashness. And yet, though Havelock attempted this very thing, there was no rashness in his enterprise. His chances of success, it is true, were small, but so complete was his knowledge of his soldiers, so perfect was their confidence in him, so thoroughly acquainted was he with the principles of his art, and so well had he calculated every contingency, that, while there remained but one faint hope of ultimate victory opposed to ninety-nine chances of failure, he felt that it was his duty to persevere.

On the 25th July the entire force with which Havelock intended to operate in Oudh had crossed over to the left bank of the Ganges. It consisted of ten guns, imperfectly equipped and manned, the Volunteer Horse reorganised and increased to sixty troopers, and the remnants of the 64th and 84th Regiments, the 78th Highlanders, Madras Fusiliers, and Brasyer's Sikhs. Few besides the sick and wounded were left in the entrenchments, but General Neill was there, a host in himself, and being able to avail himself of the reinforcements which were expected to arrive from time to time from Allahabad, this gallant officer gladly accepted the responsibility placed upon him. No one indeed urged more strongly than he upon Havelock the necessity of taking with him every available man. The little steamer which had been brought up by Lieutenant Spurgin aided materially in the passage of the river, and in the procuring of boats. But for her, the Ganges would have presented very great difficulties at the very outset. The force marched that day, the 25th, to the village of Mungulwar, five miles on the Lucknow road. Here the general halted in order to complete his dispositions for carriage and supplies. These having been arranged, imperfectly although as fully as was practicable under the circumstances, he moved forward in earnest on the morning of the 29th. After a march of three miles he came in sight of the enemy strongly posted at Oonao. The position he had taken up is thus described by the general in his despatch:—"His right was protected by a swamp which could neither be forced nor turned; his advance was drawn up in a garden enclosure, which in this warlike district had purposely or accidentally assumed the form of a bastion. The rest of his (advance) force was posted in and behind a village, the houses of which were loopholed. The passage between the village and the town of Oonao is narrow. The town itself extended three-quarters of a mile to our right. The flooded state of the country precluded the possibility of turning in this direction. The swamp shut us in on the left." Precluded thus from manœuvring, the general could only attack in front. This he did in the manner he had found so successful on the Cawnpore road. Opening with a fire from the artillery and Enfield riflemen in skirmishing order, he waited until the enemy had been driven from his advanced position and compelled to take refuge in the loopholed houses. The infantry was then brought to the front, and, after a desperate hand-to-hand conflict, the guns were captured and the enemy driven headlong from the village. The town of Oonao, however, was still before him, and the enemy was marching in dense columns to occupy it. Havelock therefore drew off his force in line on the ground he had gained between the village and the town, his guns pointing on the high road by which alone he could be attacked, and waited for the enemy's movement to develop itself. At length, formed in dense masses, they debouched from the town and halted. Havelock felt that he had them. A withering fire from guns and riflemen fell amongst their serried ranks. Unable to deploy they had no choice but to charge home or to retire. The former course would have been opposed to every principle of Asiatic warfare. Whilst, however, they yet seemed in doubt, our skirmishers, wading up to their waists in the marshes, made their presence perceptible on their flanks, and Havelock, pushing forward two guns at the same time, gave them sufficient intimation that he was determined to move the only obstacle from his path. They then gave way almost immediately, and fled precipitately, leaving their guns, fifteen in number, in our possession.

The same day, after a rest of three hours, during which the men dined, Havelock resumed his advance, and after a march of six miles came upon the enemy strongly entrenched at Busseeruthgunge. This was a walled town situated in the open, and intersected by the high road to Lucknow. In front of it lay a large pond, which, owing to the inundation, had all the appearance of a rapid river. In its rear was a still larger pond or lake, traversed by a narrow causeway. It possessed in addition a wet ditch, and the main gate was defended by an earthwork and four guns, and flanked on either side by loopholed turrets. It was just the position which Havelock could have maintained against the whole army of Oudh. Defended by Asiatics it merely afforded to the English general an opportunity of putting in practice the principles of his art. Having reconnoitred, Havelock deemed it quite practicable to cut off the enemy from the causeway in the rear, whilst he should attack them in front. The 64th were detached on this duty, and whilst wading often up to their armpits in the swamp they made a flank movement to the left of the town, Havelock advanced in his old order, against the main gate. Fortunately, the fire of the enemy was high, whilst every shot from ours told.

Under its influence the efforts of the enemy gradually slackened, and the Highlanders and Fusiliers rushing forward, forced their way, after a sharp struggle at the gateway, into the town. If the 64th had been able to reach the position assigned them, the enemy would have been entirely cut off from the causeway. As it was, he was enabled to cross his shattered forces, although not without losing a very large number of men.

But these successes, signal as they were, served only to convince the general that, with such a force as that at his disposal, it would be impossible for him to accomplish the great object of his expedition. In three days, what with fighting, sickness, and deaths from disease, his force had been reduced to 1200 men; he had no means for carrying his sick; he was marching away from his resources whilst the enemy was falling back on his; on his first march of nine miles he had had to fight two pitched battles, and attack two fortified towns, and he was aware that stronger places were before him. On the other hand, he had received intimation from Calcutta that the 5th Fusiliers and 90th Light Infantry were on their way to reinforce him. Every consideration impelled him to suspend any further attempt at an advance which had become for the moment impracticable. His resolution on this point was confirmed by intelligence which reached him during the night, that the Nana had collected a considerable body of troops and was preparing to act on his rear and cut off his communication with Cawnpore. With a heavy heart then, though convinced of the necessity for the movement, he retired on the following morning to his strong position Mungulwar. From thence he despatched his sick and wounded to Cawnpore, and informed General Neill that to enable him to reach Lucknow it was necessary that he should receive reinforcements of a thousand bayonets and another battery. He also urged the speedy completion of the bridge to connect both banks of the river, a work which he had planned before he set out on his first attempt. Into the causes which acted to delay the arrival of the reinforcements so ardently expected by the general, it is not necessary that we should enter. The disappointment, bitter as it was, only confirmed Havelock in his determination to dare everything for the relief of the Lucknow garrison. And as the diversion of those two còrps, the 5th and 90th, to other employment, seemed to intimate to him that he was to be left to his own resources, he resolved to make with those resources one more effort to rescue his beleaguered countrywomen. On the evening of 4th August, then, having about fourteen hundred effective soldiers under his command, he marched for the second time towards Lucknow. They passed through Oonao without attack, but as they approached Busseeruthgunge it became evident that the enemy lay there in force. Unwilling to risk a night action, Havelock moved back to Oonao, bivouacked there, and advanced again the following morning. He found the enemy strongly posted in the position previously described. He resolved to adopt, on a more effective scale, the tactics that had proved so successful before. Leaving the 64th, 84th, the heavier guns and the cavalry in front, he took the Highlanders, Fusiliers, Sikhs, and Captain Maude's battery to cut off the enemy from the causeway. Before, however, he could accomplish this, the enemy, seeing his design and dreading to be entrapped, bewildered, too, by the cannonade in their front, fled precipitately across the causeway. In doing this they came under the fire of the guns of Captain Maude's battery, and were mown down in numbers. They were at the same time vigorously pursued, driven from village to village, until broken and disheartened they found safety in the fatigue of our soldiers.

This victory, however, served to convince the general that he was no more capable of pushing on to Lucknow than he had been on the first occasion of his advance. Besides the losses from actual fighting, the cholera had broken out in his camp, and was hurrying off its victims in constant succession. The Nana, too, was approaching his flank, and threatened to interrupt his communications. But perhaps the most decisive intelligence of all was conveyed in the account that the Gwalior Contingent had mutinied against their Maharaja, and was moving on Kalpee. This was a position threatening to Cawnpore and menacing our communications with Allahabad. His return became through that fact no longer a matter of consideration; it was a necessity. The general felt that the maintenance of the British prestige depended upon the preservation of his army, and that its destruction would bring certain ruin on Lucknow. Impelled by these considerations he once more retraced his steps to Mungulwar.

Havelock lay at Mungulwar four or five days recruiting his men, and pushing on the construction of the bridge that was to unite both banks of the river. On the 10th, this great work, carried on under many disadvantages, was completed, and the same day intelligence was sent by General Neill that Bithoor had been occupied in great force by the enemy. Unwilling as he was to leave his position at Mungulwar, Havelock at once recognised the necessity of inflicting a signal blow upon the enemy who had dared to approach so nearly to Cawnpore, and he prepared accordingly to recross the river. Before, however, he could carry out his resolution, he learned that the Oudh rebels had taken up a strong position between Oonao and Busseeruthgunge. To dislodge them from a position from which they could have attacked him whilst crossing, became an object of imperious necessity.

For the third time, therefore, Havelock moved towards Busseeruthgunge. He found the enemy very strongly posted between that town and Oonao, and sheltered by earthworks and entrenchments. Covered as before by his artillery and skirmishers, Havelock advanced in echellon of battalions from his right. But little impression, however, was made on the earthen mounds which protected their position. An infantry charge was therefore resolved upon. The 78th Highlanders were brought on to the main road whilst the Fusiliers were moved to the right. These dashing with characteristic ardour on the enemy's left, broke it instantly, and captured all the guns at that point. Our troops instantly turned them on the main body of the enemy, who, surprised and panic-stricken, made but little resistance, but fled headlong through Busseeruthgunge, pursued with untiring energy till beyond the causeway, thus for the third time the scene of their discomfiture.

The effect of this victory was to leave Havelock free to recross to Cawnpore, without any fear of being disturbed during the operation. Accordingly, on the 13th, he moved his force across the bridge to the point whence he had started nineteen days before on his arduous campaign; during that period he had fought eight combats, in all of which he had been eminently successful. In spite of his victories, however, he had never been able to advance more than ten miles out of the fifty that lay between him and Lucknow. The overpowering numbers and immense resources of the enemy counterbalanced all the efforts of his genius, and he was compelled to feel, after each victory, that at the head of so small a force Lucknow was as distant from him as ever. General Neill, with whom he consulted on the practicability of making any further attempt to reach the beleaguered garrison, expressed his opinion at this time, that unless reinforced it could only terminate in disaster, without the possibility of relieving the garrison, and that it would be injurious to our interests in that part of India. The 14th and 15th were devoted to rest, and to preparations to check the ravages of the cholera which had broken out with extraordinary fury. On the 16th Havelock deemed it absolutely necessary to march against Bithoor. The rebels here, about four thousand in number, consisted of sepoys from the 34th, 42nd, 17th, 28th, and a few of the 31st N. I. with the 2nd regular and 3rd irregular cavalry, and some of the Nana's own retainers with two guns. They were drawn up in front of the castle of Bithoor, their communication with which was maintained by means of a bridge in their rear. Their position was strong, being defended by entrenched quadrangles filled with sepoys, and sheltered by plantations of sugarcane rising high above the head. Two villages, one on either flank, and connected by an earthen entrenchment, formed the supports of this position; they were strongly occupied. On this occasion, for the first time, Havelock had the advantage of the enemy in artillery, and he resolved to endeavour to make them feel his superiority. For twenty minutes he poured in a tremendous fire from the guns and Enfield rifles, our men meanwhile lying down. Finding, however, that he was making but little impression on the quadrangles, he ordered an advance of infantry covered by the Fusiliers. After a short conflict, in which the 42nd N. I. are said to have crossed bayonets with our men, the enemy evacuated the quadrangles, and retired to his main position between the two villages. Upon this the artillery fire was concentrated, but as here also little impression was made on the earthwork, and the enemy still kept up a galling fire from behind its shelter, recourse was again had to the bayonet. The rebels awaited the onset of our men with seeming confidence, but no sooner had these reached the parapet than their hearts failed them, and they gave way in confusion, abandoning Bithoor in their flight. Our men were too exhausted to pursue them; they bivouacked on the ground they had won, and on the following morning retraced their steps to Cawnpore. Intelligence greeted the general on his arrival at that station that another officer had been appointed to the command of the column with which he had been so gloriously associated. He received indeed no written communication on the subject. A copy of the *Government Gazette* containing Sir James Outram's appointment announced the bare fact; the reasons he was left to imagine. After all his exertions, his rapid advance from Cawnpore, the heroic efforts to reach Lucknow, his brilliant victories, the confidence with which he had inspired all with whom he had come in contact, the deadly blows which he had dealt the rebel cause, to be simply superseded seemed hard indeed. But to be superseded without a word, without an acknowledgment of any sort, the announcement first made known by the *Government Gazette*, was ungenerous and cruel. It was impossible to avoid the inference that he was superseded because he had not attained the result which was hoped for by those in power. Whatever the reason might have been, it has never yet been revealed or acknowledged. Mr. Marshman, his biographer and brother-in-law, whilst condemning it as an act inconsiderate, uncalled-for, and unjust, propounds the idea that it was an accident, the offspring of confusion and error. To the minds of others who had marked how, in that summer and autumn of 1857, success had been made the sole standard of confidence, how even General Lloyd had been maintained and supported at Dinapore because, up to a certain point, he had managed the sepoys without disarming them, another and a different conclusion appeared only natural.

However that may have been, it cannot be doubted that to the general the first announcement, no less than the manner in which it was made known, was a bitter disappointment. He was not wanting, nevertheless, on this trying occasion, to the principles which had ever guided his course. Havelock the superseded was as active, as daring, as energetic, as full of vigour as when he ruled, the unfettered commander of an independent force. Never were his great qualities more urgently required on behalf of the public service than after his return from the battle of Bithoor. Out of 1700 Europeans whom he had had altogether from the time of quitting Allahabad under his orders, but 685 remained effective. Not only was he compelled to abandon all idea of moving into Oudh, but the action of the Gwalior

Contingent at Kalpee rendered it doubtful whether he could even maintain Cawnpore. This force consisting of 5,000 men with 30 guns, was already threatening Futtehpore. To the north, the Nawab of Furruckabad had 30,000 men under him in arms, ready to take advantage of the difficulties which menaced Cawnpore. It was, besides, in the power of the rebels in Oudh, freed from the presence of Havelock's force in their own province, to detach any number of men to operate with the Gwalior Contingent, and to cut him off from Allahabad. Of all these difficulties Havelock had the fullest cognizance, yet not one of them disturbed his clear judgment. To remain at Cawnpore was, a very great risk undoubtedly, but to fall back on Allahabad unless in case of the most absolute need, would have been a calamity. Not only should we have lost the prestige and the material advantages gained by Havelock's victories, but it would have united the three then divided bodies against us, and have placed them, with more means at their disposal, in a far stronger position than that from which he had dislodged the Nana. He announced then to the new Commander-in-Chief, Sir Colin Campbell, that if he could hold out hopes of reinforcements, he would, in spite of the very threatening aspect of affairs, continue to hold Cawnpore; if not, he must retire upon Allahabad. The reply of Sir Colin entirely reassured him as to the intentions of the Government, and he resolved at all risks to hold his position at Cawnpore. He did so.

Just one month after the battle of Bithoor, the 15th September, Sir James Outram arrived with his reinforcements. With a magnanimity, for which history records no precedent but which places the chief actor on a moral pre-eminence surpassing that even of the stern warriors of republican Rome, Sir James Outram declined to take the command from one who had made efforts so noble and so strenuous to accomplish the end still remaining before them. Whilst Havelock then kept the command of the force, now increased to 2500 men, Sir James joined it as a volunteer, and in that capacity, serving with the volunteer cavalry, performed deeds of daring which, had he been a subaltern, would have gained for him the Order of Valour, but which, achieved by Sir James, were considered to partake too much of the character of the man, and to be but a too necessary corollary of past heroism, to need any peculiar distinction.

On the 20th September, Havelock for the last time crossed the Ganges, meeting little more than nominal opposition in the passage. He ascertained, however, that the enemy held Mungulwar in strength. Thither he marched the following morning, drove him out of it, and pursuing him rapidly, not allowing him time to rally, did not halt until he had gained Busseeruthgunge, and had seen the enemy in hopeless confusion beyond it. On the following morning, resuming the advance, he passed the Sye without opposition, the enemy having neglected to destroy the bridge. But sixteen miles now lay between him and the residency. The rapidity of the advance had disconcerted all the plans of the enemy, and compelled him to concentrate his forces hastily on Lucknow. But Havelock had still to push on: between him and the garrison lay difficulties which might well have seemed insurmountable, but which he at least had determined to overcome. On the 23rd, a march of ten miles brought the force to within sight of the Alumbagh, covered by an army of 10,000 men. No time was lost in attacking these. Turning their right flank, and assisting the movement by a fire from a heavy battery of 24-pounders, he quickly put them into confusion, then launching his cavalry upon them he completed their disorder, and drove them across the Charbagh bridge.

The city alone now lay between him and the residency, and to determine the plan for surmounting this difficulty, as well as to give rest to the troops, the force halted at the Alumbagh on the 24th. After long consideration it was resolved to cross the Charbagh bridge, and force their way through the intricate streets to the residency. On the morning of the 25th the troops, full of energy, marched to this desperate work. How this was accomplished, how, by dint of the most daring courage, the most splendid perseverance on the part of the men, and the most indomitable resolution on the part of the general, this, the most thickly peopled city in Asia, crowded with armed men, guarded by its narrow streets, was penetrated and forced by that small band of heroes, we cannot stay to tell. That it was successfully achieved stamps those who planned and who executed the attack as men of no common order. The difficulties to be encountered were even greater than those which staggered for so long a time the French army before Saragossa, and which the genius of the Duke of Montebello with much labour surmounted. When one thinks how easily a few determined men might have held that strong position, how a union of courage and discipline would have sufficed under a skilful leader to crush, to utterly overwhelm, the little band that dared that terrible conflict, one feels how impossible it is to admire sufficiently the courage that planned and the resolution that carried to a successful issue, an enterprise in which, regarded simply as a military operation, the unfavourable chances so largely predominated. It was because Havelock was a complete master of the art of war, because he knew so well that there are times when great principles even may be safely set aside, because he was capable of judging, and of shaping his opinions accordingly, of the effect of *morale* upon soldiers, that he determined upon, and succeeded in, an enterprise, which, viewed by a distant spectator and regarded only with reference to the disproportion of means to the end, would have been pronounced an impossibility. It is on such an occasion that the true soldier, the man who understands his profession and comprehends the most trifling action even on the part of his fellow men, stands out most brilliantly. Havelock succeeded because he felt that with the force at his disposal, he could accomplish against the force to which he was opposed, any achievement which required but the duration of four-and-twenty hours to perform. Beyond that period, numbers might overwhelm, but within it, keeping his men in constant action, and not necessitated to halt them for the purpose of food, everything was possible.

At dusk on the 25th Havelock entered the residency, so long the object of his hopes, at the head of the leading portion of his force. On the following morning Sir James Outram assumed the command, and he subsided into the position of divisional commander. But it soon became evident to himself as well as to Sir James Outram, that although the relieving force had been able to force itself into Lucknow, it was not strong enough to escort back to Cawnpore the women and children who so long and so nobly had borne the privations attendant upon the siege. It became then necessary to await a further movement from Cawnpore. This was delayed for some weeks to the great detriment of the general's health. So long as he was in the field he had been sustained by the excitement, by the great hopes he cherished, by the constant labour, mental, and bodily even, that devolved upon him. But shut up in the residency, compelled to pass the weary hours of every succeeding day within a narrow limit, certain that relief though coming was yet distant, unsustained by the hope of relieving his countrymen from danger, that reaction in his health set in, which in his tour in Germany he had looked forward to as ultimately certain. As if, too, to take away the last chance of preserving a life that England had only then recognised as so precious, he was unable within the residency to procure food of the nutritious nature requisite for the support of his system. "We eat," he wrote to his wife, "a reduced ration of artillery bullock beef, chupattees and rice; but tea, coffee, sugar, soap, and candles are unknown luxuries." Under such a regimen, and no longer under the healthful influences to which we have referred, he began gradually to lose his former vigour. The change, however, was perceptible to few besides himself, and when, after a blockade of two months, on the second and final relief of the garrison by Sir Colin Campbell on the 17th November, Havelock went out to meet him at the Motee Muhal, he was apparently in his accustomed health. Three days later it was known that he was ill with diarrhœa, although the disease had apparently yielded to the remedies applied. On the 21st he became worse, and was moved in a dooly to the Dilkoosha. On the 22nd there was little change; but he expressed a conviction that he would not recover; on that day the dooly being within the range of the enemy's bullets, he was removed in it to a more sheltered position. On the 23rd he was worse. The events of that day and the following are thus related by Mr. Marshman:—"Havelock was evidently worse, and he himself declared his case hopeless. His mind was calm and serene, supported by the strength of that Christian hope that had sustained him through life. Relying firmly on the merits of the Redeemer, in whom he had trusted with unwavering confidence through life, he was enabled to look forward to the hour of dissolution with cheerfulness. Throughout the day he repeatedly exclaimed, 'I die happy and contented.' At one time he called his son to him, and said—'See how a Christian can die.' In the afternoon, Sir James Outram came to visit his dying comrade, when he said, 'I have for forty years so ruled my life, that when death came I might face it without fear;' he enjoyed little sleep during the night of the 23rd. The next morning he appeared to revive, but at eight there was a sudden and fatal change, and at half-past nine on the 24th November he calmly resigned his spirit into the hands of his Redeemer, in the blessed hope of immortality."

Thus had lived, thus died, Henry Havelock. At the moment when his fame was at the highest, when a grateful country was showering upon him rewards and honours, when in every circle, in every town, in every hamlet of England his name was hailed with the deepest enthusiasm, his pure spirit winged its flight from its tenement of clay. He lived but just long enough to hear that England had appreciated his great services:

the full measure of her gratitude he could imagine, but was not destined to enjoy. We ought not, perhaps, to lament his fate in that particular. He died in the city which he had risked so much and dared so nobly to gain, in the full knowledge that the great object for which those unsurpassed perils had been encountered had been fully achieved. He died in the full consciousness that he had done his duty to his God, to his country, and to himself. As that long rear-guard of tender women and helpless children defiled out of the residency, it was impossible that to some amongst them the thought should not have occurred how different, but for Havelock, would have been their destiny. We can see now, even more clearly than they could then, how he had accomplished such great things. It was that successful advance from Allahabad, those intrepid marches into Oudh, and finally that noble stand at Cawnpore when he had but 600 men fit for duty, and was threatened on all sides, that had contributed far more than any other movement to that happy result. His bold attitude had paralysed the action of the rebels and had given our Government the time required to collect the resources of the nation. The very daring of his movements caused their success. It was not so much that he marched triumphantly to Cawnpore,—although not every general would have successfully accomplished that movement,—it was his conduct after he arrived there, that showed the real grandeur of his character. His three attempts to penetrate into Oudh are, as military achievements, unequalled in history: he was so overmatched in numbers, that to find the semblance of a parallel the memory travels back to the days of Thermopylæ or to the expedition of Clearchus. But that disparity was certainly not his greatest difficulty. He could not fail to see that a blow successfully executed against his force would be fraught with terrible destruction to British interests. It would involve far more than the loss of his own little army. Cawnpore would in that event have formed the point of junction for the Gwalior Contingent, the Nawab of Furruckabad, and the Oudh insurgents. Their road to Allahabad would have been open, and whether successful or not against that fortress, they would have had it in their power to accomplish enormous mischief, and would have certainly occupied our forces far beyond the time up to which the Lucknow garrison would have been able to hold out. This was a consideration which would assuredly have scared a timid commander. Its effect upon Havelock was to make him more daring, more determined. His Indian experience had convinced him that the true, the only effectual manner of coping with an Asiatic enemy, was to throw away the scabbard, to seek him out, to impress him with the moral conviction that to beat him was the inevitable result of encountering him in the field. His crossing the Ganges therefore, in the face of a province armed and ready to oppose him, though seemingly a rash act, was in reality the safest and most prudent course that a general could adopt. Although he could not reach Lucknow, he was yet able to strike such terrible blows on the rebel force as to ensure himself absolutely against molestation on that side. His profound knowledge of war, and his thorough acquaintance with men, enabled him to do that with safety, which an ordinary mortal would either have not attempted at all, or would have nullified by doubt and hesitation. Every movement of Havelock's was like the well-pronounced incision of a sharp blade ; there was no hesitation about him; no hacking bit by bit; but his blow was well aimed, well considered, and executed always with a vigour and skill not to be surpassed.

But certainly, as much to be admired, and in a military point of view at least as meritorious as his advances into Oudh, was his resolution, when reduced to 600 effective men, not to abandon Cawnpore. He came to this determination when Cawnpore, as a military position, was not tenable. Kalpee itself, and with it the command of the whole line of the Jumna thence to Allahabad, was held by the Gwalior Contingent, a compact and well-disciplined force of 5000 men. It was in the power of this Contingent at any time, to cut him off from Allahabad, and thus in fact, to isolate him entirely. He viewed the chance of any movement of this nature with far more apprehension than he regarded an advance into Oudh, and he seems to have felt strongly more than once that every military reason bound him to retire. His experience convinced him, nevertheless, that notwithstanding his false military position, boldness was his soundest policy; and, once assured that reinforcements were on their way, he clung to that policy with all the tenacity of his strong character. In this resolution, and his consequent dispositions, he displayed one of the strongest attributes of a general. He showed how capable he was of using the moral power which his victories had given him in such a manner as to paralyse, with his reduced physical power, the action of three armies, each of which would have attacked him had he given the smallest sign that he feared the encounter.

His conduct in this campaign demonstrated very clearly that he possessed all the higher qualities of a great commander. A thorough knowledge of the principles of war, improved no less by study in the closet than by practice in Burmah, in Affghanistan, in Persia, and in India itself, combined with a profound acquaintance with human nature, to place him in the very first rank of generals. The one taught him what ought to be done under all circumstances, the other how to make men do it. Thus, though a stern disciplinarian, he could at the same time inspire his soldiers with that devotion for his person that knows no limit. He impressed them with a confidence in his skill and a belief in his ultimate fortune, that made them bear almost without a murmur that terrible trial to a soldier's temper—a retreat from a victorious field. As a tactician he followed in the footsteps of the great masters of the art. He never attacked in front, when it was possible to gain his end by operating on the flanks. At the same time he would not allow himself to be fettered by the chains of even the soundest general principle. Although he knew well that it was against every rule of warfare to fight a general action with a river in his rear, he deliberately took up that position when he fought the battle of Cawnpore. The great secret, in fact, of all his movements was his thorough appreciation of the character of his own soldiers, and of the character of his enemy. This knowledge he used alike to modify a general plan of a campaign, or a disposition on the battle-field; and it was this that enabled him to attempt more and to accomplish more, than had ever before fallen to the lot of any general, with numbers so disproportionate, to achieve.

If, then, he was a general of whom his country may boast, still more may the school in which he was trained be proud to place him on her loftiest pedestal. That Indian school which produced a Lawrence, a Clive, and a Coote; which taught even Wellington how to win battles; to which the names of Lake, of Hastings, of Ochterlony, of Napier, of Pollock, of Nott have added fresh lustre; which has glorified in the triumphs of Outram and mourned the untimely death of Nicholson, and which can still point to Chamberlain, to Herbert Edwardes, to Vincent Eyre, and to Lumsden as its worthy living representatives;—that school, we say, is honoured by counting Havelock as a pupil. He lived in it, and he was of it. All his feats of war were performed under its banners, and he had grafted its principles on those general maxims which he had imbibed from a study of European warfare. With India, then and with her school of warriors, his name must ever be inseparably connected. With Clive and Wellesley, Napier and Nicholson, he stands crowned with the brightest chaplet with which fame can encircle the warrior's brow, whilst from the homes of England cries and tears of gratitude are poured out at the pedestal of the hero, who so worthily maintained his country's honour in the hour of her darkest trial.

More fortunate than most warriors, Havelock has found a competent biographer. Mr. Marshman's narrative, which we have followed in this article, is an excellent specimen of what biography should be, and we are not surprised to learn that it has met with so favourable a reception in England. To those who desire to look into the inner life of the general, to notice how truly, from his first arrival in the country to the dark hour of his departure, he adhered, in spite of all difficulties, to the *rôle* of the Christian soldier, we commend a perusal of this work. To the military student it gives, at greater length than we have been able to afford, a succinct and stirring account of his various campaigns; while, for the benefit of all, it points the moral, that unswerving rectitude of character, though clouded for years by the cold shade of neglect, will, if true to itself and proof against all temptation, inevitably find its reward.

A LECTURE

ON

HYDER ALI'S LAST WAR.*

[DELIVERED TO THE SOLDIERS OF THE GARRISON, FORT WILLIAM, 8TH APRIL, 1865.]

HYDER ALI has been styled by a French writer "the most famous conqueror India has beheld since the time of Thamas Kouli Khan." It cannot certainly be denied that he was a great and successful soldier. In that character, addressing, as I am, English soldiers, I wish to speak of him this evening. I would shew him to you as a general, who, our enemy, was brave, undaunted, persevering, fertile in expedients, ready in resources, and who never despaired; as a soldier, who though fighting against English soldiers, had the utmost respect for their discipline and valour; and finally, as a man, who, though born with a swarthy skin, never taught to read or write, is yet a striking example that great natural gifts are not confined to one single section of the human race, but are distributed in fair proportion to all. I have chosen the last three years of his

* The principal authorities consulted by me for the purposes of this Lecture are:—Wilks's 'Historical Sketches of the South of India;' Stewart's 'Memoirs of Hyder Ali Khan;' 'Journal of a French Officer;' 'East India Military Calendar;' 'Life of Sir Hector Munro;' 'The Annual Register;' Edmund Burke's 'Speeches;' and 'Inde, par M. Xavier Raymond.'

life, because, to us Englishmen, those three years are the most interesting of his long career. They were years of unremitting warfare with England, and sometimes, on his part, of successful warfare. To have compressed all the events of his life within the limits of a lecture could only have been accomplished by bestowing but a cursory notice on some of his greatest achievements, whereas, in dwelling merely upon the last portion of it, those details may be entered into which will bring, I hope, some of his deeds on the battle field vividly before your eyes. I will, however, first endeavour to set before you, in as few words as possible, a sketch of his earlier career.

Hyder Ali was born in 1718. His father, a Naik or Colonel of a thousand men, died in 1738, a period when India was in the throes of that anarchy and confusion which supervened between the death of the Emperor Aurungzebe and the establishment of British supremacy. It was just the period in the history of Hindustan, when to be an adventurer, was a profession; when, the power of the sword being supreme, he who could wield it with the greatest dexterity, was certain to rise;—a time fatal to science, to civilization, to the growth of social virtues, but well suited to the gambler,* who, with earth for his table and human bones for his dice, might hope at one throw to gain a kingdom.

It was for such a stake that Hyder Ali played. By means which, however unscrupulous, were common enough in those days, he managed in 1760, after many fluctuations of fortunè, to eject the reigning Hindoo family of Mysore, and to constitute himself virtual ruler of that kingdom. But his ambition did not stop

* His table earth, his dice were human bones.—*Byron.*

there. After increasing his territory at the expense of the Mahrattas, he joined with the Nizam in endeavouring to drive the English from the Carnatic,—the territory lying between Mysore and the seacoast,—then governed by a protégé of the English, Mahomed Ali, whose predilection for adroit baseness was always prompting him to betray his protectors. In the war which followed, Hyder Ali completely outmanœuvred the English, and dictated a peace to the Governor, on the 4th April, 1769, under the walls of Madras. The chief articles of this treaty were the restitution of mutual conquests, and the assurance of mutual aid and alliance in defensive wars.

In the following year, Hyder Ali was attacked by the Mahrattas. He called upon the English to perform their contract and assist him, but, far from doing this, they lent a moral support to his enemies. Hyder was consequently compelled to make peace at a considerable sacrifice of territory. This territory, however, he recovered in subsequent campaigns.

Hyder never forgave the English for having failed to perform their part of the treaty of 1769. He would nevertheless, on political grounds, have preferred their friendship to an alliance with the French, but he feared to trust them. In this case, as so often happens in private life, the misunderstanding was inflamed and increased by the arts of interested "whisperers," amongst whom the Nawab of the Carnatic was conspicuous.

When, therefore, ten years later, the English became involved in a war with the French, and a war with the Mahrattas, and proposed to attack the French settlement of Mahé, Hyder sent to inform them that he should consider such an attack tantamount to a declaration of war. The English paid no heed to his remonstrances, but took Mahé. They sent, however, first, Mr. Schwartz, and afterwards, in January, 1780, Mr. Gray, as envoys to Hyder's Court at Seringapatam. to soothe and pacify him. Mr. Gray was supplied with a pigskin saddle, and a breech-loading rifle, which it was vainly attempted to charge as a muzzle-loader, as presents to this Mahomedan chief. These were contemptuously returned, and when, some days later, Mr. Gray was admitted to an audience, he was addressed in language which left no doubt of the intentions of the speaker. "Formerly," said Hyder to him, "I was of opinion that the English excelled all other nations in sincerity and good faith; but from late experience I am convinced they have no longer any pretensions to those virtues." Then, dwelling with considerable emphasis on his grounds of complaint against the English, and on the impossibility of amity between the two nations, he bade Mr. Gray, "return to his employer, and tell him not to trouble him with letters or messages of any kind."

Hyder prepared to act in accordance with this lofty language. He had arranged with his three allies, the Peshwa, the Rajah of Berar, and the Nizam, that whilst he should invade the Carnatic, the Nizam should burst upon the Northern Circars, and that the two armies, effecting a junction at a fixed point, should march upon and lay siege to Madras, overthrowing any army that might attempt to stay their progress; that at the same time the Peshwa should march upon Bombay, and throw the English into the sea, and that preparations should be made at Delhi, either to obtain the cooperation of the Wuzeer of Oudh in the expulsion of the English, or, in case of his refusal, to act vigorously against him.

A plan so gigantic could scarcely have succeeded on all its points, even had there been a Hyder Ali to direct each attack. But, of all the allies, he was perhaps the only one who was bent on prosecuting the war to its avowed end. In this, certainly, he showed no slackness. He moved from Seringapatam in the direction of Bangalore in the month of June, 1780, at the head of an army of 28,000 horse, 15,000 regular infantry, drilled according to the European fashion, 12,000 irregular infantry, 28,000 local troops and tributaries, 400 Europeans under M. de Lally, nephew of the famous French general of that name, and a hundred guns,—in all, 85,000 men. Of these, the local troops and tributaries, 28,000 in number, were the least to be depended upon, but the others constituted the most efficient army ever assembled under the banners of an Asiatic leader. He had an admirable commissariat, under the direction of a Brahmin, named Poornea, one of his ministers of finance, and no arrangements seemed wanting to ensure success. Hyder commanded, in person, the main body of this army; the left wing, intended to attack the Northern Circars, was under the orders of his son, Tippoo Sahib; whilst the right wing, under one of his most trusted generals, was directed to penetrate to the south, in the direction of Madura.

In the second week of July, 1780, Hyder broke up from Bangalore, and making his way through the Ghats, burst upon the Carnatic. The fort of Chittore, on the English side of the Palamnaire Pass, offered little impediment to his progress, and on the 20th his right wing had penetrated to Porto Novo, on the coast, below Pondichery, whilst he himself had plundered the considerable town of Conjeveram, forty-two miles west of Madras. Meanwhile, the Government of Madras had made no preparations to meet the danger. They did not even believe in it, though two of their members urgently pressed it upon them. Even on the 21st July, when intelligence reached them that Hyder had forced his way through the passes, they were not at all disturbed; and it was not till the 24th, when they learned with dismay that the Mysore chieftain was within forty-two miles of Madras, that they made the smallest preparation for the defence of the territory confided to their charge.

But on the 24th it was no longer possible to question the imminence of the danger. At that time the forces immediately available at Madras and its neighbourhood for active operations, consisted of one regiment of Highlanders, the 73rd; the 1st Madras Europeans; the grenadiers of the European battalion; four native regiments; and a few artillerymen;—in all 5209 men. It was arranged, after much discussion, and in the face of many protests, that this force should march under the command of Sir Hector Munro, of Buxar celebrity, to Conjeveram; and that it should be there joined by a detachment, 2813 strong, of whom 207 were Europeans, then stationed at Guntoor to protect the Northern Circars, under the orders of Colonel Baillie. That officer was at first instructed to move westward so as to alarm the enemy about his communications, but on his own representation, these orders were modified, and he was directed to march upon Conjeveram, taking such a route as would best enable him to intercept the enemy's convoys. The policy of ordering a junction at Conjeveram under the very eyes of Hyder Ali, when it might more safely and more speedily have been effected at Madras, was protested against at the time, and there can be no doubt that it was unsound.

At the same time, Colonel Brathwaite, who commanded at Pondichery, was ordered to move with his force of 1500 men to Chingleput, and thence to Madras; whilst Colonel Cosby, with 2000 native infantry, two regiments of the Nawab's cavalry, and two guns, was directed to move northwards from the banks of the Coleroon, so as to act on the enemy's communications in the passes, but he was afterwards compelled, as we shall see, to join the main army. Meanwhile, Hyder Ali, sensible that everything depended on the celerity of his movements, pushed rapidly forwards. On the 10th of August, his advanced parties had reached St. Thomas' Mount, and had driven the European inhabitants within the fort. He deemed it necessary, however, to undertake, in the first instance, the siege of Arcot, a place regarded of great importance, as being the seat of Government of the Nawab, and the possession of which could not fail to secure to him great moral as well as material advantages. On the 21st August, therefore, he invested Arcot.

Four days later, Sir Hector Munro, at the head of the force of 5209 men, before alluded to, left Madras for Conjeveram. Here he arrived on the 29th August, and here finding himself now within twenty-seven miles of his great antagonist, he determined to wait the arrival of Colonel Baillie, expected on the following day. It is time to turn, therefore, to the movements of that officer.

Colonel Baillie had left Guntoor early in August,

and marching southwards, had encamped, on the night of the 25th of that month on the northern bank of the river Cortelaur, then nearly dry. The floods, however, descended that night, and caused the river to rise to such an extent that Colonel Baillie was detained on the north bank till the 4th September. On that day he crossed, and reached Perambaucum on the morning of the 6th. This was but fourteen miles from Conjeveram, where Sir Hector, with the main body, was expecting him. He had scarcely, however, reached the encamping ground at Perambaucum, when he found himself assailed by the enemy, in overwhelming force. This enemy consisted of the left wing of Hyder Ali's army, under the command of Tippoo Sahib. To his movements I must now revert.

It will be recollected that on the 29th August, Sir H. Munro arrived at Conjeveram, twenty-seven miles distant from Arcot, then besieged by Hyder Ali. The same day Hyder received information of the departure of Sir Hector from Madras, and of Baillie's halt on the Cortelaur. His plans were rapidly formed. Breaking up from Arcot, he moved with the main body of his force on to Conjeveram, whilst he detached his left wing, consisting of 5000 regular infantry, 6000 horse, twelve light and six heavy guns, under the command of his son Tippoo, in the direction which he knew Colonel Baillie must take. On the 3rd September he himself encamped within six miles of the English army; and, receiving intimation, two days later, of his son Tippoo's intention to attack Colonel Baillie, he took ground to the north on the morning of the 6th, as though he intended to turn the right flank of the English. Sir Hector, completely deceived, refused his right wing, and Hyder, taking advantage of this movement, continued his manœuvre, and succeeded in interposing his whole force between the English army and the only road by which Colonel Baillie's detachment, then, as he knew, about to be attacked by his son Tippoo, could receive assistance.

Meanwhile, Tippoo, who had sighted Colonel Baillie's force on the 4th and 5th, but who, from strategical reasons, had then refrained from attacking them, resolved on the morning of the 6th, to deliver the well-intended blow. It was 11 o'clock, when, at the head of the force I have already mentioned, he came in sight of the English detachment, just arrived at Perambaucum. It was not his first encounter with the dreaded English, and, though he had now made up his mind to attack them, he feared to trust to the result of a hand-to-hand contest. He accordingly opened upon them with his artillery, and was at once replied to by the English guns. From eleven o'clock to two this contest continued, when Tippoo, having lost two or three hundred men, discontinued the cannonade, and wrote to his father that it would be impossible for him to make any impression on the enemy without reinforcements. Baillie, on the other hand, whose loss amounted to about a hundred killed and wounded, felt himself utterly unable to move in the face of the overwhelming cavalry force of Tippoo, and he wrote in this sense to Sir Hector, urging him to move with his whole army to his assistance.

But this was just what the British Commander-in-Chief could not do without hazarding an engagement with the immensely superior forces of Hyder, for, as we have seen, Hyder had interposed the main body of his army between the two divisions of the British Army.

He was, besides, unwilling to leave his heavy guns and supplies, which had been stored in the pagoda at Conjeveram, a building incapable of holding out even for a day. Forced to act, however, he determined to despatch the flank companies of the 73rd, commanded respectively by the Honourable John Lindsay, and Sir David Baird,—subsequently so distinguished for his services in India and in Spain,—two companies of the European regiment, and eleven companies of sepoys,—1007 men in all,—and the whole commanded by Colonel Fletcher,—in the hope that this column might be enabled to elude the vigilance of the enemy, and that the latter would be deceived by the passive attitude maintained by the main army in front of Conjeveram.

On the night of the 8th September, therefore, this detachment marched, following a route recommended by the guides, as leading them away from Hyder Ali's encampment. But Hyder, who had watched the English force as the hunter watches his prey, and who had perfect intimation of all its movements, had only permitted Colonel Fletcher to march out, that he might ensure his destruction. He had suborned the guides, and these were directed to lead the detachment through a defile from which escape would have been impossible. Fortunately, however, Colonel Fletcher, who was an able man and a good soldier, doubted the fidelity of the guides; he had accurately reconnoitred the position taken up by Hyder's army, and it appeared to him that the road by which they were advancing must inevitably lead him into the heart of the enemy's position. Acting upon this conviction, he suddenly changed his route, and making a long detour to the eastward, passed Hyder's army unperceived, and joined Colonel Baillie early on the morning of the 9th. A dangerous and difficult manœuvre was never more skilfully performed.

This junction raised the force under Colonel Baillie to 3720 men, of whom upwards of 500 were Europeans. After resting all day, Colonel Baillie prepared in the evening to move towards his chief, then distant from him but fourteen miles. A corresponding movement made by Sir Hector would have ensured the junction, for Hyder Ali had been much disturbed by the success of Colonel Fletcher's march, and the French officers in his service regarded it as part of a masterly manœuvre to place the Mysore army between two fires. He had therefore, made every preparation, in case of any disposition to move being evinced by the main body of the English army, to retreat with his whole force to the westward. But during the whole of the 9th, Sir Hector's force remained motionless, and Hyder, at ease regarding the intentions of one English commander, and bent on crushing the other, despatched the bulk of his infantry and guns at nightfall on the 9th to join his son Tippoo, and followed himself with his cavalry and light guns at 4 o'clock in the morning.

Meanwhile, Tippoo, who, since the indecisive action on the 6th, had contented himself with maintaining his ground, was very soon aware of the march of Colonel Baillie's force towards Conjeveram. He again, however, confined himself, as on the former occasion, to maintaining a distant and desultory fire, his object being to draw his enemy into a position in which he could attack him with advantage. He counted the more on this, as the route by which the English were moving had been carefully reconnoitred, and his troops and guns had been placed in positions in which they could act with the greatest effect.

But the steadiness of the English force baffled for a time all his hopes. Though considerably inconvenienced by the constant attacks from the enemy, they pushed on for five or six miles, halting occasionally to silence the fire of the hostile guns, or else to take possession of some advantageous position which commanded the ground by which they must advance. But, after marching six miles, and being then but eight miles distant from Sir Hector Munro's camp, Colonel Baillie suddenly, and in opposition to the advice of his second in command, Colonel Fletcher, resolved to halt for the night. This fatal halt was the cause of their subsequent misfortunes, for it gave to Hyder Ali, his son, and the French officers in their service, time to concert measures for the destruction of their hated foe.

Two miles in front of the position where the English had halted, and on the road by which they must pass, was a small grove of trees, opening on to a plain, about three-quarters of a mile distant from a village. This was the position chosen by Hyder, who had been in constant communication with his son during the night, for the destruction of the English force. Three batteries, armed with fifty-seven guns, were erected, one in front of the grove, and the other two on either side of it, and the infantry and cavalry were held in reserve to complete the havoc which, it was hoped, the fire of the artillery would ensure. Ignorant of these dispositions, Colonel Baillie, who had waited till daylight of the morning of the 10th to resume his march, experienced for the first two miles but little opposition. But no sooner had he entered the grove, than a tremendous fire from the enemy's batteries opened upon him. Yet, even at that terrible crisis, though taken by surprise, and for the moment without orders, the English soldiers and their sepoy comrades shewed themselves worthy of their high reputation. Covered by their guns, which returned with steady precision the enemy's fire, the force still advanced though in crowded order, along the avenue. Suddenly from their midst, ten companies of sepoys advance at the double, and charge the battery which is playing upon their front. The battery is reached, three of the guns are already disabled, when the clouds of dust and the tramping of myriads of horsemen tell them, with a startling certainty, that 20,000 of the famed troopers of Mysore are charging to cut them off. The sepoys, however, make good their retreat, though with some loss, and again the column moves slowly on. In vain, however. Covered by Hyder's cavalry, huge masses of infantry now advance, fresh guns are pushed on, and after a short interval, from three sides,—from the front from the right, and from the rear,—from fifty different points,—a deadly cross fire is poured in on the devoted column. Still, however, the English ranks remain unbroken; still, moving slowly, in the form of a square,—the sick, the baggage, the ammunition in the centre,—they drive back every assault and continue to gain ground. Their behaviour elicits the admiration even of their enemies. "In the whole of this trying day," wrote a French officer serving under Hyder, "the English preserved a coolness of manœuvre which would have done honour to any troops in the world. Raked by the fire of an immense artillery, the greatest part of the action within grape-shot distance, attacked on all sides by not less than 25,000 horse and 30 battalions of sepoys, besides Hyder's European troops, the English column stood firm, and repulsed every attack with great slaughter; the horse driven back on the infantry, the right of our line began to give way, though composed of the best troops in the Mysore army." It was indeed true. Daunted by the unshaken firmness of the English column, and alarmed by a movement to the right in the direction of his guns which Colonel Baillie made at the moment, Hyder, who was burdened with the consciousness that Sir H. Munro could not be further off than six miles, and was probably much nearer, and might place him at any moment between two fires resolved, after a cannonade of three hours' duration, to retreat. He sent orders to Colonel Lally to draw off the infantry, and to the cavalry to cover the movement. The heroic resistance of the English had indeed produced its natural effect, when at the moment, two of their tumbrils, in the centre of their square, exploded. The effect was terrific. One entire face of the square was laid open, the guns were dismounted and overturned, their ammunition destroyed, and the entire force thrown into irreparable confusion. Hyder himself noticed the catastrophe, but before he could give orders to take advantage of it, one of his lieutenants charged at the head of a regiment of cavalry. The charge was repulsed, but the example brought down the enemy's horse in successive squadrons, whilst the infantry poured in volleys of musketry, and a little later the guns reopened at a closer range. Yet, for an hour and a half longer the unequal conflict was maintained. Closing up as their ranks were thinned, the British cohort long presented a bold front to their countless foes. At last, finding his force reduced to about 400 men, and hopeless of relief from the main army, Colonel Baillie resolved to surrender. Even then the troops desired to be led on, and to die sword in hand. Better had they done so, for no sooner had they, under a promise of quarter, laid down their arms, than Hyder's young soldiers rushed upon them, and fleshed their swords on the defenceless, the wounded, the sick. The exertions of the French officers, especially M. Pinorin and M. de Lally, put a stop to this massacre, but of the entire force of Europeans, numbering that morning upwards of 500 men, but 200 remained alive, and of these many were wounded. Of 86 officers, 36 were killed, 34 wounded; 16 only were untouched. Colonel Fletcher lay dying on the field. Colonel Baillie, mortally wounded, was brought into Hyder's presence and taunted with his defeat, but with the true spirit of a British officer, he bade the Asiatic chief not to vaunt too loudly over a victory, which,—he could appeal to his French officers,—never would have been his, but for an accident which no human foresight could prevent.

The fate of the two hundred prisoners deserves to be recorded and remembered, as one example amongst a thousand, of the folly of men with arms in their hands trusting to the promises of a barbarian enemy. Most of them were Highlanders, and of these, few could even read or write. They had, however, imbibed in early youth the faith which they had been taught by their forefathers, and from this, no temptation, no cruelty, could induce them to swerve. Fed sparingly upon unwholesome rice, exposed purposely and without covering to the burning heat of the sun by day, and to the unwholesome dews by night, seeing their companions dropping before their eyes, they were yet offered life, and liberty, and wealth, on condition of their embracing the Mahomedan faith. Yet not one of them would agree to purchase life on such terms; not one even hesitated, even at the moment when his bodily powers were weakest. They would not consent, defenceless as they were, to abandon the God of their fathers, and we may be sure that in their dying moments He did not forget them. But few survived the terrible ordeal, and those who did found in the prisons of Seringapatam a more lingering death. Another instance of English fortitude deserves to be mentioned. Among the prisoners taken was a son of Colonel Lang, commanding at Vellore, who had served with the army a volunteer. Hyder, learning who he was, sent for him, and ordered him to write a letter to his father, offering him a splendid establishment if he would give up Vellore, and stating that his own death would be the consequence of refusal. The boy at first positively refused, but, pressed with threats, he turned to Hyder, and said, in an indignant voice, in the Mysore language:—"If you consider me base enough to write such a letter, on what ground can you think so meanly of my father? It is in your power to present me before the ramparts of Vellore, and cut me in a thousand pieces in my father's presence, but it is not in your power to make him a traitor." The threats were, however, renewed, but on their proving ineffectual, the boy was consigned to the quarters of the other prisoners.

To return, however, to the battle field. Where, it may be asked, was Sir Hector Munro, whilst 60,000 choice Asiatic troops were overwhelming one of his detachments within a few miles of him? It is indeed time that we should enquire.

Sir Hector, we have seen, remained quiet at Conjeveram the whole of the 9th. At daylight on the 10th, he moved in the direction of Perambaucum, from which he was fourteen miles distant. After marching two or three miles, he saw the smoke of the action, and moved in that direction; after marching about a mile further, he saw a great smoke,—evidently the explosion of the tumbrils. Almost immediately afterwards the artillery fire ceased for a time, and a desultory fire of musketry succeeded. At this moment, considering the distances the two English detachments had marched towards one another that morning, Sir Hector could not have been more than two miles distant from Colonel Baillie. Had he only advanced, the defeat must have been converted into a great victory. This advance, in fact, was the movement Hyder feared, and which his French officers believed to be part of an intended plan. He had kept open, therefore, his communications with the west, ready to move in that direction on the first appearance of Sir Hector's columns. He, in fact, shortly before the explosion, had seen the heads of those columns, and had ordered his cavalry to threaten it in masses, with a view to cover his own withdrawal, when, to his satisfaction, he noticed its movement, to the east and subsequently to the south, back to Conjeveram. Sir Hector, on his part, had jumped to the conclusion that the cessation of firing intimated a victory gained by Colonel Baillie, and it was only after moving in every direction except that which might have altered the state of affairs, that he learned the truth from a wounded sepoy. He, at once, "for the security of his army," moved back to Conjeveram, where he arrived at 6 P.M. Deeming himself still unsafe there, he threw his heavy guns and stores into the tank, and moved early next morning to Chingleput, where, however, he only arrived with the loss of the greater part of his baggage, on the morning of the 12th. Here he was fortunate enough to meet Colonel Cosby's division, which had encountered great difficulties in its march from the south of the Coleroon, and had been compelled to cut its way through the enemy. This junction enabled Sir Hector to march north-eastwards for the defence of Madras, then at the mercy of Hyder's victorious army. He reached Thomas' Mount on the 14th, and moving next day to Marmalong, remained there with a river covering his front, till he was relieved in the following November by Lieutenant-General Sir Eyre Coote.

Meanwhile Hyder, flushed with victory, though it was a victory which had cost him some of his best troops, moved back into his former encampment in front of Conjeveram, ready to act according to circumstances. The retreat of Sir Hector from that place had left the direct road to Madras open to him, but, though sound policy and sound military strategy combined to induce him to make an attack upon the presidency, before it had recovered from the panic caused by the events at Perambaucum, he preferred the easier task of resuming the investment of Arcot, the capture of which in the crippled state of the English army, appeared to him easy. On the 19th, therefore, he moved to that place, and after six weeks' open trenches he assaulted it in two columns, one under his son Tippoo, the other commanded by Maha Mirza Khan. Tippoo's column was at first driven back, but, Mirza Khan being successful, Tippoo rallied his troops, and at a second attempt effected an entrance. The English troops, 200 in number, retired, with the 7000 men in the service of the Nawab, within the citadel, but Hyder, it is said, managed by means of the Governor, Raja Birbir, whom he had taken prisoner, to exercise such an influence on the native troops within its walls, that this citadel,—formerly so famous for its successful defence of 50 days' duration with an inferior garrison under Lord Clive,—now surrendered on the third day after the town itself had fallen. The Europeans taken on this occasion were sent to Seringapatam, where many of them were employed in drilling Hyder's new levies, formed for the most part of the native prisoners he had made during this campaign, and the Hindoo portion of whom he forced to become Mahomedans.

After the capture of Arcot, Hyder, still avoiding Madras, marched westward, and laid siege to Vellore, sending detachments at the same time to attack Amboor, Wandewash, Permacoil and Chingleput. Amboor surrendered on the 13th January, but on the 18th, certain information reached Hyder that Sir Eyre Coote had left Madras on the previous day, at the head of a considerable force, with the intention of wresting from him the mastery over the Carnatic. Hyder, on receipt of this intelligence, raised the siege of the places he was attacking, and massed his forces, apparently intending to accept a general engagement. But, hearing a few days later of the arrival of a French fleet off Madras, and believing that this intelligence would force Sir Eyre Coote to move to its defence, he moved rapidly on Conjeveram in order to cut off his enemy from the presidency. But Sir Eyre Coote, after revictualling the garrisons of the strong places held by the English in the Carnatic, had moved towards Pondichery, whither he learned, the French fleet had preceded him. He was followed by Hyder, whose march indicated an intention to move on Cuddalore. On the 8th both armies were moving in parallel lines within cannon range. On the 10th Sir Eyre Coote, pressed for supplies, which were cut off from him on the side of the sea by the French fleet, and on the landside by Hyder, offered battle to his enemy. But Hyder knew too well the advantage of his position to accept it. The situation of the British general was now desperate; he had no supplies, no means of procuring any, and he himself,—a man not given to despair,—a man who, in the famous council of war before Plassey, had given his voice with the minority for the fight,—recorded his opinion, that in all human probability the existence of that British army must be brought to a fatal close. But here again was shown the truth of that aphorism of Napoleon "that success in war lies with him who makes the fewest mistakes." Suddenly, under some inspiration of folly, the French admiral weighed anchor, and stood out to the eastward. Coote could not conceal his exultation. He at once wrote to Madras for provisions, adding significantly; "those supplied, I will manage the rest."

Sir Eyre Coote remained at Cuddalore waiting for supplies for nearly five months. Meanwhile, Hyder contented himself with occupying the passes which communicated with the interior; then, sending his son Tippoo at the head of 30,000 men to resume the siege of Vellore, he marched with the bulk of his army south of the Coleroon, and drew all his supplies of both men and money from the Tanjore territory, realising in this manner an enormous booty. His object was, if possible, to draw the English general from Cuddalore, the place that he had fixed upon as the depôt of his French allies.

On the 16th June, Sir Eyre Coote, hearing that Hyder had strongly fortified a pagoda called Chillumbrum near Porto Novo, and twenty-six miles from Cuddalore, and that he intended to use it as a depôt for the French, moved towards the place with his whole force. He came before it on the 18th, and attempted to carry it the same evening by a *coup de main.* But misinformed as to its strength and the number of the garrison, the small party he detached for that purpose was repulsed with loss. Having reconnoitred it the next day and finding it very strong, he drew off his army, and, re-crossing the Vellore river, encamped near Porto Novo.

The account of this repulse, greatly exaggerated to Hyder, emboldened that leader to make a move which he hoped would prove decisive. Quickly re-massing his scattered forces, he crossed the Coleroon, moved rapidly to the north, then making a sudden turn to the eastward, he interposed his whole army between the English and Cuddalore, having marched a hundred miles in two days and a half. On the 27th June, when Sir Eyre Coote had just made arrangements for the attack by sea and land, of the pagoda, Chillumbrum, he suddenly heard that Hyder, with his whole army, was within three miles of him.

Coote called a council of war, and this time the council resolved to fight. At 7 o'clock on the morning of the 1st July, he moved out his army, consisting of 8476 men, of whom 2070 were Europeans. Arriving in front of the enemy, computed to be about 40,000 of all arms, inclusive of tributaries, he spent a long hour in reconnoitring his position. He found him very strongly posted, occupying three villages. The ground on his front and on his flanks was intersected in every direction by deep ditches and watercourses; his left was covered by a range of sandhills which followed the direction of the coast. Embrasures for his artillery had been cut in mounds of earth, formed from the hollowing of the ditches. Behind these lay, motionless, the main body of the army.

The English general soon made up his mind. His army was formed in two lines. The second line, under General Stuart, was broken into column, and moved to the right under cover of the first line, and afterwards of the sandhills before mentioned. The columns advanced in this direction, following the coast, and thus turning the enemy's left, until they reached an opening in the sandhills, which Hyder had delayed for a day to fortify, in order that he might first make it stronger. General Stuart at once formed his men up and led them to this opening. Twice repulsed, he succeeded the third time, though not till 4 o'clock in the afternoon, in driving the enemy before him. The first line had meanwhile contented itself with a strong demonstration against the enemy's left front, but, no sooner were General Stuart's guns heard, then the feigned attack was converted into a real one, and this line also made good its position on the plateau.

Meanwhile, Hyder, who was seated cross-legged on a stool on an eminence behind the centre of his line, witnessed with astonishment and dismay the success of the advance. He instantly ordered a charge of cavalry on both lines. That on the first line was repulsed only after a most desperate encounter; that on the second was never made. Just as its commander, Meer Sahib, was about to give the order to charge, he was struck dead by a round shot, and almost immediately afterwards, an unexpected broadside from an English schooner making terrible havoc amongst the chiefless squadrons, a panic ensued, and they retreated behind the sandhills. Hyder, furious, refused to leave his stool; he would not believe that he was beaten, and declared that the heads of his generals should suffer for their failure. At last, a favourite groom, one of his privileged servants, seized him by both legs, and mounted him on his horse. Hyder then hastened from the field, and set to work to rally his beaten army, of whom 10,000 killed and wounded had fallen on this fatal day. He did not, however, lose a single gun. The English loss was 306.

Baffled, though not despairing, Hyder took a north-westerly direction, sending instructions to his son Tippoo, who was besieging Wandewash, to join him, but first to attempt an escalade of the place at all possible points. In this Tippoo was foiled by the rare sagacity of Captain Flint,—one of the unrewarded heroes of Indian history,—but he succeeded in joining his father at Arcot. Thence the combined force moved on Perambaucum,—the scene of Colonel Baillie's defeat of the previous year,—and here,—as a place of good omen,—Hyder resolved to do battle again with his old antagonist. Either from this superstitious motive, or from want of heart on the part of his troops, he neglected the opportunity of harassing Sir Eyre Coote in his march along the coast, and of hindering his junction with the reinforcements expected from Bengal. The English general was thus enabled to unite himself with these at Pulicat, adding one-third to his strength, on the 2nd August.

On the 19th August Sir Eyre Coote moved with his augmented force towards the fort of Tripasore, only a few miles distant from Hyder's encampment at Perambaucum. On the morning of the 22nd a practicable breach was reported, and the English were just preparing for the assault, when the entire army of Hyder was seen advancing to relieve it. The general instantly gave orders to storm, when, fortunately, the place surrendered of its own accord. Hyder, furious at the display of such pusillanimity in the presence of his army, sent to the English general and urged him to put to death the prisoners he had taken, and who had behaved as traitors to their master. This of course was not done, and the prisoners were released on parole.

Sir Eyre Coote, bent now, more than ever, on bringing Hyder to action, lost no time in advancing towards Perambaucum. He came in front of it on the 27th August. He found him occupying a position, which, strong by nature, had been fortified by art. His army 70,000 strong, was drawn up on the acclivities of a range of hills, at the foot of which ran several deep watercourses. On his flanks, and along his front, he had erected tremendous batteries, commanded by other batteries in the rear, and his pioneers had been employed for two days in obstructing the only road by which the English columns could advance.

This was the position which Sir Eyre Coote, with an army numbering little over 12,000 men, advanced to attack. His army was formed in two lines; the first of which, under Sir Hector Munro, was directed to advance, supported by the second, commanded by General Stuart, against the centre of the enemy's position. But the difficulties of the ground were so great, and the position so well chosen, and so bravely defended, that at 3 o'clock in the afternoon, the English had not succeeded in making any visible impression upon it.

Their further advance was checked by a strong enfilading fire from the village of Pollilore, on the left of the enemy's position. A new disposition was accordingly made. Under cover of a heavy fire from two brigades of the first line, the third brigade of which it was composed attacked and stormed the village of Pollilore, whilst the second line made a similar attack on the right of the enemy's position. At this point the battle raged with great fury, and it was not before nightfall that the English succeeded in driving their brave antagonists from the elevated plateau, which formed the key to that part of their position. During the night, Hyder, covered by his cavalry, which he had not been able to use in the action, and abandoning one gun, out of the eighty he had brought into the field, marched towards Conjeveram, thus leaving the field of battle to the English. He nevertheless fired a salute in honour of what he termed his victory, but which might more fairly be called an indecisive action. The English general, after remaining one day on the field to bury his dead, retired to Tripasore. The loss of the English is variously estimated from 421 to 600 men; that of the Mysoreans from 1500 to 2000.

After this action, Hyder, sending his cavalry under his son Tippoo to watch and harass the English, marched with the remainder of his force upon Vellore, and closely invested it on every side. He also commenced to fortify a position at Sholingur to prevent the advance of the English to its relief. But on the 27th September he was surprised by the sudden appearance of Sir Eyre Coote and his army. Unprepared to deliver battle, and yet wishing to save his guns, he hurled his cavalry under Tippoo, who had rejoined him, on the advancing

English. This attack, made with all the energy of despair, enabled him to draw off his infantry and heavy guns, and he retreated to the westward with the loss of 800 men. Sir Eyre Coote not only relieved Vellore, but also re-took the fort of Chittore at the entrance of the Palamnaire Pass.

Want of supplies, however, soon compelled Sir Eyre Coote to retire to the vicinity of Madras, and the blockade of Vellore was resumed by Hyder, with more strictness than ever. In the beginning of December, indeed, the Madras Government received information that with the utmost economy in the distribution of provisions, the place could not hold out beyond the beginning of January.

The shattered state of Sir Eyre Coote's health had induced his medical advisers to order him to return to Bengal, but, at the earnest solicitation of Government, he rose from his sick bed, to make a final effort for the provisioning Vellore. He joined the army on the 2nd January, and though struck down by an attack of apoplexy on the 5th, he rallied so far as to be carried in a palanquin with the army on the 6th. Never did he shew more skill and boldness than when he was thus, as it were, in the very jaws of death. He crossed a large convoy over the Palâr river, on which Vellore is situated, and over a swampy morass, in front of the whole army of Hyder, on the 10th January, threw three months' provisions into the town on the 11th, and recrossed the same morass on the 13th, threatened all the time by the numerous cavalry of Hyder, and under a perpetual cannonade. On the 16th, Hyder appearing again in full force, Sir Eyre endeavoured to bring him to battle, but in vain. He therefore returned, leisurely, to Tripasore. Hyder instantly took advantage of his absence. It will be recollected that in the original plan of the campaign of 1780, Colonel Brathwaite, at the head of 1500 men, afterwards reinforced to about 2500, of whom 150 were Europeans, had been directed to proceed to Chingleput, and subsequently to Madras; but, after the battle of Porto Novo, and Hyder's march to the north, he had been charged with the defence of the country south of the Coleroon. Learning that this officer lay unsupported in that position, Hyder, the moment Sir Eyre Coote had marched towards Tripasore, despatched his son Tippoo, at the head of 12,000 cavalry, 8000 regular infantry, 400 French, and twenty guns, with orders to proceed by forced marches and to surprise him. On the 16th February, Colonel Brathwaite, who was encamped in an open plain, and who had disbelieved all the announcements made to him on the subject of the approach of an enemy, suddenly found himself surrounded by this force. Unable to retreat, he resolved on a vigorous resistance. He formed his force into a hollow square, with the artillery interspersed in the faces, and the cavalry in the centre. Tippoo first played on them with his guns, and, bringing up his infantry under the cover of that fire, he poured in volley after volley of musketry. But being met by a bold and steady resistance, he ordered his cavalry to charge. On they came, the flower of the Mysore horse, but they came only to be broken and to fly. From the living sides of that square there poured upon them showers of grape and musket shot, such as even the swarthy troopers of Southern India dared not face. They charged but to reform, in diminished numbers, behind their guns.

For nearly three days this fierce contest continued,—Tippoo changing constantly his mode of attack, but changing it in vain. For nearly three days, without food, without prospect of relief, that band of heroes resisted him. At last, on the 18th, a final attempt was made. M. de Lally formed his 400 Frenchmen into close column, and supported on either flank by strong columns of Mysore troops, covered by the fire of the artillery, and with the cavalry handy, charged down with the bayonet on the devoted band. Faint and weary, they could not resist this final effort. They sank from sheer exhaustion before it. Then, as at Perambaucum, dashed in the fierce troopers to slaughter the fallen; and then, as on that occasion, did the wounded, the sick, and the wearied, owe their lives to the generous interposition of the French commander. Again, however, were the survivors reserved to a fate worse than death, being sent, loaded with irons, to the prisons of Seringapatam. Colonel Brathwaite himself was detained a prisoner in Hyder's camp.

Hyder who had been greatly depressed by the defeat of one of his detachments under Sirdar Khan at Tellicherry during the previous month, was immensely elated by this success of his son Tippoo, and learning shortly after, the disembarkation of a French division of 2000 men at Porto Novo,—being the first detachment of a powerful force under M. de Bussy,—began to re-entertain the hope of wresting the Carnatic from English influence. He speedily effected a junction with the French force, and, taking Cuddalore on the 8th April, and Permacoil a few days later, invested Wandewash. Sir Eyre Coote advanced at once to its relief, and on the 24th May offered battle to the allied armies; but these, prevented by the instructions of M. de Bussy to his French division not to fight a battle before his arrival, were unable to accept it. They retired rather to the heights around Arnee.

The English commander, having ascertained that the commandant of Arnee was prepared to give up that fort, marched against it on the 2nd June; but Hyder, divining this movement, had despatched Tippoo and M. de Lally to the defence of Arnee, whilst he himself should operate on the rear of the English army, though unsupported by his French allies. The 3rd of June both armies came in contact, but it was rather a day of manœuvring and skirmishing than a pitched battle. If, by his manœuvres, Hyder Ali foiled the intentions of the English general upon Arnee, the latter had the gratification of mortifying Hyder still more by the capture of one of his guns and eleven tumbrils, which had stuck fast in the bed of a river. Five days later, however, Hyder revenged himself by inflicting a loss on the English of 166 men and two guns by tempting them, by the display of a drove of cattle, into an ambuscade.

This was the last encounter of the two rival commanders. Sir Eyre Coote returned to Madras, and sailed thence to Bengal, broken down by ill-health, and leaving the presidency in a state which he considered all but desperate. Hyder, on his part, after several demonstrations, encamped with the main body of his army, on the high ground near the river Poni, sixteen miles north of Arcot, for the rainy season, sending his son Tippoo, with a strong force to the western coast. He had been long ailing, and on the 6th of December, feeling death coming upon him, he moved into the town of Arcot. Here, on the following day, full of years,—he was sixty-five,—and in the possession of vast resources, he died.

This man, who commenced his life as an adventurer, left behind him a territory, not including his conquests in the Carnatic, of 80,000 square miles; a revenue of two millions sterling, a full treasury, an effective regular army of 88,000 men, and the reputation of being the most energetic, the most persevering, and the most formidable enemy the English had ever encountered in India. His death was concealed for some days from his attendants by his faithful ministers, in order to give time to Tippoo Sahib, who was on the western coast, to join the army. I may add, that the war continued with varying fortune for fifteen months after the death of Hyder Ali, when it was concluded by the treaty of Mangalore (11th March, 1784), by which the restitution of all places taken by either party during the war, and the liberation of all prisoners, were stipulated. Tippoo, however, having twice, subsequently, defied the English to war, was finally slain when valiantly defending Seringapatam, —the 4th May, 1799,—and the kingdom of Mysore was restored to the family which Hyder Ali had displaced.

Time has restricted me to a bare outline of the military achievements of Hyder Ali's last war, but even these are not quite uninstructive. We have seen how, for three years,—and they continued it much longer,— the English soldiers of the last century endured without a murmur the fatigues and the dangers consequent upon incessant marches, constant exposure to the sun at the most deadly seasons, deficient supplies, treacherous allies, and an exhausted and partly hostile country; how they endured all this in the face of an enemy five times as numerous as they were, and whose great superiority in cavalry always robbed them of the fruit of their victories. We have seen them overwhelmed by numbers, yet still bearing up with a noble spirit against a countless host, animating by their example their sepoy comrades, and standing in their ranks, though without food, without water, and without hope of relief, till overwhelmed by physical exhaustion, and the weight of numbers. We have seen how cheerfully they advanced to every attack; how every privation was forgotten in the presence of an enemy; how neither superiority of force, nor strength of position, nor moral obstacles perhaps greater than these, ever damped their ardour, or rendered them less confident of victory. Yes, indeed! If England has reason to be proud of her soldiers now, she must also honour these, —she must honour the men, who, when her fame as a military nation was questioned, when she was being forced to quit her hold on those American colonies which were regarded as the brightest jewels of the Crown, fought for a new empire under overwhelming disadvantages, and who fought to win.

One word with respect to Hyder Ali. The moral of his career is indeed too significant to be passed over without remark. He rose by the sword, and he was compelled all his life-time to wield the sword. By the sword, too, his family fell. Is not this sentence, applicable as it is to the general state of India during the eighteenth century, a sufficient justification for the predominance of a power, which has prevented this incessant slaughter, which will have no military adventurers, which, though it permits to so-called independent states free action in internal affairs, yet takes from them the right of drawing the sword, which would rather inculcate on its subjects the old-fashioned principle of striving to rise, by the exercise of an honest industry, and by the orderly development of natural talents, to the places in society for which they are most fitted? Imagine what was then the fate of the Carnatic, ravaged for years by hostile armies; what the condition of Madras, with an enemy constantly at its gates, and dependent even for its supplies on the uncertain arrival of ships, liable at all times to be intercepted by a hostile squadron! Contrast the India of the last century, drawn upon incessantly for the support of the numberless armies which strove to subdue it, with the India of to-day, calm, peaceful, and prosperous under the rule of Queen Victoria, and we may then, perhaps,—Natives as well as Europeans,—feel some portion of the debt of gratitude which we really owe to those gallant soldiers, who fought so nobly, under so many accumulated disadvantages, in "Hyder Ali's last war."

SIR HUGH ROSE

[FROM THE 'CALCUTTA REVIEW' FOR MAY, 1865.]

WE seldom realise, during our own lives, the extent to which posterity will interest itself regarding the careers of those who have contributed to render illustrious the period through which we are passing. Notwithstanding that this is essentially a scribbling age, we fail to perceive that it is at all more fruitful than its predecessors in that careful biography, which lays before us, as they actually were, as they really lived and moved, those who have but lately occupied, or who are now occupying, a prominent place in the historic scene. In fact, the scribbling of the present day is of too desultory a character to be of real or permanent use. Men write, not with a view to enrich the national annals or to advance the cause of historic truth, but, too generally, to gain for themselves a fleeting renown, or to gratify a spurious sort of vanity. Not only do our library tables groan under the weight of three-volumed novels,—too numerous to read, and most of them too heavy to digest,—but we have likewise philosophical reflections and paradoxical essays,—many of them displaying, no doubt, an immense deal of ingenuity,—but wanting, almost always, in soundness, in depth, and in common sense. As we examine the majority of these "brain-sick fancies," we try in vain to realise to ourselves the cast of mind which could conceive that a man is sent into this world to act the part of the casuist and the visionary, to spend his entire life in a vain attempt to unravel problems, which it was never intended he should know, and which, if unraveled, would benefit him neither in this world nor the next. If indeed worldly wisdom be the only result aimed at, and a man be self-opinionated enough to attempt to acquire that wisdom from books,—why, a single play of Shakspeare is worth more than all the divinations of the modern school of philosophers. On the other hand if the student, before entering the world himself, should wish to see a distinguished man exactly as he lived amongst his contemporaries,—he must seek out a record of his acts, his conversation, his letters; he must pry, if possible, through his writings, into his very thoughts. To do this is always difficult, often impossible. The man himself has disappeared from the scene, and his writings are too frequently so dispersed that they can come under the cognizance of but a few. One by one, his contemporaries, those who stood face to face with him in life, follow him to the silent tomb, and the traces of his inner life become more and more obliterated. But it may be said, that at this point the biographer,—the mole of literature,—steps in. His is no path strewed with garlands. No easy honours are showered upon his progress. No present triumph stimulates his vanity or supports him under the long moments of weary labour. He has to dig and delve into forgotten documents; to search out the links of some story, all the particulars of which have ceased to be remembered; to reconcile the conflicting statements of men who are no more; to give to the dry bones of antiquated memoirs a living vitality. It is too often, in fine, a labour, which, like the wheel of Sysiphus, seems ever to recur;—a work, which, always accumulating under newly found materials, seems to defy industry, and to impose a limit even upon perseverance. The result, too, is seldom satisfactory. We have presented to us, an image certainly, the form and fashion of a man who might have lived,—but too often, the resemblance to the actual sitter for the portrait is scarcely discernible, and the peculiarities by which he was distinguished in his lifetime, are not seldom, in the picture, "conspicuous by their absence."—Not so, however, with the writer who attempts to portray a living man. This is a real representation. The artist and the sitter have lived in the same age, have associated with the same people, have taken parts,—though often very different parts,—in the same drama. The atmosphere has been alike to both, and thus, if the portrait be drawn with spirit and truth, with a sincere desire to show things as they were, it must be invested with a reality, in which the portraits of those who have lived in a distant age are necessarily deficient.

There have been few more eventful periods of general history,—none, certainly, of Indian history,—than that through which we have passed during the last seven years. In that interval many great and noble characters have risen to the surface, but what do we know of them? It is true that we have been presented with a likeness of Havelock,—that pioneer of victory. It is understood also that a life of Sir Henry Lawrence is now being undertaken by the eminent soldier-political who is best qualified to write it. But what do we know of Nicholson, that real Genius of War? So far as we are aware, not even a magazine article has been devoted to his brilliant career. Is the story of that career to die? He had friends, admirers, relations. Is there no one to come forward to give that heroic character to the world, before the eyes of those who have seen him on the scene of his exploits, and who could tell of his deeds, have been closed by death? Is the career of one who was the greatest ornament, the proudest boast of the Indian Army,—who was at once its hero and its model,—is that career to be allowed to pass out of sight unrecorded? Cannot those who have given to the world the "*copia verborum*" of their own exploits, cannot they spare a few half hours to write their reminiscences of the man to whom all are so much indebted? We never met an Indian Officer who had seen him who did not acknowledge in Nicholson the foremost man of the Indian Army. They owe it, then, to his memory, that his name should not be left to wander up and down the dull pages of some dogmatic history, but that a literary habitation should be found for it, not unworthy of the hero.

But, whilst according to Nicholson all the honour which his character and his great achievements demand, we must not forget that, in another part of this country, there were occurring about the same time events of equal moment,—events fraught with the fate of western and central India, and upon the result of which, too, the action to be taken by the princes of southern India, in all probability, depended. We will not here anticipate the story we propose to tell, in this article, of some of those events. We will confine ourselves to the remark, that there was a peculiarity in the character of the general who reconquered central India, which asserted itself on every occasion, and which materially influenced the fortunes of the campaign. This peculiarity evinced itself in a firm determination to succeed at all hazards; to recognise no such obstacle as "impossibility;" to be foiled neither by deficiencies in his own camp, nor by superiority of numbers in the camp of the enemy; to regard even disease itself, though attacking his own person, as something to be trampled upon and disregarded. It showed itself likewise in greater things than these. The general who reconquered central India had gained, either from reading, from experience, or from intuitive perception,—or, perhaps, from a combination of all three,—so complete a knowledge of the "morale" of an Asiatic foe, that, at a time when the pre-revolution tactics of the Austrian army were in fashion in this country, he never lost an opportunity of seeking his enemy where he was to be found, of beating him when he found him, and of following him up to utter destruction when he had beaten him. More than any other commander of modern days did this general realise the eloquent description, given by Sir William Napier, of the battle of Napoleon;—that it was "the swell and dash of a mighty wave, before which the barrier yielded, and the roaring flood poured onwards, covering all things." When we recall to mind that this is the general who has commanded the Indian Army during the past five years,—five years of such momentous changes that they might correctly be termed years of silent revolution,—we think we shall be performing a service, not only to the military world of India, but to the military world of Europe, if we lay before the readers of this Review, in a rapid and continuous outline, the main facts of a career which is not only full of interest, but which offers also so much that is worthy of study as does the career of Sir Hugh Rose.

Sir Hugh Rose entered the army in the year 1820, as an ensign in the 93rd Sutherland Highlanders. He obtained his commission at a very early age, and,—his father being at the time envoy at the Court of Berlin,—leave was given to him to complete his military education in,—as it was then considered,—that great military capital of Europe. He here enjoyed the advantage of the best instruction which that age was capable of affording. He was subsequently appointed to the 19th regiment, and, in consequence of the special recommendation of its commanding officer, was given an unattached majority by purchase after only a little more than six years' service. Whilst still serving in the 19th, Lieutenant Rose's name was mentioned in division orders by the Major-General commanding the district for the great gallantry he displayed in completely beating off, with only eight men, overwhelming numbers of the peasantry in the county of Leitrim, who endeavoured to take from him the gauger, still, and prisoners whom he was escorting.

Soon after obtaining his majority, Major Rose was appointed to the 92nd Gordon Highlanders, and served with them eleven years. The regiment was much employed in Ireland, chiefly in suppressing disturbances in that then distrusted country. On Major Rose devolved the duty of putting down tithe and monster meetings in Tipperary and the adjacent counties. Such was the opinion then entertained of the young field officer by Lord Vivian, Commander of the Forces, that he authorised him to collect troops from the several stations, and gave him discretionary powers as to the manner in which he should act so as to repress and put down these illegal assemblages. Major Rose accomplished this very rapidly and very effectively. He acted on this occasion, as in his after career, on the well known, though practically little accepted, principle, that he gives twice who gives quickly. He moved his troops by long marches with such celerity from one meeting to another, that the dispersion of the rioters was complete, and a few weeks saw not only Tipperary, but the neighbouring counties, freed from those vast gatherings, which had caused so much alarm in England as well as in the sister island. For his services on this occasion Major Rose received flattering acknowledgments from the Lord Lieutenant of Ireland, the Marquess of Anglesey; from the Commander of the Forces, Lord Vivian; and from Sir George Bingham, commanding the Cork district. But his conduct received even a higher recognition. The present Earl of Derby, then Mr. Stanley, and Secretary for Ireland, addressed Major Rose a letter, conveying entire approval of his conduct, and conferring upon him the commission of the peace. This was not only a compliment, but it served greatly to strengthen Major Rose's hands in the difficult duties which devolved upon him as commanding the detachments in the county of Tipperary.

Nothing occurred to break the ordinary routine of duty till the year 1840, when Her Majesty's Government determined to detach several officers of the army to Syria, to act, in conjunction with a naval force, in assisting to restore that country, made over by French influence to Egyptian rule under Mahomed Ali, to the Porte. Major Rose having applied to be employed on this service, was sent to Syria with the rank of Lieutenant-Colonel and Deputy Adjutant-General. Several other officers accompanied him,—all being under the supreme direction of Brigadier-General Michell, R.A., C.B., an officer of considerable reputation. Soon after their arrival in Syria, it happened that an Egyptian Bey attempted, at the head of a well accoutred force of cavalry, to surprise the camp of Omar Pasha at Mejdal in Palestine. Colonel Rose, who had wandered accidentally in the direction of the Egyptian outposts, having noticed the movement, hastily collected a few ill-armed Bedouins, who happened to be close by, and charged down upon the Egyptian horse. In the hand-to-hand encounter that followed Colonel Rose received two or three slight wounds, but he succeeded in completely routing the enemy, killing several of them. He himself, with his own hand, wounded and captured the leader. For this "dashing and gallant conduct," as it was described by Sir Robert Stopford and General Michell, Colonel Rose was rewarded with the Turkish order of the "Nishan Iftihar" in diamonds; he received also a sabre of honour from the Sultan; and for this and other services in Lebanon, his Sovereign bestowed upon him the military companionship of the Bath.

But a time was fast approaching when an opportunity would be afforded to Colonel Rose of showing that, dashing and gallant though he was, he possessed other qualifications for employment in the public service. Not long after the termination of the war in the Levant, General Michell died; Colonel Bridgeman, the previous second in command, had gone before him; and upon Colonel Rose devolved the command of the British staff officers and detachments in Syria. Their presence in that country however had long been looked upon with disfavour by the foreign embassies at Constantinople, and it had already been resolved that they should be recalled. But the services of Colonel Rose had been so valuable, and they had been so highly appreciated by the then Secretary for foreign affairs, Viscount Palmerston, that it was resolved that he should be retained. On the withdrawal of the other officers, therefore, Colonel Rose received the special appointment of Consul-General in Syria. This appointment conferred upon him diplomatic powers of a very extensive nature. Its duties were naturally new to him, but the qualities he had already displayed had produced in the mind of Lord Palmerston the conviction that Colonel Rose was admirably suited to the difficult task of upholding the Turkish and British policy against that of the French and Egyptian rulers in that quarter of the globe, and the result proved that he judged correctly.

The situation was by no means an easy one. To manage it, indeed, required essentially a light and steady hand, a discriminating judgment, a quick eye and an invincible firmness. The complications, foreign as well as domestic, were endless. Neither the French nor the Egyptians could forget that Syria was lost to their policy. As little could the Roman Catholic Maronites, and the half Pagan, half Mahomedan, Druses, cease to remember their hereditary feuds. To maintain an equal balance between these contending parties, to preserve Syria to Turkey, to see through and baffle the intrigues of the rival powers, were the duties that devolved upon the British Consul-General, and they were duties which demanded the most incessant watchfulness. No doubt, a well devised double-administration under the Suzerainty of the Porte would have preserved peace between the Maronites and Druses, had it been possible for France to have ceased her intrigues, and for Turkey, on such a question, to have acted with good faith. But that was not possible. Colonel Rose, however, succeeded in confining within verbal limits the feuds between these rival factions. He was particularly careful to impress upon the Maronites, whose fanaticism had been raised to a high pitch by the promise of support from France, that though the whole moral influence of that great Catholic power might be employed to better the position of her co-religionists in the East, she would never, in the face of defiant England, send a single soldier to improve that position by force. It was fit, indeed, that an official with a strong purpose should be on the spot, for a storm was brewing, and the hopes of the contending parties rose and fell with each point of the electric needle.

Colonel Rose's exertions in this difficult position were so well appreciated by the English Government, that Lord Palmerston took the first opportunity of bringing him into the regular diplomatic service, by appointing him Secretary to the Embassy at the Porte. On the ambassador, Lord Stratford de Redcliffe, going on leave, Colonel Rose succeeded him as Chargé-d'affaires of the embassy at Constantinople. In this post, Colonel Rose enjoyed many opportunities of acquainting himself with those secret springs of action, which, far more than open and avowed pressure, constitute the moving power in an Eastern Government. His quick eye soon discerned that Russia was preparing a secret blow which should render her the real mistress of Constantinople. It was by secret missions, covered though they might be by the pomp and circumstance attending splendid embassies, that Russia had always worked her way at Constantinople. During the period when Lord Ponsonby filled the post of ambassador at the Sublime Porte, the constant intrigues of Russia had demanded the incessant vigilance of that nobleman, and had proved the most powerful enemy of his repose. Yet, notwithstanding his unremitting watchfulness, the treaty of Unkiar Skelessi had been concluded without his privity. By this treaty Constantinople had been placed in such a position, that it seemed that Russia had but to give the word to take formal possession of it. And in 1853-4 every indication was given that, in the opinion of the Emperor Nicholas, the time for giving that word had arrived. A great and special embassy was despatched from St. Petersburg, headed by Prince Menschikoff, a personal favourite of the Czar, and a man of an overbearing and even insolent demeanour. Such a man was well calculated to overawe the ministers of the Sultan and to carry out the real object of Russia's secret policy,—her assumption of the protectorate of all the subjects of the Porte of the Greek persuasion,—constituting, in European Turkey, a great majority of those who owed allegiance to the Sultan. Now, as, in addition to their being the majority, these Greeks are likewise the most intelligent and the most powerful of the subjects of the Porte, the policy of Prince Menschikoff was simply the assertion of the supremacy of Russia over the larger portion of the European subjects of the Sultan,—the first and surest step to ultimate sovereignty over the whole.

More like a sovereign prince than the servant of an ally, Prince Menschikoff commenced his mission by a demand for the dismissal of Fuad Effendi,—a minister whom he regarded as belonging to the anti-Russian interest. This demand, insolently put forward,—made, in fact, with the sole view of displaying the greatness of Russia to the startled people of Europe,—was at once complied with. The obnoxious minister was dismissed, and then, Prince Menschikoff, deeming the ball at his foot, developed, perhaps rather too incautiously, the secret object of his mission. We have used the term "rather too incautiously," because it is quite probable that the Russian ambassador traded on the absence of Lord Stratford de Redcliffe from his post. He possibly thought that the fact that this determined enemy ot Russian aggression was in England, afforded him the best opportunity of pressing his master's demands upon the Turkish Government. But, if he argued in that way, he deceived himself. Not even Lord Stratford de Redcliffe, skilled as he was in foiling Russian manœuvres,— not even Lord Stratford could have watched with a keener or more penetrating glance the movements of Prince Menschikoff than did Colonel Rose. So far as the manœuvres of the insolent agent of the Czar could be fairly met, he met them. In open warfare, he was the undaunted representative of British interests. In secret manœuvring indeed, an Englishman always feels less at home than a semi-Asiatic; but in watchfulness, in promptitude, in decision,—in all the requirements, in fact, which depend upon the action of a manly mind, Colonel Rose could not have been surpassed.

But a crisis that would test all these qualities was fast approaching. Prince Menschikoff, finding that his previous demonstrations had not produced their intended effect, and seeing that the time had arrived, when, if he did not wish to be baffled, he must take a decisive step, made those demands upon the Sultan, which if complied with, would have rendered him absolutely subservient to the Russian power, and have involved, in addition, a complete infraction of the quadruple treaty of 1841, of which England was one of the guarantees. In this difficulty, the ministers of the Sultan, who had already had ample experience of the firmness and good faith of the English Chargé-d'affaires, informed Colonel Rose, that they would be compelled to give way to Prince Menschikoff, and that Russian policy must triumph, unless some positive and material guarantee were given them that England would support them in opposing the Russian demands. On Colonel Rose endeavouring to ascertain more definitely the nature of the guarantee they required, it came out, that they would be satisfied with nothing short of a material pledge, and they suggested that Colonel Rose should call up the British fleet from Malta to the mouth of the Dardanelles, or to the neighbouring waters.

This was surely a position to try a man,—to test the stuff that was in him. It should be remembered that Colonel Rose was not the appointed representative of England at the Ottoman Porte; he was acting in the absence of his chief. That chief too was a man of wide-spread European reputation, of great influence at Constantinople, where for years he had succeeded in making his will respected. The acting for such a man doubled the responsibility of the acting officer, in that a false step on his part, made during a few months' tenure of office, would be more prominently noticed by the public, when contrasted with a career that for seven years had been marked by uniform success. On the decision arrived at in this crisis depended too the issues of peace or war. Had Colonel Rose, for instance, informed the ministers of the Sultan, that, with the best will in the world, he could not take upon himself the responsibility of ordering up the fleet from Malta, the Porte would have succumbed, Russian policy would have triumphed, but there would have been no war. To order up the fleet, was to pledge England to action. It was to assure Turkey of material aid in resisting Russian aggression. For any official, especially for one only acting as a deputy, this was a very grave consideration, a very weighty responsibility,—a responsibility which would certainly have made the nights of many sleepless, and their very lives a burden.

Colonel Rose, however, never hesitated. The only responsibility he regarded was the strict performance, without fear of consequences, of that which he conceived to be his duty. With the treaty of Unkiar Skelessi before his eyes, and knowing that Russia was now demanding something more even than was conceded by that fatal arrangement, he felt that the time had arrived when, if ever, a check must be given to the encroachments of that Power. He informed the Porte, therefore, that if they would refuse to assent to the illegal demands of the Russian Ambassador, he would ask the British Admiral to assume a position with regard to Constantinople which would leave no doubt that Great Britain would not consent to the enforcement of the Russian demands. This was sufficient. The Porte, appreciating the advantage of the move, and seeing that it was a checkmate to the Russian Ambassador, delayed a reply to his demands, but at the same time, made no secret that they had asked for, and that the representative of the British Government had consented to, the appearance of the British fleet somewhat nearer Constantinople.

We may pause for a moment to consider all the circumstances attending this line of action. The importance of the crisis cannot be exaggerated. Prince Menschikoff was at Constantinople, with his grasp on the throat of the Sultan, and endeavouring to force from him his consent to an arrangement which would have been the death-warrant of the Turkish Empire. The Sultan himself appeared inclined to yield. He did not place much dependence upon England. The English ministry had, indeed, all along failed to perceive the importance of the crisis, or the proper mode of meeting it. They believed that the moral influence of England, exerted on behalf of Turkey, would be sufficient to induce the Czar to recede, and they feared that the smallest physical demonstration on our part would be regarded as an insult to the dignity, the honour, the unblemished good faith, which they publicly attributed, and privately denied, to the Russian Emperor. They dreaded, moreover, lest the Czar should seize upon any display of force as a pretext for accomplishing the great object of his ambition. It was fortunate that Colonel Rose was quite free from the delusions which paralysed the action of the British Ministry. The last movement of Prince Menschikoff had convinced him that it was absolutely necessary to satisfy Turkey, by something stronger than words, that England would not allow her to fall undefended. He felt in fact, that it was necessary not only to act, but to act on the moment,—to strike a counter-blow to this stroke of Prince Menschikoff, to commit England, as far as he could commit her, to something more than a protest against this arbitrary infraction of the common law of nations. He therefore unhesitatingly sent a requisition to Admiral Deans Dundas, then commanding the British fleet at Malta, to proceed at once to Besika Bay.

Admiral Dundas, bound to comply with the requisition of an Ambassador but not of a Chargé-d'affaires, declined to leave Malta. His refusal, however, was of no great consequence. It was the refusal of one of the machines, and not of one of the motive powers, of the English Government. The fact that Colonel Rose had sent for the fleet gave to the Turkish Government a feeling of confidence which enabled them to reply in no submissive tone to the arrogant demand of Prince Menschikoff. The certainty they now possessed of the support of England inspired the Turkish Ministers with a spirit to which they had long been strangers. None knew better than they that there were ten divisions of picked Russian troops always ready at Sebastopol for immediate operations, and they were well aware that they had nothing to oppose the disembarkation of such a force at the mouths of the Danube, or under the walls of Constantinople. Their non-compliance with his demands came, as a surprise, to Prince Menschikoff. It announced to him not only the failure of his great *coup*,—the certain success of which he had already heralded to his master,—but it discovered to him also that his attack had recoiled upon himself. This attack had indeed provoked the assurance of that material support from one at least of the great Western Powers, the possibility of which Prince Menschikoff had constantly derided. Too careless in his arrogance to look closely into matters, he had believed that the English had thrown away their last trump-card when they permitted Lord Stratford to proceed to England. His mortification, then, may be imagined, when, on leading the ace of his strong suit, he found that it was trumped by Colonel Rose.

We have stated that Admiral Deans Dundas declined to comply with Colonel Rose's requisition. In this conduct he was supported by the British ministry, but not by the British public. With a true instinct, the people of England discerned that Colonel Rose had done the right thing at the right time, and it was the common belief that the admiral's refusal to act would only the more firmly rivet in the mind of the Czar the conviction he had entertained from the outset, that the English ministry were prepared to go to any lengths to defend Turkey, except to commit England to war. Whether, at that period, the Czar had proceeded too far in his violent courses to retreat with dignity, may be doubtful; but had his judgment been sufficiently cool at that epoch to view matters in their natural light, it cannot be doubted but that the prompt carrying out by the British Government of the statesmanlike and decisive measure initiated by Colonel Rose, would have contributed more than anything to change his opinion. When, a little later, the continued aggressive conduct of the Czar opened the eyes of the members of the Aberdeen Cabinet to the policy and wisdom of Colonel Rose's conduct, and they ordered the fleet to the Turkish waters, the fatal "too late" stepped in between the order and the result they hoped for. The Czar had, in the meanwhile, pledged himself too deeply to his ambitious projects in the face of

Europe, and he could no longer withdraw from them without the loss of that prestige which he valued more than power.

But we are not writing an account of the diplomatic errors of that memorable period. Sir Hugh Rose, at all events, can look back to the part he played in those struggles with a pardonable pride. Soon after the occurrence to which we have referred, Lord Stratford returned to his post, and almost his first act, after making himself master of the events which had occurred during his absence, and after taking in the actual state of affairs, was to stamp with the approval of his vigorous intellect the conduct of his *locum tenens*. Every one knows what followed his return. When at last the scales dropped from the eyes of the Czar, and he saw that the English were prepared to fight if he did not yield; when he realised the fact that the astute Emperor of the French, apparently, and only apparently, following their lead, was resolved to support them, he had committed himself too far to retreat, and war was inevitable.

War followed. Colonel Rose, released from his purely diplomatic functions, was appointed Queen's Commissioner at the Head-Quarters of the French army. In this capacity, he and two other officers appointed at the same time,—Colonel Claremont, and Major the Hon. St. George Foley,—were the organs of communication between the British and French Head-Quarters. They were consulted by the French Generals in all matters relating to Lord Raglan's army, and were present in all the battles and operations before the enemy, being entrusted with the delicate, and often difficult and dangerous, duty, of conveying the communications between the French Marshal and the British Commander-in-Chief. To narrate each individual action in which Colonel Rose was engaged would be to narrate the history of the Crimean war. It will be sufficient to state that Colonel—then promoted to Brigadier-General—Rose was recommended for the cross of the Legion of Honour after the battle of the Alma; that he was constantly mentioned in the Despatches published in the 'London Gazette,' for distinguished conduct in the French trenches and at the battle of Inkermann, where he had two horses shot under him. It deserves to be added, that Marshal Canrobert, then commanding the French Army, recommended General Rose for the Victoria Cross for his gallant conduct on three different occasions, and that the claim was not preferred, solely because general officers were expressly excluded from this decoration. For his services in this war, General Rose received the Turkish Order of the Medjidie, was made a Knight Companion of the Bath, and was promoted to the rank of Lieutenant-General, "for distinguished conduct in the field."

But a short time elapsed before the reputation gained in the Crimea was tested in a far different field. The Indian mutiny caused a demand upon England for generals of the highest promise, and, amongst others, Sir Hugh Rose was directed to repair to the scene of warfare. He was sent to Bombay, and, very soon after his arrival there, in the autumn of 1857, he was ordered to proceed in the direction of Mhow, to assume command of the force acting in Malwa, and which was afterwards termed the Central India Field force. One division of this force under General Woodburn had marched from Bombay in June in the direction of Mhow. On arriving at Aurungabad, however, its destination seemed so uncertain to Colonel Durand, the Governor-General's Agent for Central India, and who had been driven from Indore by the mutinous troops of Holkar, that that able officer hastened to the south, in order, by his personal influence, to direct its movements. Colonel Durand met this force at Asseergurh, and so impressed his strong character on the direction of its movements, that not only was the rebellious fort of Dhar taken, but Neemuch was very seasonably relieved after two actions fought at Mundisore. These victories not only broke the spirit of Holkar's mutinous soldiers, but cowed them so completely, that at Indore they ignominiously laid down their arms before the man whose life, only a few weeks earlier, they had treacherously attempted. We would willingly pause to dilate upon this little episode of the mutiny. It is an episode which is but little known, and which the unassuming reticence of the chief actor in it has kept hidden from the outer world. It is however foreign to our present subject. We will only say of it here, that there are few passages in any history which tell of more unselfish devotion, more firm wrestling with adverse fortune, more prompt and ready action in difficult circumstances, than were evinced, from the time of the outbreak at Indore on the 1st July, to that of the battle of Mundisore in the last week of November, 1857, by Colonel Durand.

It was after the battle of Mundisore and the relief of Neemuch, which followed it immediately, that the force proceeded to Indore, and here, on the 16th December, it was joined by Sir Hugh Rose. The first instructions which Sir Hugh had received were to detach one of his brigades along the grand trunk road to Gwalior, whilst he himself should march the other brigade into Bundlekund viâ Saugor, relieving that place on its way. These two brigades were to unite at Calpee on the Jumna. Subsequently, however, it was decided that a Madras column under Sir George Whitelock should march to the relief of Saugor and for the pacification of Bundlekund, co-operating for that purpose with the little army under Sir Hugh Rose.

The force under Sir Hugh's immediate orders at this time consisted of one troop of horse artillery, one light field battery, two eight-pounder guns, two eight-inch mortars, two five and a half inch mortars, one eight-inch howitzer: of cavalry, a squadron of the 14th Light Dragoons, a troop of the 3rd Bombay Light Cavalry, and a troop of cavalry of the Hydrabad Contingent: of infantry, one European regiment, one Bombay native regiment; one regiment of the Hydrabad Contingent. The same Contingent also furnished two six-pounder guns, and detachments from two other infantry regiments. Attached to the force also were some Bombay and Madras sappers and miners.

Sir Hugh stayed a short time at Indore to organise his force, and to arrange so as to co-operate with Sir George Whitelock, but, finding that this latter officer could not be so early in the field as had been hoped, and learning that the necessities of the invested officers at Saugor were very great, he resolved to diverge from the plan of the campaign, and march himself to the relief of Saugor. On the 8th January therefore he quitted Indore, and passing through Bhopal, where he was warmly welcomed by the Begum and assisted by supplies and a contingent 800 strong, he arrived before Rathgurh on the morning of the 24th.

This fort "said to be larger and as strong as that of Mooltan," and which had resisted a very large force of Scindia for five months, is situated near the high road from Indore to Saugor, and commands the neighbouring country. It is distant but thirty miles from Saugor, and it had been occupied in force by the rebels, as the best mode of hindering the relief of that place. It is described as being very strong,—"the east and south faces almost perpendicular,—the rock scarped and strengthened by a deep rapid river running close beneath from east to west; the north face looked along the densely jungled hill, and was strengthened by a deep ditch some twenty feet wide; the west face overlooked the town and Saugor road; in this face was the gateway flanked by several square and round bastions. The wall to the north side was strengthened by an outwork looking like a second wall. Along each face were strong bastions commanding various points, and also in the four angles. Approach from the east and south was next to impossible; approach from the west or town side almost as difficult."*

Sir Hugh arrived before this place on the 24th January; and found the enemy posted in some strength on the banks of the river. Having attacked and dispersed these, he at once invested the fort, and selected sites for his breaching batteries. These were ready for opening fire on the night of the 26th, and all that night, the whole of the following day, and on the 28th, a brisk fire was kept up. On the 28th, however, the Rajah of Banpore moved forward with a force of

* *Dr. Lowe.*

revolted sepoys and Villaities,* to relieve Ratgurh. He advanced on the rear of the investing force with standards flying and with an apparent confidence seldom manifested by the rebels. The approach of this force was seen by the garrison, and their fire on the investing army redoubled. Sir Hugh, however, without for a moment relaxing his fire on the fort, detached some troops, consisting mainly of cavalry, to drive back this new enemy. The appearance of these troopers was sufficient; the rebels did not wait to be charged, but, throwing away their arms and ammunition, made off into the jungles. The garrison of Ratgurh, disheartened by the ill success of their allies, silently evacuated the fort during the night, escaping by a path, the precipitous nature of which would ordinarily be considered sufficient to deter men from using it. Their escape, regrettable in one sense, was not perhaps on the whole to be lamented, for the fort itself was so strong, that a few resolute defenders could have held it for a long time against very superior numbers.

After taking Ratgurh, Sir Hugh marched with a portion of his force to Barodia, fifteen miles distant, to complete the discomfiture of the Rajah of Banpore. He found the enemy posted on the banks of the river Bina, determined to resist his passage. But Sir Hugh, at once attacking him, drove him from all his positions, and inflicted upon him a loss of four or five hundred men. There was considerable bush-skirmishing, and the enemy fought unusually well. We lost two officers killed, and six wounded. The enemy's defeat, however, was complete, and the Rajah, wounded, was compelled to flee on foot through the jungles. The immediate

* Foreign mercenaries.

consequence of these operations was the relief of Saugor. This was effected on the 3rd February, after the place had been invested nearly eight months.

Thus had the first object of the campaign been effected. The next was the recapture of Jhansie, and the infliction of punishment for the barbarous and cold-blooded slaughter of our countrymen and countrywomen in that place.

Jhansie lies about a hundred and twenty-five miles north of Saugor. But before any movement could be made in that direction, it was necessary to capture Gurrakotta, a strong fort about five-and-twenty miles to the east of Saugor, garrisoned by the rebel sepoys of the 51st and 52nd native infantry, and amply stored with provisions of all sorts. The fort itself stood upon "an elevated angle of ground, the wide river Sonar washing the east face,—a tributary stream,—the Gidaree nullah with precipitous banks,—flowing round the west and north faces; to the south, a strong gateway flanked by bastions, and a ditch about twenty feet deep, and thirty wide. This ditch ran round the west face also." So thick were its parapets, that, when the place was attacked by Brigadier Watson in 1818 with a force of 11,000 men, and twenty-eight siege guns, he was unable, in three weeks, to make a breach in them, and the garrison was allowed to evacuate the fort with all the honours of war!

Against this place Sir Hugh Rose marched, and, surprising and cutting up a rebel picquet on his way, came before it on the evening of the 11th February. He found the enemy in some force in the village in front of the fort. He therefore, late as it was, at once took measures to dislodge them by a brisk fire of artillery. The rebel sepoys immediately formed up, and advanced at the double on our guns; but they were repulsed. Making a second attempt, however, they came close up to the guns before they were broken, but then their discomfiture was complete. Next morning the breaching batteries were erected, and a fire was kept up on the fort all day. That evening it was evacuated. The enemy, however, were pursued by the Hydrabad cavalry, and were cut up in great numbers.

Gurrakotta taken, no obstacle remained to the march upon Jhansie. About forty miles to the north of Saugor was the strongly forted pass of Maltoun, and through this it was supposed the British force must march. But there was another pass,—that of Mudanpore,—very strong and very narrow,—by which it was equally possible for the troops to advance. Between these passes and Saugor was a little hill-fort also called Barodia, held by the rebels.

In this direction the Central India force marched on the morning of the 27th. Barodia was taken on the following day, and on the 3rd March, the little army found itself in front of the passes. Finding that of Maltoun very strongly fortified and guarded in force, Sir Hugh resolved to make a feigned attack upon it, whilst he should direct his real attack upon the less strongly occupied pass of Mudanpore.

Crowning the heights with the 3rd Europeans and the Hydrabad infantry, and bringing the main body along the road, the artillery in advance, Sir Hugh soon felt the enemy in front. The skirmishers first engaged on the heights and in the jungle, but as those of the enemy were driven back, a strong fire of artillery opened from a commanding position at the other end of the pass. Our advance was for the moment checked, so hot was the fire; Sir Hugh himself had a horse shot under him, and the artillery-men took shelter behind their guns. The halt was, however, only temporary. The guns of the Hydrabad Contingent opened upon the enemy with shell, and, under cover of this fire, the infantry, reforming, dashed at them. Asiatics can stand everything but a charge of Europeans. They had here a splendid position, and a large force to hold it; but the sight of the charging Red-coats was too much for them. Men, who were brave, who certainly did not fear death, who hated us bitterly, shrunk from the hand-to-hand encounter which our soldiers offered them. They fled, and the pass was stormed. The effect of this success was very great. It so daunted the enemy, that they gave up, without a blow, the pass of Maltoun, the fort of Narut in its rear, the little fort of Serai, the strong fort of Marowra on the road to Jhansie, the fortified castle of Banpore, the residence of the Rajah of Banpore, the almost impregnable fort of Tal-Behul on the heights over the lake of that name; they abandoned also the line of the Bina and Betwa, with the exception of the fort of Chandaree on the left bank of the latter river.

After this engagement, and the formal annexation of the district, which, in consequence, came into the permanent possession of the British, Sir Hugh continued his march towards Jhansie. To the fall of this place great importance was attached by Lord Canning, Lord Clyde, and Lord Elphinstone. It was regarded as the stronghold of the rebel power in Central India, and as a place the very holding of which by the Ranee was not only a defiance to the British, but constituted the main strength of the rebels on the right bank of Jumna. It was a place, too, in which the slaughter of our countrymen and countrywomen had been accompanied by circumstances of peculiar atrocity, and where the hate to the English name had been shown by acts of the most wanton cruelty. Nevertheless, anxious as were Lord Canning and the Commander-in-Chief that Jhansie should fall and fall speedily, they were both so impressed with its strength, and the inadequacy of the force at the disposal of Sir Hugh, that they wrote to him, and offered him the option of proceeding instead towards Banda. The original strength of Sir Hugh Rose's force when he joined it at Indore, we have already seen. His first brigade commanded by Brigadier Stuart was of about similiar strength. Jhansie on the other hand was extremely capable of being defended. The city was surrounded by a granite wall, twenty-five feet high, loophooled and bastioned. On the wall large guns were mounted, commanding every approach. But the fortress was far stronger. On its south and east faces were strong towers, the guns of which were so laid as to enfilade one another, and batteries had been thrown up outside the fort, commanding every approach to it. The Saugor road had been especially cared for, and the fortress, strong naturally,—built on a high granite rock, —had been rendered to all appearances impregnable. It was garrisoned by 11,000 men, composed of rebel sepoys, Valaitees, and Bundeelas, and governed by a woman, who wanted only a good cause to be a heroine.

As if to add to the difficulties of the situation, Sir Hugh Rose learned that Tantia Topee had raised and organised a considerable force,—which he had dignified with the title of the Army of the Peshwa; that he had taken the fort of Chirkaree in Bundelkund, and that he was moving towards Jhansie with the intention of driving the English force from its walls.

With all these difficulties in his path, Sir Hugh did not hesitate for an instant. To many a man, the responsibility, kindly meant as it was, placed upon him; the offer to him to move elsewhere with his force, because Jhansie was too strong for him; would have caused terrible anxiety and hesitation. But superior men revel in responsibility. They delight in being allowed to play their own game. Far, then, from availing himself of the option of transferring his force to a less dangerous scene, Sir Hugh prepared himself, with the greater determination, to attack the rebels in their own chosen and well-fortified position. On his march to that place, and with a view to secure his left rear, Sir Hugh despatched General Stewart, commanding his first brigade, to attack the fort of Chandaree on the river Bettwa. This fort was stormed on the 17th March, after a desperate resistance on the part of the garrison, and with a loss on our side of five officers and twenty-five men killed and wounded.

Meanwhile Sir Hugh himself marched on Jhansie, and arriving before it on the 21st March, at once invested it. To invest such a place as Jhansie, four and a half miles in circumference, with the force at the disposal of the English general, was certainly a very bold measure. But boldness is often synonymous with prudence, and, in determining to adopt this mode of attack, Sir Hugh showed how well he had mastered the leading features of the Asiatic character. Investment diminishes certainly the numbers of the attacking force, but, on the other hand, it diminishes to a far greater extent, the confidence of an impressionable enemy, for it displays to him your own. It is a common remark that the English do not, and never will, understand the native character. This may be true in some of its aspects. It is not less true, however, that there are some points of the English character which the Natives can never comprehend. The Dantonic motto, *l'audace, l'audace, toujours l'audace,* contains within itself a principle which an English general can always successfully employ against an Asiatic foe;—a principle which the natives of India have never yet been able to understand. Nothing paralyzes them so much as boldness. The smallest hesitation on the other hand gives them courage. In the presence of a native army, then, a general can always risk manœuvres which he would not dare to dream of before an European enemy.

The complete investment of Jhansie, therefore, by the small force under Sir Hugh Rose, was prudent, because it was bold. The garrison within its walls read in that act the determination of the English general to take not only the place, but the garrison with it. Nevertheless, they were resolved to sell their lives dearly. The capabilities of defence were as great as the difficulties of the attack were many; and the Ranee was at the same time aware that Tantia Topee, at the head of 12,000 men with twenty guns, was marching to her relief.

The difficulties of the attack were indeed many. The fort of Jhansie, on the high granite rock,—with its three lines of works, its flanking fire, and its walls of solid masonry, presented a most formidable aspect. It was soon ascertained too that it would be necessary to take the city prior to attacking the fort, as the latter could not be breached. This involved a double labour and a double danger.

Jhansie was invested on the 22nd, and the same evening the necessary operations were effected for erecting batteries to breach the city wall. Four of these were ready on the evening of the 24th, and opened fire on the 25th. On that day, the first brigade, under Brigadier Stuart, joined from Chandaree. It was at once moved to the south of the fort, and constituted the left attack. The siege was now begun in real earnest. Our troops, however, were terribly overworked. For seventeen days they never took off their clothes, nor were the horses unbridled except to water. From the two attacks shot and shell were continually poured into the city, whilst from the whole line of wall the enemy's guns never ceased to thunder a reply. Advanced positions were taken up near the wall to enable our riflemen to fire upon the enemy's gunners. On both sides the exertions were unceasing. Women and children were seen assisting in repairing the defences of the walls, and carrying water and food to the troops on duty, whilst the Ranee herself constantly visited the troops and animated them to enthusiasm by her presence and her words.

For breaching purposes Sir Hugh had been able to spare only two eighteen-pounder guns, the remainder of the artillery being used so as to employ the enemy incessantly, and to damage the buildings inside the walls. The progress made by these two guns was, owing to the great strength of the walls, extremely slow. But on the 29th the parapets of the fort bastion were torn down from the left attack, and on the 30th and 31st further damage was made on their defences. Still, no breach had been effected; the vigilance of the enemy was unabated; their determination to resist as strong as ever; when, on the evening of the last mentioned day intelligence reached the general that a new enemy was advancing in great force from the north.

This was the army of Tantia Topee,—an army, which, collected from the materials of the force which had attacked General Windham in his entrenchments at Cawnpore, and was subsequently beaten by Sir Colin Campbell,—had been re-organised under the title of Army of the Peshwa by Tantia Topee at Nowgong, and which, taking Chirkaree en route, was now marching to the relief of Jhansie. This army crossed the Bettwa the same night, and encamped close to the English force.

The position of Sir Hugh Rose was full of peril. Before him was an unconquered fortress, garrisoned by 11,000 warriors; behind him and close to him, an army of 12,000 men headed by a sworn enemy of the British name,—one who had revelled in the slaughters of Cawnpore. It was thus a position which required in a special degree a clear head, a cool judgment, and a firm will,—a position in which a single false step would have ruined us. But Sir Hugh was equal to the occasion. Rightly judging that to withdraw the investing troops for the purpose of meeting Tantia Topee would give to the besieged a moral as well as a material advantage, Sir Hugh determined to continue to press the siege with energy and vigour, whilst he should march in person, at the head of such troops as could be spared from the actual duties of the siege, against the new enemy. His plan was to attack the enemy at day-break with about

1,000 men of the second brigade, and a less number of the first.

Learning in the night, however, that Tantia had detached a division of his army to relieve Jhansie on the northern side, Sir Hugh directed the first brigade to move against that body, whilst he himself should attack the enemy at dawn. But Tantia Topee did not wait for the dawn. Whilst it was yet dark, he moved his first line towards the British encampment, and drove in the vedettes. But, no sooner had the retreat of these cleared the line, then the British guns commenced a brisk fire on the advancing body. But the fire of a few guns was powerless to stop the onward movement of a line which extended considerably beyond the British on both flanks. The enemy had only to move straight on to come with their overlapping wings upon the investing party, who would thus be placed, literally, between two fires. Sir Hugh comprehended this in an instant. Massing then his horse artillery on his left and accompanying it with a squadron of cavalry, he directed it against the right flank of the enemy. Simultaneously, another squadron under the general in person charged his left flank. Terrified at being thus attacked on both flanks, the enemy halted, and his troops became huddled together in disordered masses. At this moment our infantry received orders to advance. Pouring in a volley, they dashed forward at the charge. The result was magical. The enemy's line at once broke and fled, in complete disorder, toward the second line, abandoning several of their guns.

Meanwhile General Stuart had been equally successful against the other division of the enemy. The two routed parties were being thus simultaneously driven on the third division, which, under the personal command of Tantia Topee, still stood its ground. The line of pursuit, however, led Sir Hugh Rose against the front of Tantia's array, whilst it drew General Stuart on to his right flank. Seeing himself thus in danger of being attacked simultaneously in front and flank, and encumbered by the crowds of panic-stricken fugitives, the rebel commander resolved to retreat across the Bettwa. To check the advance of the English he caused the jungle in front of him to be set on fire, and then, under cover of the smoke and flame, moved rapidly towards the river. He effected his passage under cover of his guns, which were remarkably well served, but he did not find himself the safer. He was closely followed by our horse artillery and cavalry, which had dashed at a gallop through the flaming jungle, and the pursuit was continued until every gun in his possession had been captured. Tantia himself fled to Calpee. He had lost, in this action, fifteen hundred men, and his force had been completely dispersed. Never was a victory more complete.

Fatigued and exhausted, but with their *morale* increased as much as that of the enemy had been depressed by the events of the day, the victorious little army returned to their position before Jhansie, on the evening of the 1st. Sir Hugh was determined to take prompt advantage of the discouragement which the defeat of the great army of the Peshwa had produced among the garrison. He therefore continued to pour in a heavy fire all that night and the day following,—when, deeming the breach in the city wall just practicable, though only just practicable, he resolved to attempt the storm of the place the next morning. He made his preparations accordingly. His plan was to make a false attack on the west wall, with a small detachment. On the sound of their guns being heard, the main storming party was to issue forth and attack the breach, whilst on the right and left attempts should be made to enter the city by escalading.

At 3 A.M. on the morning of the 3rd April. the storming parties moved to the positions marked out for them to wait for the signal from the western side. No sooner was it given than the main storming party, consisting of the 86th Foot and the 25th Bombay native infantry, dashed at the breach, covered by a strong fire from the artillery. The resistance here was but trifling and the breach was entered with but small loss. The right attack, however, was not so successful. Consisting of the 3rd Europeans, some Hydrabad infantry, and Madras and Bombay sappers,—the ladders on the shoulders of the last,—they marched forward at the signal, but on debouching into the plain in front of the city wall, they were met by a heavy fire from artillery, and the discharge of rockets, stinkpots, stones, blocks of wood, and other missiles. Moving straight on, however, they planted their ladders against the wall, but some of these were too short, some broke down under the weight of the stormers, and the officers who succeeded in gaining the wall on the others were cut to pieces before they could receive assistance. Still our men pushed on, and very opportunely, a shout from the main column, showing that the breach had been stormed came to assist them. The opposition in their front then slackened, and the rampart was gained. The attempt at escalading on the left had been successful, and the three columns, uniting, poured into the town. But resistance was not yet over. Covered by the fire from the fort, the enemy showed a determined front, and each house and street were contested with a fierce obstinacy. Colonel Turnbull, commanding our artillery, was shot in this street battle.

Nevertheless our troops pressing steadily onwards made way, and drove the enemy into the palace,—the place he had fixed upon for his most resolute resistance. Here the conflict was desperate. Every room was defended with the most determined fury. But it was of no avail. From chamber to chamber were the rebels driven with great slaughter, until at last the palace was our own. Even then the contest was not over. The Ranee's Body Guard, some fifty in number, still held the stables. Rushing into the stable-yard to attack them, exposed as it was to the fire of the fort guns, several of our men were in the first instance cut down. The rebel troopers, after firing their carbines from behind their horses, mounted, and charged sword in hand. Some of their comrades at the same time fired the stables. A terrible confusion followed. The glare and heat of the flames, the fury of the excited combatants, the fire of the fort plunging amid friends and foes, the small space for the contest, all combined to make a scene such as has been seldom witnessed. It was not till every man of that Body Guard had been cut down that order was in some degree restored.

All that night, and throughout the following day, desultory fighting continued,—the enemy being either slaughtered, or driven under the shelter of the fort guns. But on the night of the 4th, the Ranee, despairing of further resistance, evacuated the fort with all her remaining followers. Sir Hugh occupied it early on the following morning, and detached a party in pursuit of the enemy. Of these two hundred were cut up. Our loss in the storming of Jhansie and the action of the Bettwa amounted to 343 killed and wounded, of whom thirty-six were officers; that of the enemy was about 5000.

Sir Hugh's object now was to march on Calpee. This was the main arsenal of the rebels, and it was well provided with artillery and other warlike stores. Its distance from Jhansie is one hundred and two miles in a north-easterly direction. The capture of this place would enable Sir Hugh to co-operate with the left rear of Lord Clyde's army, and, coupled with the fall of Jhansie, it would set the seal to the extinction of the rebellion in Central India.

Having rested and re-organised the force, wearied with seventeen days' incessant labour, during which few of them were allowed the luxury of a change of clothes, and having placed a sufficient garrison in Jhansie, Sir Hugh prepared to carry out his plans on Calpee. The appearance, however, of the rebel garrison of Kotah in the neighbourhood compelled him to send a detachment after that enemy, and he awaited its return before he moved. He had meanwhile been joined by a weak wing of the 71st Foot, but this reinforcement did not fill up the gaps which had been caused by casualties, and by the necessity which existed for leaving a garrison in Jhansie. At last, on the 25th April, having previously detached a flying column under Colonel Orr, to clear away the remnants of the rebels, who might otherwise imperil the communications between his own force and General Whitelock's, and then to co-operate with him against Koonch, Sir Hugh marched in the direction of Calpee. Meanwhile the Ranee of Jhansie, the dispossessed Raja of Banpore, and Tantia Topee had united their followers, and, impressed with the necessity of saving Calpee, had resolved to do battle for that place at Koonch, about forty miles south-west of Calpee on the Jhansie road. The heat of the weather, unusually great, had made them determine to harass the Europeans as much as possible in the day time. Leaving then but a few troops in Calpee, they marched with the remainder to Koonch, where they drew up under cover of the fort, and threw up entrenchments and cut ditches across the road in their front. They also occupied the small fort of Loharee, which, so long as they were allowed to hold it, would play upon the flank of an advancing enemy.

Against this position, Sir Hugh Rose moved on the 6th May. The heat was terrific, but the whole district being studded with forts it was necessary to advance with great caution. It was long past sunrise, therefore, when Sir Hugh, having mastered the enemy's position, arrived so near it as to be able to direct Major Gall to proceed with a detachment to storm the fort of Loharee. This service was gallantly executed with a loss on our side of four officers and nineteen men; on that of the rebels, of all their number. This impediment to an advance removed, Sir Hugh directed the 1st brigade,—co-operating with Colonel Orr on the other side of the Bettwa,—to make a feigned attack on the enemy's position, whilst he himself, with the 2nd brigade, should make a flank march round their left, and attack them. The enemy did not wait for the full execution of this manœuvre. Alarmed by the presence of the 1st brigade in their front, and the movement of the 2nd brigade round their flank, threatening to cut them off from Calpee, they gave way, after firing a few rounds, and retreated. Koonch at once fell into our hands, and troops were at once sent in pursuit of the enemy. They were followed up for sixteen miles, and pursuit only ceased where they had lost all their guns.

Although the resistance made by the rebels on this occasion was feeble on the field of battle,—a result owing probably to the fear entertained by their leaders of being cut off from Calpee,—yet in the execution of their retiring movement the gallant bearing of the infantry,—consisting of some regiments of the Gwalior Contingent,—called forth the admiration of the English officers. This retreat was covered by a line of skirmishers two miles in length, resting upon supports of masses of thirty or forty men at stated intervals. These skirmishers retired for a long time in perfect order keeping up a brisk fire, and it was only when they were taken in flank by our cavalry and artillery that they were compelled to double up and give way.

Our troops suffered on this occasion far more from the sun than from the enemy. The thermometer showed 120° in the shade. The force had been marching from daybreak, and the pursuit was not over till nine o'clock at night. Twelve men of the 71st Foot were struck dead by the sun. Sir Hugh himself was struck down three times, and, Dr. Lowe informs us, "while the action was going on, dhooly after dhooly was brought into the field hospital with officers and men suffering from sunstroke, some dead, others prostrated, laughing and sobbing in weak delirium." The sufferings from fatigue, thirst, and exposure were terrible. To all, however, the general showed an example which inspired his soldiers; thrice struck down, he each time forced himself to rally; he personally directed the attack and pursuit; he exposed himself as much as the meanest soldier; and the privations he endured were not less than those to which all ranks were subjected.

Pressing on, as soon as possible, after this successful action, Sir Hugh established himself with the 2nd brigade at Golowlee, on the right bank of the Jumna, seven miles from Calpee, on the 15th. Golowlee is not on the direct road from Koonch to Calpee, but Sir Hugh, having been informed that that road had been strongly fortified, made a flank march across country to his right, leaving the 1st brigade to make a feint upon the direct road. By this means Sir Hugh was able to open communications with Colonel G. V. Maxwell,—who, with the 88th Foot, some Sikhs, and the Camel Corps, was on the left bank of the Jumna,—and also to threaten Calpee in an unexpected quarter. Unfortunately the exposure suffered by the troops told upon them with terrible effect, and the deaths and admissions into hospital increased at an alarming rate. The condition of our troops in this respect was well known to the enemy. Indeed, a general order issued by the rebel commander on the subject was, about this time, intercepted. This order stated that "as the European infidels either died or had to go into hospital from fighting in the sun, they were never to be attacked before ten o'clock in the day, in order that they might feel its force." To add to his anxieties, information reached Sir Hugh at this time that the Nawab of Banda, who had recently been defeated by Sir George Whitelock, had joined the rebels at Calpee with a large force of very efficient cavalry,—the remnants of our mutinous regiments,—and with some infantry and artillery as well.

On the 16th, 17th, and 18th May there was constant skirmishing between the two armies, in which the enemy were invariably driven back. On the night of the 19th Sir Hugh concentrated both brigades at Golowlee, and receiving on the following day from Colonel G. V. Maxwell a reinforcement of two companies of the 88th, the Camel Corps, and 120 Sikhs, he prepared for a general attack upon Calpee.

The attack presented great difficulties. Calpee is situated on a high rock rising from the Jumna, and is surrounded by miles of deep ravines,—forming in themselves not only strong natural obstacles to an attacking party, but offering to an enemy well acquainted with the country means of making sudden attacks, and of cutting off small detachments. These difficulties however only inspired the general with a determination to overcome them. His plan was, that while Colonel Maxwell should shell Calpee, in reverse, from the left bank of the Jumna, he should clear the ravines himself, and then attack the left face of the fort.

In pursuance of their plan to attack our men in the heat of the day only, the enemy had come down in force on the 20th, and attacked our right flank. To save his men for the grand assault he was meditating, Sir Hugh had contented himself with merely repulsing this attack. Next day Colonel Maxwell opened on the town and fort, and shelled them without intermission. On the following morning, information was brought to Sir Hugh that the rebels had resolved to attack him with all their force on the 23rd; that their plan was to make a feint on his left, whilst, stealing up the ravines with their main attack, they should suddenly burst upon his right, which they calculated would be weakened to support the left.

The plan was a good one, and in a military point of view, well deserved to succeed.

It will be understood that our force lay in the ground between the road from Calpee to Banda and the Jumna, —the left nearly touching the Banda road, and the right resting on the ravines near the river. In pursuance of their plan, then, to compel us to weaken our right, the rebels marched out in masses about ten o'clock along the Banda road, and commenced an attack upon our left. This attack, headed by the Nawab of Banda, and Rao Sahib, nephew of the Nana, though intended only as a feint, soon made itself felt, and the left was heavily engaged. Still Sir Hugh, confident in his information as to the real object of the enemy, did not move a man from his right. The attack on the left continued, the feigned attack became a very real one, but Sir Hugh still kept his right in position. It was well he did so. Suddenly, as if by magic, the whole line of ravines became a mass of fire; guns opened, and the enemy's infantry, climbing up from below, poured in a musketry fire upon the right of our line. The suddenness of the attack, the numbers of the enemy, and the terrible heat of the day gave them a great advantage. Another point, too, was in their favour. Many of our Enfield rifles had become affected by constant use, and the men, after the first discharge, found it impossible to ram down their cartridges. Numbers of them likewise were struck down by the sun, and many more were disabled by its force. When, therefore, the rebels, starting up in great numbers from the ravines, poured in volleys, which our men could but feebly reply to; when they saw that each discharge from our line became weaker than the former; they began to gain confidence.

Moving on with loud yells, and finding less and less opposition as they advanced, seeing in fact that our men rather gave way, they at last came on with great determination, and driving all before them, came charging towards our guns. General Stuart, seeing the infantry driven back, dismounted from his horse, and drawing his sword bade the gunners defend their guns with their lives. Still the rebels advanced with frantic cries, and it seemed as though, from their very numbers, they must prevail, when Sir Hugh, to whom information of the desperate nature of affairs on his right had been conveyed, brought up the Camel Corps at their best pace, then, dismounting them and leading them forward at the double, without a moment's hesitation, charged the advancing foe,—who were then within thirty yards of our guns,—his men cheering as they did so. For a moment the enemy stood, but only for a moment. To waver, to turn, to flee back into the ravines, followed almost naturally. Not only was the attack on the right thus repulsed, but the victory was virtually gained. For the left charged the enemy at the same time with so much vigour and determination, that they broke and fled with precipitation. Those readers who have followed the career of Sir Hugh Rose thus far with attention will not have failed to notice that he was never content with merely gaining a victory, but that he always improved it so as to disperse and damage his enemy to the utmost. So it was on this occasion. Not satisfied with driving the rebels from the field, he followed them up so closely, that he cut off a great number of them from Calpee. The same night the enemy evacuated that fort. They were pursued however by our horse artillery and cavalry, until they lost their formation, and dispersed. All their guns, stores, and baggage were taken from them. Even the Ranee of Jhansie, who fled with them, was compelled, for want of a tent, to sleep under trees.

Calpee was entered on the morning of the Queen's birth-day. It was found to contain warlike stores in great abundance; cases of English rifles and swords unopened; shot, shell, and every description of ordnance.

Dr. Lowe thus describes the condition of some of the heads of departments when they entered Calpee. From it an idea may be formed of the manner in which the officers and soldiers of the force generally were suffering: "The General," he says, "was very ill: his chief of the staff, Colonel Wetherall, C.B., was in a raging fever; his quartermaster-general, Captain Macdonald, worn out; the chaplain of the force had lost his reason, and was apparently sinking fast." Truly the men who composed this force, who fought so nobly, and who suffered so severely, deserved the best gratitude of their country!

The taking of Calpee completed the plan of the campaign which the Government of India had drawn out for the Central Indian force. Marching from Mhow in November, that force, in five months, had traversed Central India; from the banks of the Seepree and Kala Sind it had marched to the Jumna, and had there effected a junction with the troops under the orders of Lord Clyde. It had been compelled, it is true, to contest the whole country which it traversed; it had been its lot to encounter, on several occasions, armies vastly superior in number, and led by men whose rancour against the British name incited them to the most determined efforts for our destruction; it had undertaken sieges, the success of which alone would have made the reputation of a general. These deeds had been accomplished, too, during a season, the terrible heat of which far surpassed the heat of corresponding seasons, and under a sun which proved more deadly even than the enemy. Yet, moving steadily onwards, regarding difficulties as "obstacles to be overcome," letting nothing beat him, showing himself equal to every emergency, Sir Hugh Rose had marched his force to the destined goal. Every impediment to his advance had been swept away or struck down. Careless of himself, knowing that to him the representative of his Sovereign, and that Sovereign herself, looked for the successful issue of the campaign, Sir Hugh had shown himself foremost whereever there was danger, kind, sympathising, and attentive wherever there was suffering. His care of his soldiers has never been exceeded. To look after their comforts, to see that, after a hard-fought action, the wounded were attended to, and after a long and tedious march, that provisions and water were abundant, was with him a sacred duty. The kind word, the sympathising enquiry, were never wanting to the weary, the wounded, the suffering. If on the battle-field he demanded all their energies, all their capabilities; if, for seventeen days before Jhansie, he required them to give every faculty of mind and body to the carrying out of a great end, and even to forego every comfort,—at least, when the necessity passed away, he did for them all that it was in the power of a man in his situation to do. No man could have done more. The same sun that struck down the soldier did not spare the commander; the same dangers that they encountered he dared likewise; if they did not spare themselves, neither did he; and yet with all the cares of the command upon him, with despatches to write, reports to listen to, sketches of the country to examine, he managed to find time to attend to their concerns. The great interest taken in the soldier during his tenure of the office of Commander-in-Chief has not always been regarded in an appreciatory spirit. Yet that interest will not be regarded as extraordinary by those who have had practical experience of the splendid fighting qualities of our men, and who have learned from experience on the field and by the sick-bed that, however much it may suit the conscientious pharisaism of some writers to place them on a level with the brute creation, it is yet possible by kind and judicious treatment to kindle within their breasts a strong yearning after that which is good and elevating and pure. Without sympathy on the part of a commander, soldiers may indeed be led, but they will never show that enthusiasm which is so great an incentive to gallant actions. It was doubtless an element in the success of the Central India force that this sympathy was evinced in an eminent degree by Sir Hugh Rose.

The campaign was now virtually over. The junction had been effected. Rajpootana, Bundelkund, Jhansie, had been relieved from the presence of the rebels, and Sir Hugh, worn out with fatigue, was preparing to return to Bombay. He had issued a farewell order to his troops, when suddenly the intelligence reached him that the rebel army under Tantia Topee and other chiefs, amongst whom was the Ranee of Jhansie, had attacked Scindia at Bahadurpore, nine miles from Gwalior; that Scindia's whole army, with the exception of his body guard, had deserted in mass to the enemy; that Scindia had fled to Agra; and that the rebels had instantly taken possession of the fort of Gwalior, containing artillery and munitions of war in abundance.

Sir Hugh Rose had previously detached a portion of his force under Brigadier Stuart in the direction of Gwalior, with a view to overawe the rebels; and, immediately on the receipt of this intelligence he followed with the remainder. Setting out on the 6th June, —the thermometer 130° in the shade,—he moved by forced marches towards his destination, and, overtaking Brigadier Stuart at Indoorkee, on the 16th reached Bahadurpore, the scene of Scindia's defeat. The same day having been reinforced by Brigadier-General Napier and Brigadier Smith, he marched with General Napier's brigade and some of his own men upon the Morar cantonments, five miles distant, occupied in force by the rebels, and drove them out after an action which lasted two hours. As a part of the same movement Brigadier Smith advanced from the east upon Kotah-ka-serai, about seven miles from Gwalior, a point at which communications could be opened with Sir Hugh Rose. The brigadier succeeded in occupying that position, but as the enemy threatened him in considerable force, he deemed it right to attack them. An action ensued, which resulted in the retirement of the enemy, and in the taking up by the brigadier of a position not unassailable by the enemy, but sufficiently strong. The most important occurrence of the action, however, was the death of the Ranee of Jhansie, who fell fighting at the head of her troopers, whilst endeavouring to repel a gallant charge of the 8th Hussars. "Although a lady," writes Sir Hugh in his despatch, "she was the bravest and best military leader of the rebels." At the same time that these movements were taking place,

Major Orr advanced upon the Seepree road to the direct south of Gwalior, whilst Colonel Riddell was moved so as to complete the investment on its west side.

Sir Hugh now prepared for the final stroke. His plan was, having completed the investment, to attack Gwalior on its weakest side, that by which Brigadier Smith had advanced. Leaving therefore Major Orr and Colonel Riddell to guard the outlets on the south and west, and directing General Napier to remain at Morar, Sir Hugh himself marched with the bulk of his forces, on the morning of the 18th June, to join Brigadier Smith at Kotah-ka-serai. The distance was twenty miles, and the march was extremely harassing. The heat of the sun was intense. More than a hundred men of the 86th alone were compelled to fall out, although it may be added that these gallant soldiers were not deterred by sickness from joining on the following day in the assault. Sir Hugh found Brigadier Smith, who had advanced nearer Gwalior, in a very cramped position, in a pass between two ridges of hills, one of which, on the left of our force, had been occupied by the enemy, another body of whom were also in force in the gorge about two miles in rear of our position. In front of him was a very deep canal cut out of the rock. Sir Hugh conceived the idea of cutting off both these bodies from Gwalior. The only obstacle to such a manœuvre lay in the difficulties presented by the canal. These, however, could be overcome. By sunset or a little later a bridge or dam could have been constructed, and over this Sir Hugh might have marched a force which should interpose between Gwalior and the rebels, whilst another brigade should occupy them in front. The movements of the enemy, however, compelled

Sir Hugh to abandon this project. Fresh troops poured out of Gwalior and made a serious attack on our left flank, resting on the canal, the point where we were weakest. To meet this attack, Sir Hugh detached Brigadier Stuart's brigade with orders to cross the canal, and crowning the heights on the other side of it, to attack the enemy on their left, whilst at the same time Brigadier Smith should advance obliquely, under cover of the ground, against their left front. This attack on their left at once had the effect of making the enemy desist on his right, and no sooner did they find that their left was turned by the movement, than they fell back in haste, abandoning their guns. They were pressed hard by our troops, and driven into the city, and our line advancing at the same time took possession of the highest range of heights above Gwalior. From these heights "the slopes descended gradually towards the town; the lowest one commanding the grand parade of the 'Lushker,' which was almost out of fire of the Fort and afforded an entrance into the city." *

Gazing from this position on Gwalior, thus lying at his feet, seeing the enemy's infantry and cavalry debouching from the city, but apparently without the resolution to attack him, Sir Hugh Rose resolved to strike at the moment, and endeavour to gain possession of the place that same day. Having formed his battle array, accordingly, he gave the order to advance. The 1st Bombay Lancers, under Colonel Owen, had been ordered to descend the hills and occupy the road which led to the grand parade of the Lushker. This they did in gallant style, not only clearing the parade but pursuing the enemy into the very streets of Gwalior.

* *Sir Hugh Rose's Despatch.*

They were then withdrawn, and the infantry, taking their place, marched right up to Scindia's palace without meeting much opposition,—the enemy retreating through the town with great rapidity. Brigadier Smith, who had been detached in pursuit, succeeded, however, in cutting up great numbers of them, in the face of a fierce resistance offered by their artillery. The remainder fell into the hands of General Napier at Morar, who killed between three and four hundred of them.

The old and new cities thus fell into our hands; but the fort was still unsubdued; indeed throughout these operations it had maintained a constant, though not very effective, fire upon our troops. On the morning of the 19th, however, at an early hour, Lieutenant Rose, of the 25th Bombay native infantry, and Lieutenant Waller, with a party of the 25th and some police, crept up the rock, burst open the main gateway of the fort, and, taking the enemy by surprise, forced an entrance through an archway connected by a narrow street with the interior defences. Here they had to maintain a fierce hand-to-hand encounter with the garrison, urged to desperation by the knowledge that they had no retreat. The gallantry of Lieutenant Rose and his companions prevailed, however, over the fury of these desperate men; they were all either shot down or cut to pieces, and the fort was ours, though in gaining it Lieutenant Rose sacrificed his own life.

Thus ended the Gwalior episode of the Central Indian campaign. Forming no part of the original project, it was yet forced upon the general by the unexpected rebellion of the troops of our ally. Taken by itself it would have been regarded as a brilliant feat of arms, but looked upon as an unexpected call upon strength and resources which had undergone no mean trial, it may well be regarded as an achievement of no common character. The service was one of the last importance. The promptness, the suddenness of the blow,—a striking characteristic of all Sir Hugh Rose's movements,—alone prevented Gwalior from becoming a second Delhi,—a rallying point for all the parties of rebels who were scattered over India. Of the conduct of our soldiers their commander was the best judge, and thus he speaks of it. "As commander of the troops engaged," wrote Sir Hugh in his despatch, "it is my duty to say, that though a most arduous campaign had impaired the health and strength of every man of my force, their discipline, devotion, and strength remained unvarying and unshaken, enabling them to make a very rapid march in summer heat to Gwalior, fight and gain two actions on the road, one at Morar cantonments, the other at Kotah-ka-serai; arrive at their posts, from great distances and by bad roads, before Gwalior before the day appointed, the 19th June; and, on that same day, carry by assault all the enemy's positions on strong heights and in most difficult ground, taking one battery after another, twenty-seven pieces of artillery in the action; twenty-five in the pursuit; besides the guns in the fort; the old city; the new city; and finally the rock of Gwalior, held to be one of the most important and strongest fortresses in India."

Sir Hugh made over command of his force to General Napier on the 29th June, and proceeded to Bombay.

We now approach that which may be termed the third division of Sir Hugh Rose's career. Appointed Commander-in-Chief at Bombay, he was transferred, on the departure of Lord Clyde from India, to the higher appointment in Bengal. This appointment he took up in the month of June 1860, and he held it till the end of March of the present year,—a period of nearly five years. We do not propose to follow step by step each act of Sir Hugh Rose as Commander-in-Chief. In such an appointment the value of an officer's services is to be tested, not by any one particular measure, but by the tendency and result of the line of policy he may pursue. If that line of policy be based upon sound principles, if the measures he attempt to carry into effect be just and fair to all whose interests are touched by them, then the result must be advantageous. Yet it must by no means be imagined that all that a Commander-in-Chief has to do, is to wish to act well; that he has only to carve out a policy to himself, and adhere to it. On the contrary, there is probably no appointment emanating from the Crown of England, in which the hands of the holder are so tightly bound as that of the Commander-in-Chief in India. Nominally an independent appointment, it is really an appointment the independent action of which is jealously watched and carefully restricted. Formerly indeed, the powers which might, under certain circumstances, devolve upon a Commander-in-Chief were not very accurately defined: but from the day when the Marquis of Dalhousie snubbed Sir Charles Napier into the resignation of his command for presuming to crush mutiny in the bud, without cousulting the Marquis who was at sea, or the Council which was at Calcutta, the relations between the Commander-in-Chief and the Government have become, practically, somewhat clearer than they were before. The decision of the Home Government and of the Duke of Wellington upon that important question announced, not the predominance of the Civil Power,—for not even Sir Charles Napier ever questioned that,—but, that not so great a peril as the prospect of a mutiny would justify even the temporary assumption by the Commander-in-Chief of any portion of that power which was vested in the Government alone. From this some idea may be drawn of the very delicate and difficult position which a Commander-in-Chief would occupy, who, full of zeal and energy, revolving plans of reform and improvement, should find himself in the presence of a superior power by whom all his intentions might be frustrated and all his reforms nipped in the bud. We do not intend to assert that a dead-lock of this nature is even within the bounds of probability. We only allude to the subject, in order to show, that even should a long tenure of the office of Commander-in-chief produce no results, it is not necessarily to be attributed to indifference on the part of the head of the army.

We have written to little purpose if we have failed to impress upon the minds of our readers that Sir Hugh Rose was a man of deep convictions, strong will, and great tenacity of purpose. Yet in the diplomatic training he had enjoyed in Syria and in Constantinople, he had had many opportunities of observing that the most common solution of even the weightiest affairs was a compromise. With all his strong convictions he was far too clear-headed, he had mixed too much with the world, to imagine, that he could expect every other man to agree with him on every subject. He knew well that, in his new position, he would have to encounter men of different and differing schools,—men who looked at affairs from a point of view widely diverse from his own,—and he had associated too much with the world to think that these men would give in to his opinions, simply because he held them. Whilst therefore perhaps no man ever occupied the office of Commander-in-Chief more strongly satisfied of the soundness of his own ideas, of the necessity for putting them in practice, and more determined to hold to and carry out those views, if it were possible to do so, no one perhaps was at the same time more impressed with the sense of the delicate and difficult nature of his position, and of the wisdom of accepting a part, if he were unable to gain the whole.

The state of the army when Sir Hugh Rose assumed command of it was peculiar. The European portion of it was just reposing after the triumphs of the mutiny. They were reposing, however, in buildings which had been intended for half their number, and the wretched state of existence which had always made the life of a soldier in India proverbial, had been rendered even more wretched by the crowded state of the barracks and the deficiencies of the hospital accommodation. The men of a section of that European force too,—that section which, formerly under the Company, had been transferred to the Crown without being made over to the Horse Guards, were known to consider themselves aggrieved, because the option of bounty or discharge had not been offered to them on the occasion of their transfer. As for the native army it was in a state of chaos. Of the seventy-four native regiments of which the Bengal Army consisted before the mutiny, but eight or ten existed. There were officers without regiments scattered all over the country. There were police corps irregular corps, local corps, doing military duty in various districts and stations, raised no one knew how, and subject one scarcely knew to whom. There were hosts of claimants for appointments, men who had lost all in the mutiny, who had no regiment to go to, and who were conversant only with the military duties to which they had been brought up. The mutiny had annihilated all the old regulations, and none had come to replace them. The officers of the old Company's army, deprived of their old employments, looked anxiously to the future. Each man knew that something was coming, yet no one knew what to expect. At this time the Home Government, in opposition to the written opinions of Lord Clyde, Sir Hugh Rose, Sir William Mansfield, and other high authorities, had determined to maintain the Indian Army as a separate army, subject to the Secretary of State and not to the Horse Guards, but as to the manner in which it would be reorganised or officered not a syllable had transpired.

The objects, then, which Sir Hugh just proposed to himself on taking the command of the Indian Army, were these. He wished, first, to improve the condition of the European soldier; to see that he was not only properly lodged, well tended in hospital, and well fed, but likewise that he should be provided with that which all previous reformers had failed to secure for him,—occupation during the long and weary hours of the day. Few men had had better opportunities than Sir Hugh of seeing what the European soldier could do if he were only, we will not say encouraged, but allowed, to do it. In that terrible Jhansie campaign the soldier had always been ready to do more than his mere duty; he was not then fanciful about his rations, nor did he disdain the hard earth for his bed. The Commander-in-Chief had witnessed his exertions, his privations, his devotion then, and he was resolved that, now that the fight was over, those comforts and those opportunities for profitable employment should be given to the European soldier, which no one more than he had nobly earned.

At the same time discipline was to be maintained, and though discipline had not been openly violated, there were symptoms even then that the pressure of a firm hand might be required, and that a lesson might be needed. To those signs of the times Sir Hugh was fully alive; though it was still hoped, that by a cautious and prudent line of conduct, the danger might be averted.

Then, again, there was the condition of the native army. The question of the reorganization of this army generally was a matter for the consideration of the home authorities, but there was a point connected with it which did come within the jurisdiction of the Commander-in-Chief, and that was, to raise the tone of those numberless officers, who, having lost their regiments, were either absolutely without employment, or were reduced to that most painful of all positions to men who once had a regiment and a home,—that of doing general duty in some large station.

This last task was that first undertaken by the new Commander-in-Chief. The course he adopted was somewhat carped at at the time, but experience has testified to its wisdom. To ascertain among a crowd of applicants who are the fittest for military employment is for a new Commander-in-Chief a very difficult matter. It may be said that he can trust to his staff. But that is the rock upon which the reputation for fair and just dealing of so many previous Commanders-in-Chief has been wrecked. The statement made before the Committee of the House of Lords, by an Adjutant-General, whose patronage had been extremely advantageous to his own personal friends, to the effect that those officers whom he had not selected for employment where the "refuse" of the Army, has not yet been forgotten. In the dark and weary days of the mutiny, those who composed this "refuse" had fought at least as well as their more favoured comrades. In some cases, indeed, the *élite* had not altogether come up to public expectation. For a new Commander-in-Chief, then, to go back to the old ways, to rely for the selection of men on whose conduct would mainly depend the efficient carrying out of his own views, on the reports of the Adjutant-General, was not a plan likely to find favour with one whose views of discipline were so rigid, and whose sense of responsibility was so marked as was the case with Sir Hugh Rose. To his mind it appeared that one great public test was far better than all the private recommendations. And though this test might not operate quite evenly, though it might exclude deserving officers, yet, being open, it was a test the fairness of which, all, he thought, would be ready to acknowledge, and which even those who suffered from it would declare to be preferable to the secret system which had, by its unjust action, soured many a noble spirit. Acting upon this principle, Sir Hugh Rose officially declared, as soon as possible after his assumption of the office of Commander-in-Chief, that the staff appointments in his gift would be bestowed, without favour or affection, upon those officers whose services in the field and whose general good conduct, testified to by those under whom they had served, gave them the greatest claim upon the country. This was a test, open, clear, and incapable of being misunderstood.

It was liable certainly to act hardly upon officers who had not seen service; but it was nevertheless the best test that could be devised. In all stations of life there are inequalities. Fortune showers her favours with bounteous hands on some; she withholds them, in a niggard spirit, from others. To those who, perhaps, hardly seek for them, she gives frequent opportunities; to those who would walk bare-footed from one end of India to another for one single chance, she often rigidly denies that chance. We see this in every career, in every station of life. If, then, this rule bore hardly upon those who, from no fault of their own, had not fleshed their maiden swords, it was, after all, one of the chances of existence. It had upon them, besides, this other effect, that, shut out from military employment, these men where induced to turn their energies to the performance of those departmental duties under the government of India for which military service was never considered a necessary qualification.

We have said that this new test proposed by Sir Hugh Rose was rather carped at when it appeared. But it was carped at simply because very few believed that it would be strictly and rigidly adhered to. Declarations of the same sort had been made by others; yet, with the exception of Sir Charles Napier and General Anson, they had seldom been acted up to. Practically the officer who had no interest had had but a slender chance. The Indian public therefore were slow to believe that any change in the system which had effectually provided for the relations and friends of the staff of the army would follow even the emphatic declarations of the new Commander-in-Chief.

Yet, at the close of a five years' tenure of office by

Sir Hugh Rose, we find that he never swerved from that declaration. It is now an admitted axiom, that public service is the test for promotion. Sir Hugh has impressed that principle on the military administration. Loud, doubtless, have been the lamentations over "the good old times." But what a few private individuals have lost the public has gained. The tone of the officers is far higher than it was before. Men have ceased to care about letters of introduction or relationship to officials. A system has been introduced which has made every man who has done good service feel that his claim upon his country will be satisfied. It is our conviction that Sir Hugh never gave away an appointment to any one who was not, in his opinion, the best qualified amongst those unemployed, to fill it.

He, like his predecessors, has no doubt had his temptations. People, "with a certain influence," are always upon the *qui vive* to obtain something good for Charlie or Frank. Yet it was the great merit of Sir Hugh Rose, and that which has stamped his administration, that if Charlie and Frank had been his own sons, he would have given them nothing, if he believed that other men had a prior and a better claim.

The increase to the allowances of commandants, and of seconds in command; the appointment of wing officers and of paid doing duty officers,—measures recommended by the Government of India and sanctioned by the Secretary of State,—gave to Sir Hugh Rose many opportunities of providing for deserving officers. It is quite possible that the critic may point to this or that officer, and say that the appointment was not a good one; that a better might have been made. Even admitting this for the sake of argument, it was at least recognised that that man was appointed who, in the opinion of the Commander-in-Chief, had, from public services, the best claim. No one has ever dreamt of asserting that private interest ever influenced the decisions of Sir Hugh Rose in this respect. Conflicting claims must be balanced by one man. The great thing is, to feel confidence in the impartiality of the adjudicator, and, though men may have differed from Sir Hugh in his estimate of the value of services, every one will admit that his decision invariably gave the actual conclusion at which his mind had arrived.

With respect to the European soldier, Sir Hugh had a more difficult task. In a very few months after his arrival in Calcutta, the discontent which was even then lurking in the minds of the European soldiers of the Indian Army culminated in acts of open mutiny. In dealing with this mutiny Sir Hugh displayed that tact and decision which had characterised his campaigns. He was prompt to strike, severe to punish the ringleaders, but merciful to the many who had blindly followed the few. This danger averted—the snake not only "scotched" but killed—Sir Hugh was soon after summoned to Calcutta to take part in introducing the great measure which was the consequence of that mutiny,—the amalgamation of the two armies.

It was whilst this measure was being discussed, that Sir Hugh found time to introduce one of his great remedial measures for the improvement of the condition of the soldier,—the establishment of soldiers' workshops. In these the soldier was encouraged to develop the knowledge he had acquired in his early youth by working at the trade to which he had been brought up. Every facility was afforded him. A workshop, tools and materials were supplied, and the soldier was permitted to dispose of the results of his industry. A certain class of officers who believe only in the drinking faculties of the European soldier, who regarded him as a mere brute to be lashed into obedience, laughed at the simplicity which could devise so inoperative a measure. We are bound to add, however, that by the Indian Press, it was warmly received and applauded. Its greatest opponents were the officers of the old school, wedded to the ideas of their boyhood. But Sir Hugh had great confidence in the experiment. He put it in force, and the result has been the redemption of the well-disposed men in the barracks; it has proved a death-blow to that listless idleness which has been the greatest enemy of the European soldier; it has enabled men to save money, which they have invested not in "drink," but in the education of their children; and it has, in many places given a stimulus to local trade such as its supporters never anticipated.

Similarly with soldiers' gardens. These, nominally existing before, have been improved and increased during the last four years. The vegetables supplied to regiments are in many cases grown by the soldiers themselves, and the European residents in stations are often indebted to those gardens for their supplies.

It was quite impossible that a man of Sir Hugh Rose's strong convictions and determination to do what he believed to be right without respect of persons, could avoid coming in contact with some of the many departments of army administration which abound in this country. We cannot be surprised to find, therefore, that his endeavours to improve the rations of the soldier brought him into collision with the department which is entrusted with the supply of food to the army. It must be admitted that in the course of the correspondence on this subject charges were brought against the department, which could not afterwards be sustained before the Commission appointed by Government to enquire into the subject. It is always the fate, however, of an ardent reformer, who occupies a high position, to find his sentiments and opinions exaggerated by some of those about him, and certainly many of the charges against the commissariat were very extravagant. That department has always been one of the best arranged and best organised in the Indian service. And if it may be said that it is liable sometimes to become too much of a bureaucracy,—to be a service within a service,—the appointment as its chief, of an officer untrammelled by its traditions, and unfettered by its precedents,—a course which has lately been adopted by the Government,—will always tend to remedy that evil.

It was the opinion of the late Commander-in-Chief that the commissariat department should be placed under his orders, instead of being a department under the Government of India. But we think the Indian Government acted very wisely in adhering to a system which, under every exigency and under seemingly insuperable difficulties, has always worked well. The Government of India would be mad if it was not as anxious as the Commander-in-Chief for the lives and health of the European soldiers serving in India; it would be culpably negligent, if it were not to enforce upon its agents, charged with the supply of food to the soldier, the necessity of seeing that those supplies were of the very best quality. We cannot refrain from expressing our opinion that in this branch of commissariat arrangement the Government of India has nobly done its duty. No reasonable expense is spared to make the supplies for the European troops equal to the best procurable in the market. The officers of the commissariat department are equally interested in seeing that the wishes of Government in this respect are carried out. We believe that it happens far more often that the men reject what is good from an over-fastidiousness than that the commissariat officer sympathises with the contractor in the tender of an inferior article. A curious incident bearing upon this subject, happened in the cold weather of 1856-7 in Lucknow when that city was visited by General Anson. On the morning of the general's arrival, the regiment quartered there had rejected the bread tendered by the contractor. The same bread was accepted, as usual, by the messes. Dining at one of these the same evening General Anson remarked on the excellence of the bread, and he then learned to his surprise that it was the very bread which the men of the regiment, and a committee of their officers, had that morning rejected.

It is in our opinion a positive advantage that the commissariat should be under the Civil Power. In the first place, it assimilates in that respect to the English system. Then again, as a disbursing department, it is properly placed under the control of the Government. But, we believe, it is advantageous in the mere executive arrangement of the department, and in the interest of the troops themselves. A Commander-in-Chief could not get more out of the commissariat officers than do the Government now. He could not hang them by reason of the badness of the supplies,—though Sir

Harry Smith after Buddiwal, in buffoon-like parody on the Duke of Wellington, threatened to do so. He could only turn them out of their appointments, and he would find it then difficult to supply their places with superior men. But so long as the commissariat is under the supreme Government, the Commander-in Chief possesses a power in reality far greater and more effectual. We allude to the power of reporting an officer to the supreme Government. To be turned out by the Commander-in-Chief would not be nearly so great a punishment to an officer as to be turned out by the supreme Government on the report of the Commander,-in-Chief. In the one case the Commander-in-Chief is the accuser and the judge, and the moral effect of a sentence against the accused would, in that case, be comparatively small. In the other, the tribunal is absolutely unbiassed, and an adverse decision would be disgrace or ruin.

Nevertheless, the course adopted in this respect by Sir Hugh Rose was prompted by a pure and sincere desire to benefit the soldier. He had no private interests to serve. He sought solely that the men who had fought for us might not only be well fed, but that they might be fed as well as the country could feed them. And he succeeded. It is true the Government did not adopt his views, yet he did not the less, though by other means, obtain the result at which he was aiming. The constant stirring of this question called constant attention to the subject. It became the first interest of the commissariat officers that the supplies should be of a character such as none could object to; and though objections were occasionally made,—for it is the nature of Englishmen to grumble and object,—yet they were generally pronounced frivolous. The main result however was, that during the command of Sir Hugh Rose, the rations attained a variety and an excellence such as had never been before equalled; and this, as we understand it, was the practical result at which he aimed, when he first agitated the subject.

Similarly with respect to punkahs and tatties for barracks, to soldiers' cots, and to every other article on which the soldier's comfort depends. No toil was too great, no hours were considered thrown away, which were devoted to improvements on these matters. On some of them, as on the question of soldiers' cots, Sir Hugh showed himself far in advance of those even who were considered specially qualified to report on them. There was this also about Sir Hugh, that he was by no means wedded to his own theories; he was always ready to receive suggestions, no matter whence they came. When satisfied that a man was in earnest, he at once was attracted towards him. Confident in the purity of his intentions, he cared as little for hollow-hearted ridicule as for foolish applause. He worked straight to an end, and allowed no considerations to deter him from carrying out that end to the extent of his power. His regulations for cholera camps, and his rules for the efficient sanitary care of the various cantonments were excellent. He was especially anxious to see that officers attended to their men during times of epidemic sickness. No remissness, in his opinion, was equal to that which kept officers from the hospital at a time when their men were struck down by hundreds, from a mere fear of catching the disorder. He would have disrated his own brother had he found him guilty of a dereliction of duty of this nature. Many officers, no doubt, needed no stimulus to induce them to pay proper attention to their men at such seasons. We believe, indeed, that sickness especially calls into active operation the sympathies of brave men. Yet it is equally possible that the knowledge, that the Commander-in-Chief regarded backwardness on such occasions as second only to backwardness on the field of battle, was not without its effect on some.

We have now glanced hastily at the effect of Sir Hugh Rose's administration on the position of two classes,—the European officers and the European soldiers. With respect to the native soldier little remained to be done, except to regulate the conditions of good service pay, and to invent for him a dress more suited to him, and to the climate of the country of his birth, than that worn by the old Pandy regiments. The first, in concert with the supreme Government, was accomplished; the second Sir Hugh Rose attempted. We believe he had a dress made up somewhat in the style of the dresses worn by the Turcos and Zouaves, and submitted it to the Government of India. Whether it was accepted we are not informed. It certainly is not worn at the present time. Those, however, who have seen the Turcos on guard at the Tuileries, with their clean neat cloth dresses, well adapted for any work, and who have contrasted them with the ill-fitting, slovenly, dirty-looking uniform worn by our Indian sepoys, will not fail to hope that the suggestions of our late Commander-in-Chief in this respect will yet be carried out.

It may not be out of place to allude here to those other qualities by which the character of Sir Hugh Rose was marked. We have spoken in the earlier part of this article of his own personal bravery, and of his conduct on the field of battle. It may be said that on those occasions, it was necessary that he should not spare himself. Yet, when the necessity did not absolutely exist, he spared himself as little. To make himself master of the topography of the Punjab frontier, he rode sixty and seventy and eighty miles a day, and thought nothing of it. To acquaint himself with the nature of that frontier was, in his idea, as much an act of duty, as it was to inspect the condition of the troops, and he therefore did it. Small wits have sneeringly alluded to his dandy-like appearance,—and there can be no doubt but that Sir Hugh Rose felt a pride in appearing on every occasion as a gentleman and a soldier,—but those witlings would have felt extremely uncomfortable if they had been challenged to accompany the dandy Commander-in-Chief on one of of his frontier rides. He possessed indeed an energy and a pluck which enabled him to defy fatigue.

Sir. Hugh Rose loved a brave man. Words cannot describe the absolute contempt he felt for a coward. His hospitality was unbounded. He was totally devoid of pretentious vanity. He strove, as he said in his farewell speech in Calcutta "to do his duty." His manners were distinguished by a refined courtesy to all. For real, earnest men, whatever their rank or station, he always testified a special regard. That he had faults is perfectly true. But they were faults, which, weighed against his great qualities as a general, his earnest persistence as a military reformer, his impartiality and heartfelt desire to do what was right, without care for the consequences, deserve but little consideration.

Our task is now finished. We have endeavoured to place before our readers an impartial sketch of the Commander-in-Chief who has just quitted us. Such an attempt, at an earlier date, would have been impossible. But if, whilst a great public character is in India, his enemies and detractors may say their worst of him, it is surely permissible to those who may entertain for him a genuine admiration, to describe his career, after his final departure for Europe, in language which the incidents of it in their opinion demand. Sir Hugh Rose has indeed played no ordinary part in the world. We have seen him as a young soldier gaining the approval of one, who, at the time a young statesman himself, has twice been Prime Minister of England. We meet him then, gaining on his first essay in arms in a foreign country a sabre of honour and other marks of distinction from a foreign Sovereign, and the highest approval from his own commander. Had the Order of Valour then been instituted, there can be no doubt but that the Victoria Cross would have been awarded to Colonel Rose for his gallantry in Syria. We see him again, transferred to the diplomatic line, earning the warm approval of the greatest Foreign Minister of the nineteenth century,—the present First Minister of the Crown. Transferred to Constantinople, to give him a wider scope for his abilities, we find him there, with a fearlessness of responsibility which too many would have shrunk from, deciding the policy of his country at a critical period, and engaging her to set bounds to Russian ambition. A little later, attached in a semi-military, semi-diplomatic capacity to the Marshal commanding the French Army in the Crimea, we hear of him again in the front rank, doing deeds which, but for his high rank, would have secured for him the coveted Cross. There is then an interval of rest, and he comes in the hour of danger to Hindostan. That romantic campaign of Central India,—romantic from its many incidents, its constant marches and combats, its deeds of glory,—for the double victory of Jhansie, and the "crowning mercy" of Gwalior, showed clearly to all who have studied war, that England yet possessed a general. That determination,—so rare in the present day,—to move forwards; that energy,—so uncommon in all ages,—not * once witnessed in the five years' course of the American War,—to turn a defeat into an utter, a ruinous, rout; that self-possession under all circumstances,—that noble self-confidence which hugs to itself responsibility, that directness of mental vision which keeps a man firm to his original object,—all combined to show indeed that in Sir Hugh Rose England possessed a Captain of a very high order of military ability.

Then again, in his final career as Commander-in-Chief, we see the same qualities developing themselves in another form. The care for the men who had fought so nobly under his eyes; the efforts to wean the officers from looking to any other than a soldier's career; the strong sense of discipline and regard for their men which he impressed upon the generals and the colonels, the captains and the subalterns of his army, were, throughout that career, most strongly marked. His own careful inspection of the troops, of the frontiers, his personal examination of officers, convinced every one that the Commander-in-Chief was in earnest; that he only asked from officers that which he had done and was ready to do himself. At the same time his generous hospitality and his courteous demeanour to all were worthy,—the one of an officer occupying so high and distinguished a position; the other, of the Chief of an Army in which

* This was written before the result of the final battles before Petersburg was known.

chivalry, it has been well stated, "has found her last refuge." To say that he had faults is only to say that he was mortal. But whilst we admit those faults, we would call attention to the higher virtues, the larger qualities by which the smaller failings are almost entirely overshadowed. We live, it is true, in a cavilling age; in an age when all the acts of a public man are laid open to the public view, when much that is good is lost sight of, whilst all that is bad is repeated and exaggerated; yet, even in this age, we believe that there are few who study the military character and achievements of Sir Hugh Rose, and who examine his public acts as Commander-in-Chief, but will join in the eloquent eulogy pronounced by Mr. Seton-Karr, and endorsed by the community of Calcutta, on the occasion of the farewell entertainment on the evening before His Excellency left Calcutta for the last time; and will realise the conviction, that "in the long experience, tried sagacity, and well known forethought" of our late Commander-in-Chief, "our country possesses a solid and effectual guarantee for the adequacy of our national defences, for the inviolability of our coasts, for the protection of the fair homes of England,—for everything, in short, within the scope of his command and the limit of his observation, that shall concern the peace of the subject or the honour of the Crown."

THE END.